Modernism in Practice

D1572502

# Modernism in Practice

## AN INTRODUCTION TO POSTWAR JAPANESE POETRY

Leith Morton

University of Hawai'i Press
Honolulu

09   08   07   06   05   04   6   5   4   3   2   1

**Library of Congress Cataloging-in-Publication Data**

Morton, Leith.

    Modernism in practice : an introduction to postwar Japanese poetry /
Leith Morton.

      p.  cm.

    Includes bibliographical references and index.

    ISBN 0-8248-2738-4 (hardcover : alk. paper)—ISBN 0-8248-2807-0
(pbk. : alk. paper)

    1. Japanese poetry—20th century—History and criticism.  2. Modernism
(Literature)—Japan.  I. Title.

PL733.82.M577M67  2004

895.6'109112—dc22                                    2003022765

Designed by The University of Hawai'i Press production staff
Printed by The Maple-Vail Book Manufacturing Group

# Contents

# Preface

 I have to thank many people and institutions without whose support and assistance this book would never have been written. First and foremost I must express my gratitude to the postwar poets discussed in detail in the book. I have met most of these poets personally, and the few I have not met I have corresponded with. All these poets have been extremely generous in offering support and cooperation, and their active encouragement has made the drudgery usually involved in research almost disappear. They deserve my heartfelt gratitude.

Research has been carried out at a number of institutions in Australia and Japan: in Australia, most prominently at the universities of Sydney and Newcastle; and in Japan, at Kwansei Gakuin University, Tokyo Metropolitan University (Tōkyō Toritsu Daigaku) and the International Research Center for Japanese Studies (Nichibunken) in Kyoto. To all the staff in these institutions who have been most generous with their time and resources and also for the financial and other support provided, I offer my deepest gratitude.

Some individuals have played more prominent roles than others in helping me to research modern poetry in Japan over the past decade and a half, and to these people I must express my most sincere thanks; in the Japanese name order of surname first (titles have been omitted and names are in alphabetical order): Awazu Norio, Ellis Toshiko, Fukuda Junnosuke, Hokama Shuzen, Ichihara Chikako, Inaga Shigemi, Iraha Morio, Itō Hiromi, Kokai Eiji, Kusano Shinpei (lately deceased), Nakahodo Masanori, Nakajima Yōichi, Nakamoto Masachie (lately deceased), Shinkawa Kazue, Shiraishi Kazuko, Soh Sakon, Suzuki Sadami, Takahashi Junko, Tanikawa Shuntarō, Wada James, and Yoshihara Sachiko.

Outside Japan, I have particularly to thank (in alphabetical order and with titles omitted) Hugh Clarke, Thomas Fitzsimmons, Van Gessel, Phil Hammial, Mabel Lee, Michael Marra, Matsui Sakuko, John Ramsland, Tom Rimer, and Catherine Runcie. Also, I am grateful to the two anonymous readers for the University of Hawaiʻi Press for their advice, and to my editors at the press for the work they have put into the book. Finally, as always, I wish to thank my family: my wife Sachiko and daughters Aya, Yae and Chiyo who have given me more love and support than any man is entitled to.

Early versions of two of the essays included here have been published previously. Chapter 2 was published in an earlier form in Japanese in the journal *Arishima Takeo kenkyū* (vol. 1) in 1997. An earlier version of chapter 4 was published in the *Journal of the Association of Teachers of Japanese* (vol. 31, no. 2) in October 1997. This journal is now called *Japanese Language and Literature*. My grateful thanks for permission to republish.

# Introduction

*Naranja, poma, seno, esfera al fin resuelta*
*en vacuidad de estupa. Tierra disuelta.*
—Octavio Paz, "Renga"

*On the very idea of a conceptual scheme*
*dogs set up a sort of barking, underneath*
—John Forbes, "On the Very Idea of a Conceptual Scheme"

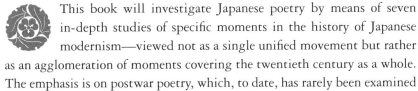This book will investigate Japanese poetry by means of seven in-depth studies of specific moments in the history of Japanese modernism—viewed not as a single unified movement but rather as an agglomeration of moments covering the twentieth century as a whole. The emphasis is on postwar poetry, which, to date, has rarely been examined in detail in English. The book also has a clear emphasis on language as the chief mediating element of modernist poetry. Therefore, the individual chapters are linked by a focus on the twin themes of modernism and language rather than by a continuous historical narrative.

Discussion of individual books of poetry and poems will take predominance over discussion of theoretical manifestos, although some analysis of such declarations will be undertaken. In addition, one of the chapters will focus on contemporary Okinawan poetry, an area of research as yet in its infancy in the West.[1] Some reference will be made to postmodernism, but, in this study, postmodernism refers to a type of art and poetry created by the avant-garde from the late 1960s or 1970s onward, namely, a particular mode of writing, or of language.[2] Hence, as the analysis that follows will demonstrate (especially in chapter 6), postmodernism is viewed as part of the larger Modern movement.

The volume is divided into two parts. The first part consists of two chapters that provide a prologue to the development of postwar poetry by examining two important early examples of modernist verse. Chapter 1 investigates the modernist experiments of Yosano Akiko (1878–1942) and her husband Tekkan (1873–1935) in the *tanka* genre of traditional poetry, which, in content, led to the birth of a modernist aesthetic and to the creation of the "new woman" in literature.[3] Chapter 2 conducts an analysis of the novelist Arishima Takeo's (1878–1923) only collection of poetry, *Hitomi naki me* (Eyeless eyes, 1923), which here is read as an early modernist experiment and linked to similar experiments elsewhere.

The second part of the volume comprises five chapters, which represent different approaches to postwar poetry. Chapter 3 examines the poet Soh Sakon's (b. 1919) poetry collection about World War II *Moeru haha* (Mother burning, 1968) from the perspectives of language and theme. Chapter 4 is a detailed analysis of rhetorical strategies in the poetry of three major contemporary women poets: Ishigaki Rin (b. 1920), Tomioka Taeko (b. 1935), and Itō Hiromi (b. 1955).

Chapter 5 is a study of contemporary Okinawan poets and their struggles with modernist language, with the main focus on the Okinawan poet Ichihara Chikako (b. 1951) and her 1985 poetry collection *Umi no tonneru* (Tunnel through the sea). Chapter 6 reads the contemporary poet Asabuki Ryōji's (b. 1952) collection *Opus* (1988) as an exercise in late modernist or early postmodernist rhetoric, with discussion of some theoretical issues. Chapter 7 seeks to locate the poet Tanikawa Shuntarō (b. 1931) in the context of contemporary debates over language and poetry and makes explicit reference to those debates occurring throughout the 1990s in the magazine *Gendai shi techō* (Contemporary poetry notebook). Thus the investigation of these seven moments in literary history attempts to trace a genealogy of one dominant thread of twentieth century modernist poetry in Japan.

A strong emphasis on language, a strategy that hardly needs justification when treating poetry, demands a much more intense yet historically mediated approach than biographies of individual poets can provide, no matter how excellent they may be. Similarly, treatments of movements focusing on two or three poets, especially if they belong to a sharply delineated movement, are subject to similar constraints of space and time in that the attention to the movement under investigation prevents a wider examination of the broader linguistic and thematic issues, and sometimes restricts detailed consideration of the verse produced by such movements.

In that sense, this book represents a break from existing scholarly practice in this field and proposes a different way to approach Japanese literary history. The focus on linguistic usage is also a strategy justified by the historic importance of language to literary modernism: in a very real sense, I will argue, language is modernism in practice. This approach results in the close readings of the many individual poems that are found throughout the book. As numerous commentators have noted, translation is the ultimate form of scholarly exegesis, and so I have translated a large number of individual poems not merely to provide the ground on which my arguments proceed, but also because most of the poets discussed here are rarely translated.

No single theoretical or conceptual approach will be followed in this book. Reading strategies will be entirely pragmatic. The purpose of interpretive or conceptual frames should surely be to help elucidate the meaning and significance of the texts under examination. Consequently, this study makes use of a wide range of theorists in its attempt to trace a possible outline of modernist poetry in Japan, only one of many such possible outlines. I will also make use of a number of leading Japanese critics and commentators in my investigation of the several themes or threads that combine to make up the book and define the particular historical moments under examination. In addition, I will use the insights of several Western theorists and commentators. This technique allows cross-cultural comparisons to be made and brings to the study the specific advantages to be gained by an investigator working from a perspective outside the language and culture of the poets themselves.

In this study, for the most part, "poetry" means *shi* or Western-style free verse, which was introduced into Japan in 1882 with the publication of the volume *Shintaishi shō* (Selection of poetry in the new style).[4] This genre of poetry became the dominant mode of modernist verse. And, as the name suggests, it was always associated with the birth of the "new" in the minds of the reading public and poets alike. But other modes of writing will also, from time to time, come under examination, at least in part because poetry was not written in a vacuum and drew on various genres of prose for inspiration. In addition, the traditional genre of *tanka* will be considered in the early chapters dealing with the first part of the century, since at this time *tanka* competed with *shi* for dominance as the preeminent poetic art.

The choice of the verse of Yosano Akiko and her husband together with the poetry of Arishima Takeo to represent the early steps toward the development of a modern aesthetic in Japanese verse was made primarily on the basis of two separate arguments. The first is that this aspect of Akiko's significance as a poet, while generally acknowledged by Akiko specialists in

Japan (as seen in chapter 1), has not been taken up to any great degree by Japanese literary historians of the avant-garde, especially those who work in the area of modern poetry. Nevertheless, my contention is that her contribution to modern verse is precisely where Akiko's influence and legacy are most striking. The significance of Arishima's verse, in contrast, arises initially from the fact that it is almost completely unknown, whether in Japan or elsewhere.[5] Yet Arishima is an excellent example of a prewar author who absorbed and understood the lessons concerning the modernist experiments in verse conducted by his compatriots during the first two decades of the twentieth century. Hence his poetry has an intrinsic interest over and above the very specific relevance it holds for insights into his own life and death.

There have been a number of significant English-language studies (mostly in the form of biographical analyses), and many studies in Japanese, of prewar poetry in Japan that map the history of that period in some detail. By comparison, however, there have been few studies of postwar poetry.[6] One of the problems is whom to select for examination from among the many hundreds of poets who have published (and, in the case of contemporary poets, are continuing to publish) in this era. A glance at five representative sets or collections of postwar poets will illustrate the difficulty of the task.

The fifteen-volume [*Zenshishū taisei*] *gendai Nihon shijin zenshū* (Collection of modern Japanese poets [complete poems for each poet]), published between 1952 and 1955, purports to contain the complete collected poems to that point in time of sixty-four important modern poets. The thirty-four-volume *Nihon shijin zenshū* (Collection of Japanese poets), issued between 1966 and 1967, and the thirty-volume *Nihon no shiika* (Japanese poetry), published between 1967 and 1970, both contain selections from individual books of poems, from roughly the same eighty modern poets. The latter two collections were the result of a "mini-boom" in poetry publishing at the time. The literary historian Shimaoka Shin writes that single volumes of the *Collection of Japanese Poets* (produced by Shinchōsha) sold over one hundred thousand copies.[7]

The continuing series Gendai Shi Bunko (Library of Contemporary Poetry), which commenced publication in 1968, is divided into three sets and has published 180-odd volumes, each devoted to a single poet, but a number of poets have two or more volumes in the set. Thus, the total number of modern poets represented adds up to about 140 or so poets, many of whom are still active. Finally, a rival series called Nihon Gendai Shi Bunko (Library of Contemporary Japanese Poetry) that began in the late 1970s has published ninety or so poets, but very few individuals overlap between the two series.[8]

Thus, the poetry of well over two hundred postwar Japanese poets is available in print in these collections, and, naturally, these poets represent just the tip of the iceberg, with many more poets having published poetry in the postwar era. The question remains as to how to select poets for sustained scrutiny from among so many. The issue of translation is moot, as only a tiny minority of these poets have been translated into English. Subjective factors must enter the equation if only to allow for the actual number of poets who have been read by the investigator: in my case, the poets I have managed to read over the decade and a half that I have been engaged in research on Japanese poetry (including most, but not all, of the poets collected in the sets mentioned above).[9]

My selections of postwar poets have been made on the basis of a number of factors: most important, the concern with language, especially in a modernist sense, displayed by the particular poets under examination; familiarity with and admiration of the work of the individual poets; and, last but not least, the judgment of those poets by contemporary Japanese scholarship (which represents Japanese readers). One concrete expression of the way in which these poets have been evaluated in contemporary Japan is the large number of literary awards garnered by most of the individual collections examined in this study.

In addition, I have tried to focus on major poets whose verse is not as well known as it should be—a relatively easy task as so few postwar poets have had any extended treatment of their verse in English. As noted above, this also provides a justification for the large number of translations contained within this book. The only exception to this rule is the chapter on Tanikawa Shuntarō: no discussion of postwar poetry would be complete without a consideration of his work, since he is the dominant poet of his era. Early versions of some of the essays included here have been published before, but all have been rewritten for this volume to accord with its overall design and aims. Other chapters have been written specifically for the study.

The translations have been made with a deliberate attention to the aural aspects of the verse forms favored by many of the poets. An emphasis on the musical or rhythmical elements of verse has been characteristic of modern Japanese poetry (shi) since its inception in the Meiji period (1868–1912). The early experiments of the pioneer translator and poet (better known as a novelist) Mori Ōgai (1862–1922) with end rhyme in his 1889 volume of verse translations *Omokage* (Vestiges) have been echoed by such postwar poets as Tanikawa in his book *Kotoba asobi uta* (Word-play songs, 1973) and, in recent years, by rhyming poets associated with the magazine *Nakaniwa* (Inner garden) such as Umemoto Kenzō and Inaba Michio.[10] Matsumoto Kyōsuke is one of the latest poets to try his hand at rhyming verse with his 1993 volume titled *Ōinteikeishishū: Nihongo henro* (Fixed rhyme poetry collection: Japanese-language pilgrimage).[11]

The metrical schemes used by postwar poets encompass many more devices than rhyme, and thus to communicate the rhythms and cadences of these poems in English, the translator must have recourse to a wide variety of similar or related techniques. Apart from such poets as Tanikawa and Asabuki, few prominent contemporary Japanese writers are actively involved in "sound poetry" where, as Steve McCaffery explains, "the primary goal [is] the liberation and promotion of the phonetic and subphonetic features of language."[12] However, the ear as well as the eye (and, naturally, the cognitive faculties) is important in reading and comprehending postwar Japanese poetry, and so I have made a concerted effort to try to reproduce as best as I can the aural effects and affects of the poets whose verse is translated here.[13] Such sound-oriented poetry falls primarily into the category of "performance poetry."

The scholar Takahashi Seori argues that the 1970s saw a fundamental split between performance poets like Terayama Shūji (1935–1983) and elite print-oriented poets who rejected this trend, writing ever more obscure and difficult "language" poetry.[14] Terayama created verse dramas for underground theater, produced videos, and composed radio poetry. In 1960, when he was only twenty-four, Terayama wrote a famous essay titled "Kōi to sono hokori—chimata no gendaishi to action poem no mondai" (Action and its boasts—the issue of the fork in modern verse and action poems) in which he criticized poets' obsession with print media. He characterized jazz poetry and graffiti in public toilets as "action poems" that were "revelations of life overflowing in forks in the road."[15]

In the late 1960s and 1970s, poetry recitals and performances became extremely popular. Shimaoka cites Terayama's 1973 action poem "Jikanwari" (Timetable)—a sketch of how to experience poetry by drawing in chalk a square on a concrete footpath and dividing it into various zones—as typical of the kind of verse (or performance) activity that Terayama championed.[16] While Terayama explored the motifs of "clowning," "laughter," and "deconstruction" in his poetry, poets of an opposing persuasion developed verse in a direction similar to abstract art—this kind of poetry Takahashi calls "conceptual art," poetry exemplified by Asabuki Ryōji's 1989 collection *Misshitsuron* (Closed room treatise).[17]

It can be argued that "conceptual" poets focus at least as much on the eye as on the ear. In Japan, modern poetry that emphasizes visual qualities has had a long history. The modernist poet Hinatsu Kōnosuke (1890–1971), who was active in the prewar period, is a good example of an author whose work stressed the visual surface, in his case using recondite Chinese characters for their artistic (and also phonetic) effect. The well-known avant-garde poet Takiguchi Shūzō (1903–1979) was also renowned for his "plastic" poetry that accentuated the visual nature of his work.[18] These two poets are but a small sample of a large number of Japanese poets who have written as much for the eye as for the ear. The tradition of these poets has continued to the present, with numerous Japanese multimedia poets active on the Internet and in other venues.

Unfortunately, the limitations of space do not permit a thorough consideration of more than a few authors. Consequently, the emphasis here is on poets whose work can be more easily comprehended in translation rather than on multimedia artists whose achievements extend beyond the printed page and thus demand a larger dimension of understanding than can be conveyed by the medium of print alone. Nevertheless, poetry circles in Japan are particularly close and so, despite the factionalism of the various poetry coteries organized around a leading poet and in-house journal, it is fair to say that Japanese poets are well aware of each other's publications. This is borne out by the many examples of one volume of modern poetry influencing a host of others—as can be seen in the numerous *"monogatari shi"* (tale poems) produced in the 1960s.

This collection of essays thus attempts to sketch out one version of postwar Japanese literary history, only the beginning of a larger history yet to be written. The postwar poets chosen for investigation are all important authors, and the themes of their work speak not only to Japanese readers but also to readers everywhere. However, there has been little writing on or analysis of these poets (or postwar Japanese poets in general) in any language other than Japanese.

It is important to note that the notion of the postwar has faded in the minds of many Japanese. Several Japanese critics, like Kokai Eiji, would argue that the era of "postwar poetry" is over, as Japanese literature has entered a different phase of development where many of the issues that arose in the two decades or so after the end of the war are no longer relevant or meaningful to contemporary Japanese.[19] However true this may be for Japanese readers, it is certainly not the case for a non-Japanese audience, as the historical map sketched by this volume is terra incognita for most Western readers. Furthermore, the authors included here represent not only poets who came to prominence in the 1950s and 1960s such as Soh Sakon and Tomioka Taeko, but also poets whose writing became famous much later, for example, Itō Hiromi and Asabuki Ryōji. I hope the chapters to follow will open up new territory and lead to further exploration by both scholars and readers in the West.

I

# THE DEVELOPMENT
# OF MODERN
# JAPANESE POETRY

# Chapter 1

# The Birth of the Modern

## Yosano Akiko and Tekkan's Verse Revolution

*Certain kinds of knowledge leave the field of*
*all possible experience, apparently to enlarge*
*the sphere of our judgements beyond the limits*
*of experience, by means of concepts to which*
*experience—even after we've made up our minds*
*about its blaze of nothing—can never supply*
*any corresponding objects.*
—John Forbes, "Love's Body"

*Let us admit it. There are powers*
*No border can contain. They sit with us, the uninvited guests,*
*Wherever our table is laid,*
*Accepting a different coffee,*
*Awaiting the end of the story.*
—Harry Clifton, "Where We Live"

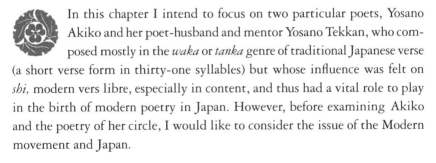 In this chapter I intend to focus on two particular poets, Yosano Akiko and her poet-husband and mentor Yosano Tekkan, who composed mostly in the *waka* or *tanka* genre of traditional Japanese verse (a short verse form in thirty-one syllables) but whose influence was felt on *shi*, modern vers libre, especially in content, and thus had a vital role to play in the birth of modern poetry in Japan. However, before examining Akiko and the poetry of her circle, I would like to consider the issue of the Modern movement and Japan.

## The Modern Movement and Japan

In an essay published in 1994, the scholar Toshiko Ellis asked exactly what is Japanese modernism?[1] Ellis' essay is an attempt to rewrite accepted views of Japanese modernism that commonly locate the birth of the movement in the avant-garde of the 1920s, when the word "modernism" (*modanizumu*) was introduced to Japan.[2] Ellis is careful to distinguish the notion of the "modern" from the movement called "modernism," while not denying that links exist between them. But Western commentators on modernism like Marshall Berman, Malcolm Bradbury, and James McFarlane argue that such a distinction is fraught with difficulty, as a relationship between history and sensibility, however complex, nonetheless exists. Both Berman and Bradbury and McFarlane (the latter two writing jointly) argue that a modern sensibility in art and literature extends, in the West at any rate, as far back as the middle of the nineteenth century.[3] Earl Miner, addressing the same question as Ellis, cites a well-known Japanese dictionary to argue that the notion of the "modern" *(gendai)* begins with the Meiji Restoration of 1868, stressing how much Japanese notions of modernity are in some senses reactions to the incursion of Western imperialism.[4]

What, then, is to be made of Toshiko Ellis' most important question? Ellis wishes to rewrite the existing script in order to broaden the category of "modernism" in Japan to encompass writers other than those who were self-proclaimed modernists. My study is also one important step in such an argument, dealing as it does with poetry. The notion of the modern or of modernity *("kindai"* or *"kindaishugi")* is also useful in helping to define "modernism," as such a label is frequently applied, for example, to prose written in Japan from the late nineteenth century onward. The literary critic Karatani Kōjin in his well-known 1982 book *Nihon kindai bungaku no kigen* (Origins of modern Japanese literature) locates the birth of the modern in the prose fictions of Kunikida Doppo, which were published in 1898.[5] The scholar Mizutani Akio takes a historical perspective and finds the birth of the modern in literature to have occurred between 1885 and 1889, from the time of the adoption of the cabinet system to the promulgation of the Meiji constitution, although he also argues that modernity frequently encountered setbacks, and thus, this early period as a whole is confused, and the notion of modernity is not by any means straightforward.[6]

Suzuki Sadami in his book *Nihon no bungaku gainen* (The concept of "literature" in Japan, 1998) argues that the word *"kindai,"* or modern, is quite old and can be found as far back as the thirteenth century, but at that time it simply meant "recent." The first use he finds in the sense of "modernity" or relating to what is now called modernism is in 1911 in an essay titled "Kindaishugi no eigen" (The origins of modernism) written by the critic

Kaneko Chikusui (1870–1937).[7] Suzuki also refers to the postwar debate in Japan over the notion of the modern, at that time one of the major ideological battlegrounds between left and right, and he contends that the term is now hopelessly colored by ideology.[8] Nevertheless, even admitting that this is true does not negate the value of reexamining the notion of modernity in order to expand current conceptual paradigms to take account of the Japanese experience—following the example of Earl Miner—and to subject to scrutiny, and possibly revision, existing Japanese models of literary modernism.

In Japan, the modern concept of literature assumed that literature was esteemed socially (earlier in Japanese history, literature was often held in low esteem) and also depended on the idea of Japan as a unitary nation-state, a relatively late development in Japanese political thought. In his 1998 book, Suzuki Sadami spends much time tracing and historizing the debate over modernity in Japan—focusing on realist fiction as a putative marker of modernity—to find that it is much confused by ideology and ignorance. He singles out for criticism the notion that Japanese literature can only be defined as that which borrows heavily from Western models of literary modernity, a notion promoted by the distinguished literary historian Nakamura Mitsuo (1911–1988).[9] Suzuki finds that authors were beginning to doubt the notion of modernity by the early 1900s—so well known was the concept of modernity—which confirms his periodization of between 1900 and 1910.[10]

Historians of the avant-garde generally support Toshiko Ellis' assertion that in the 1920s modernist poetry, referred to using the Western loan word *"modan"* rather than the Sino-Japanese compound *"kindai"* (which is of much older origins), came to dominate older models of verse. Chiba Sen'ichi in his 1998 book *Modanizumu no hikakubungakuteki kenkyū* (A comparative study of modernism) cites numerous examples of the term "modernism" *(modanizumu)* drawn from journals and magazines published between 1915 and 1930.[11] Although Chiba cites more examples relating to fiction than to verse, nevertheless, his research appears conclusive. Suzuki has argued a similar case centering on the word *"kindai"* as a marker of modernity. Is there, then, an argument to be made that differs from these previous models?[12]

The prime reason for rejecting the accepted view that modernism begins in the twenties lies in the connection between the romantic movement in literature and modernism. In general, Japanese scholars follow Western commentators in identifying romantic views of selfhood as fundamental components of the shift in sensibility in the late nineteenth century that is referred to as the Modern movement. The critic Shimamura Hōgetsu (1871–1918) writing in 1908 remarked that Japanese naturalism overlaps with romanticism, thus, as Ken Henshall notes, clearly drawing a line of demarcation between French and German versions of naturalism and the Japanese version.[13] The novelist Tayama Katai (1872–1930) described Japanese naturalism in 1908 in language distinctly reminiscent of literary romanticism: "One result has been the emergence of the individual with a strong sense of self-awareness. The author tries to touch upon truths of human life, destroying old morality and convention, and tries to establish individuality. This is the basis of self-consciousness on which naturalism has developed."[14] Although Yosano Akiko is usually viewed as an opponent of the naturalist ascendency in Japanese letters, nevertheless, Tayama's statement could just as easily describe the program that she and Tekkan advocated, which is generally called Myōjō romanticism, named after the journal Tekkan started.

Before embarking on a detailed examination of what such Myōjō romanticism signifies in the poetry of Akiko and Tekkan, let me briefly clarify what the Meiji era conceived of as romantic. I have made an extensive examination of the notion of romantic love *(ren'ai)* elsewhere: in summary, my contention is that romantic love as received and interpreted by Meiji intellectuals from the 1880s onward is conceptually quite distinct from earlier notions of love originating from within Japanese tradition and represents an accommodation to Western notions of romance that were imported from Europe and the United States at this time. The proof I adduce for this argument largely arises from a study of the notion of *"ren'ai,"* or romantic love, as it was developed by a variety of authors in the *Taiyō* (The sun) magazine from 1895 to 1905, a crucial period in the history of Japanese (especially middle-class) sensibility.[15] The sources of the romantic as far as the West was concerned are neatly summarized by Earl Miner thus: "The European Literature that assisted in bringing about naturalism in Japan . . . was not what is usually thought modern European literature but literature Victorian or co-eval with it in other countries."[16]

The nature of that literature has been investigated by several scholars, most recently by Camille Paglia in her 1990 book *Sexual Personae.* Paglia identifies a number of distinct strands that characterize the romantic in her two chapters on "High" and "Late" romanticism. One that is found in the poetry of Tekkan and Akiko is "a tremendous emphasis on cruelty, brutality and violence" that some may find antithetic to an expression of love but that derives, in Paglia's words, from "a conflation of soul images, mirrored self-love."[17] The second strand common to the Japanese experience identified by Paglia is that romanticism is "a mode of self-projection."[18] Paglia takes this argument further, contending that it "arises from the artist's desire to vivify and eternalize his or her emotional but socially forbidden identity."[19]

These two strands Paglia discovers in late Victorian authors like Théophile Gautier (1811–1872), Charles Baudelaire (1821–1867), Emily Brontë (1818–1848), Samuel Taylor Coleridge (1772–1834) and A. G. Swinburne (1837–1909). The impulse behind such Victorian writings Paglia locates in earlier classic romantic exemplars like Goethe (1749–1832) and Lord Byron (1788–1824). In her chapter on the visual art generated by the romantic movement, Paglia nominates pre-Raphaelite artists like Dante Gabriel Rossetti (1828–1882) and Sir Edward Burne-Jones (1833–1898) as chiefly embodying the stage she describes as "Late Romantic." Such Japanese scholars as Haga Tōru and Isoda Kōichi, both writing from a comparative perspective on the impact of fin-de-siècle art and letters on Meiji writing and especially on Akiko, in books that have subsequently been acclaimed by scholarly opinion (as is evident in the many reprintings of these volumes), have already demonstrated the profound influence of this particular group of artists, as well as some of the Victorian authors, on Myōjō aesthetics.[20]

The use of the word "romanticism" to describe the *Myōjō* magazine occurred as early as 1911 in an article by the leading poet Kawai Suimei (1874–1965), and the link may well predate Kawai.[21] But the literary movement associated with the Tōkyō Shinshisha, or New Poets Society, which published the journal, was "Shinpa *waka*" or "New Style" *waka,* a movement to reform the traditional Japanese genre of verse that Tekkan and Akiko wrote.[22] The effect that Myōjō romanticism had on later Japanese literature is undeniable. For example, in November 1902 the critic Higuchi Ryūkyō (1875–1929) wrote that their two collections had jointly inaugurated a revolution in poetic language. This declaration came less than a year after the publication of Yosano—or rather Hō—Akiko's (she did not marry Tekkan until October) first poetry collection, *Midaregami* (Tangled hair), in August 1901 and Tekkan's companion collection *Murasaki* (Purple) in April 1901.

Later Japanese critics agree with Higuchi's judgment. Itō Sei in his magisterial history of the Japanese literary world noted in 1960 that *Myōjō* was the center of the "new romanticism," a view later echoed by the scholar Yano Hōjin, who declared in 1973 that Meiji romanticism begins with *Myōjō* and reaches a climax in Akiko and Tekkan's poetry.[23] The poet Ishimoto Ryūichi in 1996 argued that without the romanticism created by the New Poets Society, that is, *Myōjō,* later Japanese poets of the stature of Kitahara Hakushū (1885–1942) and Ishikawa Takuboku (1886–1912) would not have emerged.[24] In 1998, Watanabe Sumiko, a leading feminist scholar, reiterated Yano's words in her biography of Akiko, stating that the two collections were the "cradle" of Meiji romanticism.[25] Thus, a consensus developed over time within the Japanese scholarly community that has not been seriously challenged.[26]

The dominant image produced in the verse of these two poets was of a kind of romantic love never before expressed in Japanese poetry and also of a new kind of woman never before seen in Japanese letters. The effect of these images on later generations, and for the future course of Japanese literature, cannot be overestimated. Many scholars see Myōjō romanticism as leading to symbolist verse, which laid the foundation of the modernist revolution in poetry.[27] The scholar Wada Hirofumi sums up the thesis thus: "By liberating romantic love and carnal desire, fin-de-siècle and early twentieth century [Japanese] romanticism created the interior face of modernity."[28] Shimaoka Shin, in his 1998 history of modern Japanese verse, published in the same year as Wada's statement, divided the romantic movement in Japanese poetry from 1896 to 1907 into two distinct currents: decadent romanticism or symbolism, and antiromanticism or naturalism.[29] Akiko's and Tekkan's verse falls into the category delineated by the first current, as the analysis that follows will demonstrate.

Suzuki Sadami argues that the notion of romantic love as a literary representation of the figure of the "new woman" of the Meiji era who subverted the existing order is the driving force behind modern Japanese fiction.[30] Although he does not relate this notion directly to Akiko's verse, nonetheless, her poetry comprised the most significant and celebrated expression of romance and the female. Watanabe Sumiko claims that the historical significance of Akiko's poetry is enormous, since it celebrated female subjectivity by using male sexuality as an instrument for the satisfaction of female eros.[31] In fact, the connections between Akiko's vision of womanhood in her poetry and the emerging women's movement are rarely questioned by contemporary Japanese scholarship. Tekkan has his supporters also, with the scholar Iwasaki Yukinori declaring that Tekkan rather than Akiko played the major role in

FIGURE 1. The poet Yosano Akiko and her husband Hiroshi, known at the time by his pen name Tekkan. Ca. 1901. Courtesy of the Library of Modern Japanese Literature (Nihon Kindai Bungakukan)

creating the Myōjō romantic school.[32] I will subject these competing claims to careful scrutiny below.

## Romance as Modernity

Yosano's real name was Hiroshi; he adopted the literary name "Tekkan" between 1895 and 1905. *Myōjō,* the journal he established to publicize his views, carried an important statement in the sixth issue, published in September 1900.[33] In this issue, Tekkan declared: "We will publish poetry about our own egos *(jiga no shi)*. This will not imitate the poetry of the past but will be our poetry, or rather, the poetry we have created individually."[34] He renames "new-style" poetry *(shintaishi),* the Japanese version of vers libre based on translations of Western poetry, *"chōshi"* (long poems). The traditional genre of Japanese poetry in which he also worked—*tanka*—he renames *"tanshi"* (short poems). Finally, he names the new, modernist poetry he wishes to promote *"kokushi,"* or "national poetry."[35] No clearer statement can be found of the revolutionary intent of Tekkan's program of verse reform.

Modernity manifests itself in Yosano Tekkan's *Purple* in a variety of ways. The proud expression of individuality and the equally strong rejection of the past—here indicating the poetry of the previous age—feature strongly in *Purple,* Tekkan's fifth collection of verse. The collection itself consists of 310 *tanka* and 10 long new-style poems. Thus, like the three collections that immediately preceded it, the book is a mixture of traditional and Western-style poetry. The volume, more than any other of Tekkan's collections of verse, embodies the ideals of the New Poets Society, namely, to create a new kind of poetry for a new age. The volume portrays the poet at times as a Japanese equivalent to Goethe and Byron, two favorite culture heroes of the Myōjō group.

In a typically impatient mood, Tekkan asks the following question in the second stanza of his new-style poem "Yarebue," or "Broken Flute."

| | |
|---|---|
| Yo mijikaki ni | Time is short |
| Gētē iden ya | Will Goethe appear? |
| Bairon idenya | Will Byron appear? |
| Wakaki ko no mae | How foolish to ask if my poems will last |
| Nagaki uta tou gu nari | Before youthful poets[36] |

His rhetorical question is an answer itself: the poet has such complete confidence in his verse that it can bear comparison to Goethe and Byron.

The very first poem in this collection, a *tanka,* despite the pessimism of the last line, expresses the same confidence:

| | |
|---|---|
| Ware onoko | I am a man |
| Iki no ko na no ko | Of vitality of name |
| Tsurugi no ko | A sword |
| Shi no ko koi no ko | A poet a lover |
| Aa modae no ko | Ah sick at heart[37] |

In his previous collections, Tekkan had already established a reputation as a strong, highly individual poet gifted with brio and daring, who in his verse demanded that females be the new women of the new age, not the submissive wives and mistresses of old. In *Tekkanshi,* the collection of verse published a mere month before *Purple,* the opening two lines of the first stanza of his new-style poem "Hito wo kouru uta" (A poem of longing for someone) had already become exceedingly famous:

| | |
|---|---|
| Tsuma wo metoraba | If you take a wife, choose one with |
| sai takete | abundant talent |
| Mime uruwashiku nasake aru | A fair face and tender heart[38] |

Tekkan's stance here confirms the contemporary view of a man for a new age who will choose a wife on the basis of her intellectual skills and talents, a position utterly contrary to Neo-Confucian ideals of wifely obedience in which the proposition that a woman should be taught to read was considered outlandish.

Tekkan's persona here and in other poems from the collection is very much a version of the romantic hero; the element of posture, of a self-conscious narcissism, has many affinities with its European counterparts. One can even see the mannered melancholy associated with Goethe's young Werther in poems like the following:

| | |
|---|---|
| Yume wa koi ni | My dream is of love |
| Omoi wa kuni ni | My thoughts are for my country |
| Mi wa chiri ni | My body is dust |
| Sate wa hata tose | For twenty years |
| Sabishisa wo iwazu | Never did I speak of my loneliness[39] |

This is the third poem in the section titled "Seikyō" (Innocence and madness) that begins *Purple.* The first poem in the book is the "I am a man . . . A sword" cited earlier. The second poem is as follows:

| | |
|---|---|
| Ono ko ware | I am a man |
| Momoyo no nochi ni | Whose poetry may |
| Kieba kiemu | Vanish in a thousand years |
| Nonoshiru kora yo | Those who condemn my verse |
| Kokoro mijikaki | Your minds are tiny[40] |

As many commentators have pointed out, such verse is revolutionary in its modernist intent; it throws down a clear challenge to the established tradition of Japanese poetry. That such a carefully constructed persona is emblematic of modernity is undeniable; that it arises out of the importation of like modes of thought, especially romantic thought, from Europe seems unproblematic. One can recognize in these poems "the primary romantic concerns with consciousness, with self-object relationships and with intensified experience"—a comment referring to European romanticism that can equally well be applied to Tekkan's verse.[41]

Japanese critics like Ōta Seikyū argue that much of the poetry in *Purple* reads like an adaptation or translation of Western verse. Ōta cites the following two *tanka* to illustrate his contention:

| | |
|---|---|
| Hana wa ki ni | The flowers are golden |
| Kusa wa midori ni | The grass is green |
| Futo mireba | Suddenly I see |
| Ware wa mashiroki | Myself enfolded |
| Tsubasa no naka in | In snow-white wings[42] |

And:

| | |
|---|---|
| Shiroki uma ni | God riding |
| Shirogane no fue | On a white horse |
| Toreru kami | Blowing a silver flute |
| Maboroshi naru yo | Is a dream |
| Niji usureyuku | A rainbow fading away[43] |

Tekkan himself argued against Western influence in the first of these *tanka,* claiming (a year or so after the poem was composed) that it represented a pictorial vision of an Eastern paradise.[44] However, the image of angelic wings has convinced most commentators that Tekkan was somewhat disingenuous in his comments and that the painterly quality of both verses originates in Western art or literature.

The critic Ueda Hiroshi finds the aesthetic heights reached by both these verses to be outstanding but reads the angelic vision as essentially a narcissistic, almost mystical apotheosis. The poet himself is a veritable god consorting with the angelic host.[45]

Another poem from *Purple* where the same troping reappears is the following verse:

| Hito futari | I saw |
|---|---|
| Masshiroki tsubasa | Two people |
| Ou to mishi | With snow-white wings |
| Yuri no sono u no | How I long for |
| Yume natsukashiki | The dream of the lily garden[46] |

The air of fantasy, of an ethereal longing, also stamps this poem as a complex mixture of the personal and the imported, with the angelic wings once again making an appearance. T. S. Eliot remarked of the poetry of A.G. Swinburne that "the object has ceased to exist, because the meaning is merely the hallucination of meaning, because language, uprooted, has adapted itself to an independent life of atmospheric nourishment."[47] Tekkan's verse does not go quite this far, but the same sense of subliminal, almost mystical eroticism does characterize various of his poems from *Purple,* and thus by drawing on many of the same sources that Swinburne drew upon, Tekkan has made the same journey as Swinburne, a journey to romance and the modern.

## The New Woman

Yosano Akiko in her first collection of poetry, *Tangled Hair,* published only three months or so after *Purple,* traveled even farther along this path than her husband-to-be, for while her verse is explicitly narcissistic, there is little of the self-conscious posturing of the romantic hero found in Tekkan's writing.[48] Akiko, like her mentor, drew heavily on the Western romantic tradition in constructing a new image of womanhood for Meiji Japan. By examining some samples of verse from *Tangled Hair* that display the same interest in biblical troping found in Tekkan, one can begin to formulate an aesthetic that can accommodate both.

Akiko wrote in 1912 that, as a child, she read the Bible and studied Christianity, but the use of Christian motifs in *Tangled Hair* appears, for the most part, to be a deliberate play on imported notions of religiosity.[49] Like Swinburne and other romantic poets whose work tended toward the decadent, Akiko wielded Western notions of the numinous as a symbol of the modern, at times adopting an attitude that could be taken as blasphemous. However, these poems stand cheek by jowl beside other verse that clearly is personal in its inspiration, as seen from the following two *tanka:*

| | |
|---|---|
| Fuchi no mizu ni | The Bible that |
| Nageshi seisho wo | I hurled into a deep pool |
| Mata mo hiroi | Once again I retrieve |
| Sora aogi naku | Staring up at the sky, weeping |
| Ware madoi no ko | I am a lost child[50] |

And:

| | |
|---|---|
| Seisho daku ko | I who embrace the Bible |
| Hito no mioya no | Bowing at the grave |
| Haka ni fushite | Of his parents |
| Miroku no na wo ba | In the evening called upon |
| Yūbe ni yobinu | The name of the bodhisattva Maitreya[51] |

Both these poems are included in "Hatachizuma" (A young wife of twenty), the last of the five chapters of *Tangled Hair,* which consists solely of verses written in the *tanka* genre, some 399 poems in all. This chapter, more than the previous four, is viewed by commentators as treating the life of Akiko and Tekkan after they had publicly declared their love for another. The first poem, therefore, could quite possibly be autobiographical, dealing with some crisis of faith in Akiko's life. The second poem cited, refers, according to the Akiko authority Itsumi Kumi, to a visit by Akiko and Tekkan to pay their respects at the grave of Tekkan's parents.[52] The reference to the bodhisattva Maitreya appears to originate in the fact that Tekkan's father was a Buddhist priest.

The following five verses are typical of many in *Tangled Hair* that could be deemed blasphemous, as they portray Tekkan as Akiko's god and revel in the sinful pleasure of adultery.

| | |
|---|---|
| Kami koko ni | Now her god |
| Chikara wo wabinu | Has lamented of his power |
| Toki beni no | The blind maiden |
| Nioi kyōgaru | Maddened by |
| Meshii no otome | The scent of liquid rouge[53] |

| Muro no kami ni | In our bedchamber |
| Mikata kaketsutsu | I covered my god's shoulder with |
| Hire fushinu | The kimono of burning carmine |
| Enji nareba no | I wore last night |
| Yoi no hito kasane | And collapsed at his feet[54] |

| Ma ni mukou | I kissed his five fingers |
| Tsurugi no tsuka wo | Too slender |
| Nigiru ni wa | To grasp |
| Hosoki itsutsu no | The hilt of the sword |
| Miyubi to suinu | Of Satan facing him[55] |

One recalls here the poem in *Purple* where Tekkan referred to himself as "a sword."

| Sono nasake | Do not direct |
| Kakemasu na kimi | Your love to me! |
| Tsumi no ko ga | Tell me you will watch |
| Kurui no hate wo | What becomes of this sinful child |
| Mimu to iitamae | In the extremes of her passion?[56] |

| Uta ni kike na | Ask of poetry |
| Tare no no hana ni | Who can deny the crimson |
| Akaki inamu | Of the flowers of the field? |
| Omomuki aru ka na | They have their own charm |
| Haru tsumi motsu ko | Sinful children of spring[57] |

This last poem is the second *tanka* in *Tangled Hair* and the first link in a chain of poems connecting the images of flowers and sin. The reference to the flowers of the field has reminded many commentators of Matthew 6:28–30: "Consider the lilies of the field, how they grow; they neither toil nor spin; yet I tell you, even Solomon in all his glory was not arrayed like one of these."

Isoda Kōichi has attempted to trace the history of this image as it filtered into Japanese verse in the Meiji era, to discover what the Japanese sources were for Akiko. He traces its lineage from poets of new-style verse like Shimazaki Tōson (1872–1943) and Susukida Kyūkin (1877–1945), who, I have

FIGURE 2. Yosano Akiko and her friend the poet Yamakawa Tomiko. Ca. 1900.
Courtesy of the Library of Modern Japanese Literature (Nihon Kindai Bungakukan)

argued elsewhere, had a decisive influence on Akiko's poetic diction, and he
also cites the novelist Tayama Katai's novel *Ya no hana* (The flowers of the
field), published in the same year as *Tangled Hair.*[58] Nevertheless, however
the influence was mediated, it clearly arises from Western sources. And the
mocking use of the "sinful" foregrounds Akiko's purpose—to create a dic-

tion that was fresh and new, in other words, modern: as far removed from the language of traditional poetic rhetoric as possible.

At times, Akiko's verse even appears to mock Tekkan's poetry, although such *tanka* can also be read as one part of a complex daisy chain of linked verse, where Tekkan and Akiko, and later Akiko's intimate friend and erstwhile rival for Tekkan's affections, Yamakawa Tomiko (1879–1909), weave an intricate tapestry of poetic exchange.[59] One example of a poem that appears to mirror directly Tekkan's opening verse in *Purple*—where he declares he is a "man of vitality of name"—is the following:

| | |
|---|---|
| Michi wo iwazu | I do not speak of the way |
| Ato wo omowazu | I do not think of the future |
| Na wo towazu | I do not inquire of my name |
| Koko ni koi kou | Here I love I love |
| Kimi to ware to miru | We stare at each other you and I[60] |

This poem, rather than focusing on the agonies of love, emphasizes the thrill, the risk, and the passion of love, and this type of verse, more than any other, distinguishes *Tangled Hair* as heralding a new kind of erotic rhetoric. The intricate metanomia created a narrative of love in the verses exchanged between Akiko and Tekkan (subsequently rewritten and reedited when they were published in the respective collections of the two poets) that became for their contemporaries the most striking aspect of these two collections. They also did more than any comparable work of the time to create a new, modern notion of romantic love.

## The Ideology of Romantic Love

Herman Bahr, in his celebrated series of studies on the modern (that commenced in 1890), defined modern literature as that which achieves "a synthesis of naturalism and romanticism."[61] Writing nearly seventy years later, Cyril Connolly in his 1965 book *The Modern Movement* claimed that modernism owed everything to Flaubert and Baudelaire.[62] One can see here an implicit link between a modern sensibility in art and what Camille Paglia calls "Late Romanticism": the evolution of romance into a conception of love that focuses on the illicit, on adultery.

Just as Flaubert wrote of the joys and sorrows of adulterous love in *Madame Bovary,* so in Japan the leading naturalist novelist Tayama Katai burst onto the literary scene with a famous novella called *Futon* (The quilt, 1907), which was an examination of illicit desire.[63] The naturalist impulse toward confession (as Dennis Washburn puts it) is an "assertion of the self against ethical or social conventions . . . an act of individuation . . . [that] disrupts authority, stasis and repetition."[64] Again, such a perspective links individuation with rebellion and, further, finds individuation arising from amorous desire. This kind of logic appears, however, to contradict the late-nineteenth-century veneration of marriage as the supreme expression of love, a veneration especially noticeable in Japanese journals of the day like *Jogaku zasshi* (The woman's magazine).[65]

Whether one agrees with Denis De Rougement's argument for European literature that romanticism exalts adultery as an almost mystical manifestation of unrequited longing and thus is manifested as the epitome of romantic love, one cannot deny the power of the ideal of conjugal love as a rallying cry for romance.[66] But, as the philosopher Irving Singer points out, even admitting the apotheosis of longing as an important element within romantic thought, the final consummation of such longing is invariably seen as "the attainment of a permanent and stable union."[67] Moreover, Singer notes that this yearning for the unattainable other is often "an attack on conventional or forced marriages that were still common in the nineteenth century."[68] Thus, adultery is preferred to a loveless marriage. Both longing, and consequently illicit desire, and the ideal of conjugal love are treated in the exchange of poetry between Tekkan and Akiko.

When one compares the Japanese discourse on love to the European, both similarities and differences emerge. Recently, Nakamaru Nobuaki has used the historian Edward Shorter's notion of a "romantic ideology"—derived from his study of the family in Europe—to argue that an analogous ideology was at work in fin-de-siècle Japan.[69] Nakamaru claims that this ideology was the basis of the naturalist novel and was instrumental in the formation of literary modernity in Japan.[70] Yet he also claims that illicit romance was an important part of this ideology.[71] Saeki Junko argued in 1996 that the Meiji notion of romantic love incorporated pre-Meiji concepts of eros, thus stressing the contradictory nature of romantic love.[72] Saeki elaborates on these observations in her 1998 book on love and eros in Meiji Japan, where she points to the vast gap separating male and female conceptions of love, and notes how complex and various such concepts were.[73]

Such confusion and uncertainty, typical of this era when Japan was undergoing rapid change, provided fertile ground for these daring new Western ideas relating to romantic love to flourish. Takumi Hideo claims that, despite Akiko's and Tekkan's notoriously poor knowledge of foreign languages, *Myōjō* held a preeminent role in introducing Western romanticism and modernism in general to Japan, as I have argued earlier.[74] He further observes that the best example of the adaptation of Western art and literature in Japanese literature at the time was the poetry of Yosano Akiko.[75] In this instance, he is thinking of the romantic narrative woven by Tekkan and Akiko.

There is no doubt that Tekkan was acutely aware of the revolutionary nature of the program for poetry reform that he advocated in the *Myōjō* journal. He was equally conscious of the importance of the rallying cry or, to borrow Shorter's term, the ideology of romantic love in this program. This is demonstrated vividly in two poems from *Purple:*

| Koi to iu mo | We have not yet exhausted |
|---|---|
| Imada tsukusazu | This thing called love |
| Hito to ware to | Myself and one other |
| Atarashiku shinu | Have made new |
| Hi no moto no uta | The poetry of Japan[76] |

And:

| Yo no sue ni | At the end of the world |
|---|---|
| Kakaru koi ari | Such a love as this |
| Uta mo ari | Such poetry as this |
| Tsuyoki mitari wo | Three strong poets were |
| Higashi ni uminu | Born in the east[77] |

This verse refers to all three poets: Tekkan, Akiko, and her rival in love and friend Yamakawa Tomiko.

There is an earlier, even more explicit linkage between romance and poetic revolution in the following *tanka* from Tekkan's collection *Tekkanshi,* published only a few months before *Purple.*

| Yo no uta wo | I sneered at |
|---|---|
| Azawaraishi wa | The poetry of our age |
| Kinō nari | That was yesterday |

| Ima wa koi sae | Now even romance itself |
| Kimi to waga te ni | You and I hold in our hands[78] |

Here Tekkan uses *"koi"* the older word for romance, but his point is obvious.

Love is painful and cruel; its uncertainties push the individual ego to extremes. This picture of a violent and tormented eros, and a tormented ego, is found in several poems by Tekkan and Akiko. First Tekkan from *Purple:*

| Akugarenu | I longed |
| Sozoro ni narinu | I was lost |
| Namida guminu | I wept |
| Utate nayamu ka | Must I suffer? |
| You ka kuruu ka | Shall I drown my sorrows? Go mad?[79] |

The following poem from *Purple* seems to revel in a perverse trope; as Itsumi implies, perhaps it celebrates Tekkan's consummation of his relationship with Akiko.

| Yo ni tatan | Oh, to be successful in the world |
| Hae yo chikara yo | Glory and power! |
| Kimi ni yorite | From you |
| Kyō waga etaru | Today I received |
| Utsukushiki muchi | A beautiful whip[80] |

Two other poems from *Purple* seem to refer to the same event, a flower-viewing party held on 5 November 1900:

| Akikaze ni | Shall I give you |
| Fusawashiki na wo | A name appropriate |
| Mairasemu | To the autumn breeze |
| "Sozorogokoro no | "You of a restless heart |
| Midaregami no kimi" | and tangled hair"[81] |

And:

| Ana samu to | How cold |
| Tada sarige naku | You said |

| Iisashite | So casually |
| Ware mo mizarishi | Not glancing at me |
| Midaregami no kimi | Your hair so tangled[82] |

Love can turn quickly from cold to hot. The following two poems from *Purple* Itsumi believes to have been written after Tekkan and Akiko had made love for the first time. Illicit desire and desire consummated contend with one another, as they do elsewhere in both poets' work:

| Obashima ni | The willow trails |
| Yanagi shizurete | Down the railing |
| Ame hososhi | Fine rain falling |
| Yoitaru hito to | She is intoxicated |
| Kyō no yama miru | Together we view the Kyoto mountain[83] |

And:

| Ware ni soite | Beside me |
| Beniume sakeru | On the Kyoto mountain |
| Kyō no yama ni | Red plum-flowers blossoming |
| Ashita ori[ta]tsu | A lovely goddess |
| Kami utsukushiki | Has descended this morning[84] |

Akiko's poetic response in *Tangled Hair* is the following *tanka*:

| Shiorido ari | A wicker gate |
| Beniume sakeri | Red plum-flowers blossom |
| Mizu yukeri | A tiny stream |
| Tatsu ko ware yori | Standing beside me |
| Emi utsukushiki | His smile lovelier than mine[85] |

A different figurative pattern arising most probably from the same event can be seen in the following *tanka* from *Purple:*

| Tabi no asa | On the morning of our trip |
| Hito no beni sasu | I took |
| Fude torite | Your rouge brush |

| You ko tokoshie | And wrote, "A woman intoxicated |
| Haru zo to kakinu | With love is forever young!"[86] |

Akiko's mixed response to the intertwining motifs of eros and its representation found in Tekkan's verse can be divined from the following two poems from *Tangled Hair:*

| Uta fude wo | His poem-brush that |
| Beni ni karitaru | I borrowed for my rouge |
| Saki itenu | Was frozen at the tip |
| Nishi no miyako no | So cold was the |
| Haru samuki asa | Spring morning in Kyoto[87] |

And:

| Haru samu no | In the spring cold |
| Futahi wo kyō no | For two days on the Kyoto mountain |
| Yamagomori | Hidden away |
| Ume ni fusawanu | Unlike the plum blossoms |
| Waga kami no midare | My hair all a-tangle[88] |

A more intimate portrait of the two days in Kyoto is provided by the following three *tanka,* anticipating perhaps the joy of conjugal love, which was soon to become a reality. First, Tekkan's poem from *Purple:*

| Furikaeri | I turned |
| Sate wa waga fude | And put |
| Soto okinu | My brush aside |
| Netaru ko okosu | My poem was not worth |
| Uta ni araji yo | Waking my beloved[89] |

Next, Akiko's two *tanka* from *Tangled Hair,*

| Midaregami wo | The morning in Kyoto |
| Kyō no Shimada ni | I changed my tangled hair |
| Kaeshi asa | To the Shimada style |
| Fushite imase no | I should say, "Don't rise" |
| Kimi yuriokosu | But shook you awake[90] |

and the following poem in its original form as expressed in a letter from Akiko to Tekkan dated 2 February 1901:

| Kimi saraba | With you alone |
| Awata no haru no | In the springtime at Awata |
| Futa yo zuma | I was your wife for two nights |
| Mata no yo made wa | Until we meet again in the world to come |
| Wasure itame | Forsake, forsake these memories[91] |

This was altered in the final version published in *Tangled Hair* to

| Kimi saraba | With you alone |
| Fuza no haru no | In the springtime of our tryst |
| Hito yozuma | I was your wife for one night |
| Mata no yo made wa | Until we meet again in the world to come |
| Wasure itame | Forsake, forsake this memory[92] |

After Akiko had moved to Tokyo to live with Tekkan, the tone changes once again, as seen in the following *tanka* from *Tangled Hair:*

| Futo sore yori | Quite by chance |
| Hana ni iro naki | A spring has come |
| Haru to narinu | When the color of my flower has faded |
| Madoi no kami | God of doubt |
| Madowashi no kami | God of confusion[93] |

Another *tanka* from *Tangled Hair* is written in a similar key, although it precedes the move to Tokyo.

| Ushiya ware | How bitter! |
| Samuru sadame no | I pray that I may never wake |
| Yume wo towa ni | From my dream |
| Same na to inoru | That is destined to end |
| Hito no ko ni ochinu | Yet I return to myself[94] |

There is a similar verse in *Purple,* although opinion is divided over whether it refers to Akiko or to Tekkan's first love, Tomiko:[95]

| Waga koi wo | Asked about |
| Hito ni towarete | My love |
| Kokoro ni mo | I gazed upward |
| Aranu kanata no | At the distant star |
| Hoshi aogi mishi | No longer in my heart[96] |

This poem resembles the following poem from *Purple,* which expresses an even stronger sense of disillusionment with the "star" ideal, a complex metonym for a whole host of related ideas arising from the many-layered fantasia of eros and its consequences, constructed jointly by Tekkan and Akiko.

| Waga te toru wa | The one who takes my hand |
| Kuroki katsugi no | Robed in black |
| Shi no mikami | Is Death |
| Tanomishi hoshi mo | The star on whom I depended |
| Chiisaku narinu | Has grown small[97] |

## Modernist Heirs

The question may be asked why this remarkably early manifestation of modernist writing is generally not linked by Japanese critics and literary historians to the articulation of modernist motifs by avant-garde authors a decade or so later. The answer appears to lie in two factors. First, of all the Japanese literary genres, *tanka* was the most conservative. Even when the reforms began by Tekkan and Akiko had been taken up by later poets like Masaoka Shiki (1867–1902), Ishikawa Takuboku, and a mass of avant-garde *tanka* poets, rarely was the diction of traditional *waka* (the old name for *tanka*) challenged.[98] It took nearly a half a century of literary experimentation before *tanka* poets could write freely using colloquial rather than classical grammar. And even then many traditionalists sought refuge in archaic diction.

The debate continues to the present day. The fact that *waka* is the oldest of traditional Japanese literary genres, with a history going back to the seventh century and before, represents a huge barrier to radical change. The many millions of fine *waka* written throughout Japanese history create such a large variety of possible models that originality is difficult to create. Also, that *waka* was considered the mainstream of Japanese literature, its status institutionalized by imperial authority and its prestige ensured through the several imperial anthologies of poetry, adds even more weight to an already formidable historical burden.

The second factor lies in the introduction of two new genres of writing in the Meiji era that, in the beginning at least, were essentially translations from Western literature. These two genres were the novel and free-style colloquial verse, or *shi*. The fact that both genres had (in essence) little precedent in Japanese literary tradition meant that both were free to innovate and experiment. Indeed, innovation was the foundation of any original novel or free-style poem written by Meiji authors. This point is not made to gainsay the long and complex process of adaptation that accompanied the introduction of these new modes of writing. I have argued elsewhere that Akiko's verse, and this argument can be extended to Tekkan's verse too, played a pivotal role in demonstrating how new ideas from Western literature could be adapted to existing literary genres.[99]

The new genres had no real enemies, no defenders of existing types of writing or traditional practitioners to contend with in their development. In contrast, *tanka* reforms, in Tekkan and Akiko's time as for later generations of *tanka* poets, had a powerful entrenched establishment to compete with. Opponents of the Myōjō style were legion, and attacks on Tekkan and Akiko's innovations began very early. To a large degree, both poets themselves retreated from the radical experiments in diction and theme that they had indulged in during the period from 1898 to 1905. Nonetheless, their legacy lives on, as much among free verse poets as among *tanka* poets.

Later free verse poets, not only those of the symbolist persuasion, learned their trade while they belonged to the Myōjō circle.[100] Tekkan's revolutionary vision encompassed all genres of poetry, so perhaps it is not unexpected that this vision should be fulfilled in the works of later generations of poets rather than those of the pioneers themselves. However, the evidence for the proposition that Tekkan and Akiko were pioneers of various aspects of what was later to be known as modernism is undeniable.

# Chapter 2
# The Expression of Despair
## Arishima Takeo's Modernist Poetry

*Windstille, sternlose Nacht.*

—Georg Trakl, "Sommer"

*We all live in the past now. And so the children*
*must still hang on somewhere, though no one is quite sure where or how many*
*or what paths there are to be taken in darkness. Only the fools, the severed*
*heads, know.*

—John Ashbery, *Flow Chart*

 Nietzsche links the love of life and death thus: "Love of life should make us wish for an altogether different death, a free and conscious death, one which is no accident and holds no surprises."[1] Maurice Blanchot uses this quotation in his 1955 book *L'éspace littéraire* to argue that death creates possibilities. The possibilities that Blanchot enumerates are complex and contradictory. One possibility suggests itself as pertaining to the novelist, critic, and poet Arishima Takeo's (1878–1923) tragic death. Arishima hanged himself in a double suicide with his lover, the well-known journalist Hatano Akiko (1894–1923) in June 1923, an event that shocked 1920s Japan. Arishima was a widower when his relationship with her began, while Akiko was married to a much older businessman called Hatano Harufusa who was a notorious womanizer.[2]

## The Space of Death

Another of these possibilities pertains to the death or at least the limits of language. In Blanchot's words: "He who kills himself is the great affirmer of the *present.* I want to kill myself in an 'absolute' instant, the only one which will not pass and will not be surpassed. Death, if it is arrived at the time we choose, would be an apotheosis of the *instant;* the instant in it would be that very flash of brilliance which mystics speak of. . . . And surely because of this, suicide retains the power of an exceptional affirmation."[3]

The notion of the "apotheosis of the *instant*," the "flash of brilliance which mystics speak of," strikes several chords for a reader of Arishima. The second line of Arishima's powerful yet puzzling poem "Shi wo" (Death!) reads: "Death the incandescence of life."[4] The notion of "incandescence" *(shōten)* is a burning point that somehow both denotes and even centers both life and death. This terrifying ambivalence controls every line of this poem, and it is not the only poem in Arishima's sole collection of verse, *Hitomi naki me* (Eyeless eyes, 1923), to display simultaneously both attention to and revulsion for death.

Arishima's poetry collection and its modernist influences form the subject of this chapter, but I want to approach that subject by a circuitous route. Several detours from the poetry itself will be necessary to understand what Arishima might have been trying to express in the final few months of his life.

Arishima seemed to find the possibility of happiness in his death. In the letter he left to his mother, he wrote: "I approach my fate with my heart full of joy."[5] In the letter he left to his brothers and sisters, Arishima wrote: "Since falling in love with Akiko, for the first time since my birth, I have come across true life."[6] And, finally, in his farewell letter to Morimoto Kōkichi (1877–1950), his closest friend while at college and the man with whom he once contemplated suicide, he wrote: "We approach death at the peak of our love."[7] Contradiction gives birth to paradox as "joy" and "fate" (here meaning death) are juxtaposed, "true life" means death, and finally love at its peak is equated with death. Blanchot's remarks about death as an "apotheosis of the *instant*," an "exceptional affirmation," could not be referring to a historical event as tragic as the suicide of Arishima and his lover Hatano Akiko. And yet, among the possibilities he lists, this kind of occurrence seems to be the most apposite.

Perhaps one reason even to consider the notion of congruence is that Blanchot's ideas are expressed in words, and the conception of Arishima's suicide, the interpretation he himself placed on it, is only knowable in the words quoted earlier. In other words, it is a literary congruence rather than a real-life congruence, as Arishima's and Akiko's death is beyond words, indeed beyond literature. However, the letters Arishima left behind are not an event outside one's capacity to grasp; rather they form part of a literary pattern described in letters, novels, poems, and plays that make up an expression of despair, in this case, an especially perverse despair.

In Arishima's last work, the strange dialogue-novel *Dokudansha no kaiwa*

(The conversation of a dogmatist), written only a month or so before his suicide, he put into the mouth of the character "A" the following words: "A beautiful power like a magnet gathering all its energy into one spot, come quickly and save me!"[8] This story ends with these words and, as I will describe later, critics as diverse as Akita Ujaku (1883–1962) and Endō Yū have singled this line out as pregnant with possibilities, hinting at something beyond the text.[9]

The juxtaposition of love and death, or at least of death and passion, occurs more than once in *Eyeless Eyes* and also in the *tanka* poetry Arishima wrote in his last days. In the poem "Death" directly following the use of the word "incandescence" is the line "Death which sought me out in the midst of youth" and later "Death which compensates beyond my sight for all my humiliation." These two lines imply that the narrator has a deep sympathy with death or perhaps that death has a deep sympathy with the narrator; in any case, a deep bond, a passionate bond, seems to be in evidence.

If this free verse poem can be read as a projection of some aspect of the author, while not inferring any direct identification of author with narrator (perhaps the critic Wayne Booth's notion of "implied author" is useful here), then the examples of verse written by Arishima in the *tanka* genre of traditional poetry seem to assume an even more direct expression of feeling.[10] The expression of feeling and feeling itself are two different things: the former is a clear construction or projection; the latter is a subjective state that cannot be perfectly communicated. Nevertheless, some *tanka* seem to come tantalizingly close to breaching the barrier between the sensibility suggested by words and the sensibility created within ourselves as a result of these words.

The following two *tanka* contain the most affecting possibilities concerning the terrible cost of love and the consequences to life itself exacted by the burden of love. The first one is also the first of a group of poems captioned "These nine poems were found in Arishima's study after his death" published in the Arishima memorial issue of *Izumi* (Fountain), the journal he founded to publish his own writings. It introduces the theme of fire:

| | |
|---|---|
| Yo no tsune no | If my love |
| Waga koi naraba | Were ordinary, and of this world |
| Kaku bakari | Never would I burn |

| Ozomashiki hi ni | In so terrible |
| Mi baya yaku beki | A fire[11] |

In the next poem, the seventh in that group, the fire becomes cloud as the road ahead for the anguished lover is obscured, but his love is no less strong.

| Kumo ni iru | Like an osprey |
| Misago no gotoki | Flying into a cloud |
| Hito suji no | Because I know |
| Koi to shi shireba | Love's straight road |
| Kokoro wa tarinu | My heart is full[12] |

## Nihilistic Fire

The dramatist and critic Akita Ujaku in his memorial to Arishima "Buronzu no te—Arishima Takeo kun Tsuitō shuki kara" (The bronze hand—from Arishima's Notes of Lamentation), published in the magazine *Josei kaizō* in August 1923 soon after Arishima's death, quotes the line from *The Conversation of a Dogmatist* cited earlier, asking, "What is the beautiful power that he writes of?"[13] Akita also notes that another poem from *Eyeless Eyes* possesses an "astonishing power."[14] This poem—"Sekitan no kakera" (A lump of coal)—Akita sees as representing a "new fire" shining out of the darkness cast by the despair he finds in the other poems in the collection. The poem reads as follows:

### A Lump of Coal

A lump of coal unearthed from the Arctic Ocean,
Without flinching from the eternal cold, holding fire.
Black, holding fire.
Supple white hands play with it,
Amethyst eyes wet with spring stroke it.
Abstain from mischief.

Don't put your burning red lips too close to coldness and blackness,
Don't press your cheeks filled with temptation sideways against the
    roughened surface,
Abstain from mischief.

Coal is fire.

Fire is destruction.

Abstain from mischief![15]

    (7 APRIL)

The fire in this poem is held in check, yet the potential, the possible dangers, is ever-present throughout the three stanzas. Not merely does fire have the potential to burn, but in this poem it is plainly put that it has the potential to destroy. It is, as Akita Ujaku remarks, a "new fire," but it contains within itself the incandescence of death. The reading outlined above works from simple analogy and is quite transparent, but more interesting perhaps is the seductive allure of "coldness and blackness" *(tsumetasa to kurosa)*. Coal could stand for many things: for an illicit passion, like that of Arishima and his married paramour Akiko; for death itself, the "absolute instant," as Blanchot puts it; or it could not so much stand for something as imply something more than mere symbol: it could imply matter, the hard, cold material reality that exists outside language. I will return to this notion later.

The nihilism that Akita finds to be the chief feature of *Eyeless Eyes* is also present in abundance in this poem. Numerous scholars have found ample evidence of a dark despair, in his letters especially, during the last few years of Arishima's life. Egashira Tasuke, for example, examining Arishima's last works, cites letter after letter where Arishima pours out his anguish. Egashira also cites the three *tanka* that Arishima sent his friend Asai Mitsui (1897–1969) in September 1920 as illustrative of his mood.[16]

The first of these three poems could not be described as "nihilistic," but even as a conventional expression of sadness, it is quite melancholy.

| Umayaji no | The flowers on the grasses |
|---|---|
| Kaya no nokiba no | On the eaves |
| Kusa no hana | Of the post road |
| Aki sarikureba | When autumn deepens |
| Shiore yuku ka mo | They will wither[17] |

The withering here hints at a certain austere beauty, the beauty of the changing seasons, the beauty of death. However, the last of the three poems implies a different kind of death altogether.

| Ono ga tsumu | Among the |
|---|---|
| Mashiroki ito no | Pure white threads |
| Naka ni shite | Woven by the silkworm |
| Ko no goto ni mo | Like the silkworm itself |
| Ware wa shinamashi | I too wish to die[18] |

Here the death that the narrator desires is the silent death of absolute safety. A pristine, virginal cocoon surrounds the narrator; death is an absence, an absence of love, but also an absence of fire. The infantile regression—the return to the womb—implicit in the central trope of the poem can, even if only tenuously, be linked to the absolute annihilation of self intrinsic to the notion of nihilism.

Three or so years later, in *Eyeless Eyes,* Arishima, or, rather, an implied Arishima, contemplated another beautiful object—the bronze hand given to him by the poet Takamura Kōtarō (1883–1956)—and found not only a kind of austere, stark beauty but also the absolute silence of nihilism. Both in terms of a portrayal of a kind of beauty and of death as absence, affinities emerge between the earlier *tanka* and the later poem.

### Hand

(Gazing upon the bronze of the left hand sculpted by Takamura Kōtarō)
Solitary, lonely mystery . . .
a hand . . . a single hand . . .
Gazing upon it, the hand is strangely set free from flesh, spirit.
The majesty and falsity of existence—God?—Nothing?
Gazing upon it,
All things leave hands and vanish,
In the infinity of space,
There is only a single hand left.
Look at your left hand!
Now, in the light by which you read this, your own left hand, gaze upon it!
The lonely crowd of five fingers,
What are they thinking?
What do they do?
What is there to point at . . . What is there to grasp? . . .
. . . . . . . . . . . . . . . . . . . . . . . . . . . . . . . . . . . . . . .
The hand is struggling unto silence.[19]

    (9 MARCH)

The third and fourth lines describe a disembodied hand—which is exactly the state of the bronze bust. But, this disembodied state by its very nature—whether imagined as disembodied as a poetic fancy or contemplated physically as a bronze object—points to an absence. By being disembodied, the hand is robbed of all meaning, "strangely set free from flesh, spirit." Pictured here is a falsity and meaninglessness, which, in the very next line, the narrator applies to existence itself and finally to God *(kami)*. The last interrogative of this line is the most powerful interrogative of all—*mu* (nothing?). Whether Buddhist or Christian in origin, the profound doubt enacted here imitates the state of *nihil,* the very essence of nothingness. The last line returns to the cocoon of Arishima's *tanka;* the hand is struggling toward "silence" *(chinmoku):* the silence of the womb? Or the silence of a total absence?

## Absences

Arishima's characterization of existence in his one-line poem "Jinsei" (Life)—where "life" appears close to "existence" in meaning—is equally nihilistic; merely an idle phantom *(namaketa gen'ei).* The poem reads:

Life

The idle phantom that can be seen among the wanderings of biological life[20]
(10 MARCH)

Arishima's "idle phantom" bears only a slight resemblance to the distinguished modernist poet Nishiwaki Junzaburō's (1894–1982) later "phantom man" *(gen'ei no hito).* This image appears frequently in Nishiwaki's 1947 collection *Tabibito kaerazu* (No traveler returns), but if there is a resemblance, it may be in the ephemeral nature of both phantoms.[21] If Nishiwaki's phantom has ties with Buddhist metaphysics, then Arishima's phantom (which may also have Buddhist links) is closer to the aesthetics of extinction of the self, possibly inspired by his reading of Schopenhauer or Nietzsche.[22]

One also recalls here the modernist aesthetic of the father of modern Japanese poetry, Hagiwara Sakutarō (1886–1942), set out in the celebrated preface to his first collection, *Tsuki ni hoeru* (Howling at the moon, 1917): "No matter what the circumstance, when people attempt to express their emotions perfectly, they find that this is no easy matter. In this situation, words are of no use whatever. . . . Poetry explains what cannot be explained in words. Poetry is language beyond language *(kotoba ijō no kotoba)*."[23] Hagiwara mistrusted words and, instead, sought deep structures of meaning in the musical qualities of language, another characteristic response to the modernist dilemma that focused on the fact that the building blocks of meaning are themselves composed of words, leading to a distrust of language itself, and thence to an engagement with nonmeaning or nothingness. In the poem above, Arishima discerns this dilemma in the essence of existence itself.

From *Eyeless Eyes* the poem "Densha no me ga mita" (What the train's eye saw) also points, as does the last line of "Hand," to silence and emptiness. The poem reads:

**What the Train's Eye Saw**

The eye of the train flickering down the railway embankment,
An eddying of people below the embankment that the eye sees,
A heat haze appearing and disappearing,
Cigar smoke tossed by the breeze,
Slipping sideways vanishing.
Nothing,
Don't people want to live happily?
That prayer slips sideways vanishes . . . vanishes flickering.[24]

    (10 MARCH)

The prayer for humans to be happy vanishes. This last line is echoed in the last line of "Omoi" (Thoughts), where the thoughts generated by books, perhaps an allusion to learning or even civilization, "scatter in disarray." The full poem reads:

**Thoughts**

Falling from a book that contains beautiful pictures
Two missing pages swept away by a sudden gust of wind.
One high,
One low.
Exchanging glances,

Losing sight of each other
Once more exchanging far-off glances,
They scatter in disarray.[25]
    (2 APRIL)

Nevertheless, the nihilism, the absence, the emptiness depicted in these poems is primarily aesthetic. The absence occurs within the context of the contemplation of a beautiful bronze or of a book with lovely pictures. The same complex contradiction that Blanchot identifies as a distinguishing feature of the self-representation, the artistic representation of death, is as much, therefore, a part of these poems as that last brilliantly contradictory and enigmatic line from "Death" where death is characterized as "that enigmatic life!"

The nihilism that Akita finds in *Eyeless Eyes* is not simple despair or an unalloyed destructive urge. It is more positive than that, as absence implies presence but an open presence, a future presence, a presence undefined at present. This undefined presence may be a gesture toward the spiritual—whether conceived in Buddhist or Christian terms—or it could be something much simpler: a hope that the process of writing itself may suggest or actualize a solution to the emptiness depicted in these poems.

## Modernist Expression

Here I turn to the notion of expression in an attempt to identify the aesthetic object of Arishima's journey to an unknown absence. The focus on aesthetics rather than spirituality is justified by the emphasis that Arishima himself placed on aesthetic and literary questions, as demonstrated in his writings during these last years, quite apart from his own loss of faith in Christianity, expressed most cogently in the autobiographical memoir contained in his *"Ribingusuton den no Jo"* (Preface to *The Life of Livingstone,* 1919).[26]

Arishima had clearly signaled his interest in avant-garde art in his major philosophical treatise *Oshiminaku ai wa ubau* (Love, the generous plunderer), published in June 1920. In chapter 21 of this long, ambitious work, Arishima applied his notion of "love" to art, arguing that poetry occupied a higher place than prose in the hierarchy of art. He also expressed his frustration at his own "lack of sensitivity" and noted that if he had been more sensitive, he might have "run with poetry."[27] He declared his preference for futurism *(mirai-ha)* in the world of art, believing that it would come to dominate his time.[28]

By January 1922 in his essay "Geijutsu ni tsuite omou koto" (Thinking about art), Arishima had shifted to expressionism *(hyōgenshugi),* which he felt would form the basis of world art.[29] After expressionism, an entirely new form of art would appear: the yet-to-be-born art of the proletariat *(daiyonkaikyū).* Virtually at the same time, in his interview-article "Daiyonkaikyū no geijutsu" (The art of the proletariat), he reiterated his personal dilemma of being trapped as a bourgeois in the doomed paradigm of bourgeois art, although, he declared, he would be able to find within his instincts, a "common chord" between himself and the proletariat.[30] However, this hope had evaporated a year later, when Arishima wrote in "Bunka no matsuro" (The end of art): "I realize now that it is pointless to inherit the culture of the common people to whom I have come to belong." He followed this declaration of defeat by remarking: "My life must collapse."[31]

Three months later, in April 1923, in "Shi e no itsudatsu" (A new start with poetry), Arishima focused on artistic expression, perhaps the key issue for him in his role as a writer, given that his failure to write creatively—his writer's block—which had begun in 1920, was continuing. Using the analogy of the dilemma of the lover trying to express his love, Arishima wrote: "Love is the incandescence of life, and death is its destruction. What manner of contradiction is this!"[32] This linking of love and death becomes even more explicit in the next sentence: "But among all the steps by which people seek out their existence; while negating everything, only death can just manage to approach the insatiable passion of lovers."[33] Here Arishima explores the boundaries of the absolute of death that negates all and the absolute of passion that does the same. And yet something remains, something is still unsatisfied.

This paradox of absence and presence has been encountered before as the paradox of the notion of *nihil,* or self-annihilation, that is the major theme of *Eyeless Eyes.* In this essay, the paradox is placed directly at the heart of love, the same love that Arishima apotheosized in *Love, the Generous Plunderer.* Most interesting of all is that in "A New Start with Poetry" Arishima examines this paradox within the context of artistic expression.

It is as if Arishima the essayist, the poet, and the man has constructed an artificial space—the space of literature, or, more precisely, the theoretical space of expression—in which the crises engulfing him in every aspect of his life can be reduced to a single puzzle, although an immensely complex one.[34] In other words, the issue of his adulterous relationship with Hatano Akiko, his continuing writer's block, and his despair over the political path down which Japan was being led have been reduced metaphorically or symbolically to the notion of expression, which deals with the creation of writing out of nothing but the author's imagination, itself a metaphor for birth, the birth of new ideas and possibilities.

The last line of "Death" is the perfect embodiment of this dilemma, "Ah, you tread down life without mercy, this enigmatic life." The second line of the poem, probably written a matter of weeks before "A New Start with Poetry," is a restatement in verse of the contradiction expressed in the prose: "Death the incandescence of life."

The expression of the absolute, the paradox of love and death: where do these ideas arise? Why does Arishima focus so sharply on poetry? What is the relation of futurism and expressionism to these notions? The answers to these questions do not lie in Arishima's thought alone, for they are ideas that were taken up by many artists, poets, and thinkers, especially those belonging to the artistic avant-garde.

## Futurism and Anarchism

Chiba Sen'ichi has documented the history of the futurist movement in Japan in meticulous detail.[35] The original futurist impulse ignited in Paris by F. T. Marinetti in 1909 by 1913 had given birth to a remarkable work of poetry, a verbal-visual collage by Blaise Cendrars and Sonia Delaunay called *La prose du transsiberien et de la petite Jehanne de France,* which celebrates, in part, the Russo-Japanese war.[36] But, as Chiba notes, the Parisian origins of this new artistic movement, which spread like wildfire all over Europe, created no barrier to its export to Japan.

At the same time introductions to futurism were published in Japanese in 1909 and 1913 by the novelist Mori Ōgai and the artist Kimura Shōhachi (1893–1958), respectively. The poet Yosano Hiroshi (by this time he had abandoned the pen name Tekkan) returned to Japan in 1913 after three years in Europe, principally in France. He had absorbed the new avant-garde art and literature exploding like anarchist bombs all over the European continent and had met in person many of the leading members of the avant-garde, including the poet Apollinaire.[37] In 1914, Hiroshi published translations of many of the leading French and Italian futurist poets in his translation volume *Rira no hana* (Lilac flowers).

According to Yasukawa Sadao, Arishima and Yosano Akiko first became acquainted during 1915 and 1916, probably through Arishima's younger brother, the painter and novelist Ikuma (1882–1974).[38] Even if Arishima did not know Hiroshi personally from his acquaintance with his wife, it is likely that he would have heard of or glanced at *Lilac Flowers*.[39] By 1921, Arishima was receiving so many literary journals in the mail that he could hardly read them, as he noted in his preface to Yamamura Bochō's (1884–1924) poetry collection *Kozue no su* (A nest of twigs), where, incidentally, Arishima remarked: "I don't really understand . . . poetic form."[40] Apart from his access to these publications, it is probable that Arishima had heard of the futurists and indeed met them, as well as other avant-garde artists, through Ikuma's intimacy with the leading members of these movements.

Chiba has also documented Ikuma's involvement with the avant-garde. In April 1915, Ikuma translated a chapter from an Italian work on futurism for the art magazine *Bijutsu shinpō*. This article apparently inspired the leading avant-garde artist of the time, Kanbara Tai (1898–1997), to take up the futurist banner.[41] Sasaki Yasuaki has explored Arishima's links with the anarchists, especially with the working-class activist Yoshida Hajime (1892–1966) and the celebrated terrorist poet Nakahama Tetsu (1897–1926), a member of the infamous "Guillotine" terror group (Girochinsha).

Before examining this connection in a little more detail, it is important to note that Arishima's own interest in anarchism as an intellectual doctrine dated from as early as 1907, if not well before.[42] In that year Arishima visited London, where he met Prince Peter Alexeyevich Kropotkin (1842–1921), the famous anarchist and social reformer, whose political ideas already held some attraction for him. Evidence exists that Arishima's hidden links with the Japanese anarchists began to be forged from about this time.[43]

The association between anarchist ideals and art was made in Japan as early as 1910 by Arishima's friend Takamura Kōtarō in his article "Midori no taiyō" (A green sun), which appeared in the April issue of the journal *Subaru*. Takamura noted: "[Japanese anarchism] is not the anarchism of the anarchists."[44] Later, contrasting his own anarchistic tendencies as an artist (he wrote earlier: "I seek absolute freedom in the world of art") with the famous Western-style painter Kuroda Kiyoteru (1866–1924), he noted, "I tend toward anarchism, but [Kuroda] is a monarchist."[45] As I will show, in some ways, Takamura's and Arishima's views were similar.

Yoshida Hajime borrowed funds from Arishima to attend the 1922 Comintern meeting in Moscow, where he had an encounter with Lenin. Nakahama Tetsu, who probably met Arishima only once, was so inspired by him that he wrote a number of poems that eulogized Arishima with lines like "Our respected friend Arishima Takeo/Died in battle on the front line of romantic love."[46] Nakahama's apparent lack of poetic talent was more than compensated for by his revolutionary ardor, which resulted in a plan to assassinate the Prince of Wales during his trip to Japan in 1922. Such activities eventually led to his execution in 1926.[47]

As Sasaki Yasuaki demonstrates, artists like Kanbara Tai, who had anarchist connections, were deeply involved with radical political movements because of the radical nature of their art.[48] Echoing Takamura Kōtarō, Kanbara Tai himself declared in his 1920 manifesto that "art is absolute freedom."[49] The prominent futurist poet Hirato Renkichi (1893–1922) in May 1922, quoting B. Diebold, declared: "Thus Expressionism is one specific possibility of art: a specific crisis—the underground that gives birth to a specific art. . . . The expressionists . . . through their indwelling spirit gave body to real existence."[50] This definition and these words echo Arishima's own aesthetic dilemma as revealed in "A New Start with Poetry."

The art and poetry of the avant-garde—whether the futurists, the expressionists, the dadaists (who were often the same people)—was revolutionary in intent, linked to proletarian political movements. Could dada, the most inherently destructive wing of the avant-garde, have been the new art that Arishima prophesied would emerge from the proletariat? As Tsuji Jun (1884–1944), the dadaist poet, wrote in June 1922, "Naturally dada is fermenting widely among the proletariat, but it is important to note that the mode of expression employed by all the proletarian poets is close to dada."[51]

Scholars of modernist verse like Kikuchi Yasuo and Komata Yūsuke quote poem after poem by the avant-garde that embody much of the same complex confusion, the same obsession with death, the same aesthetic urge to test the absolute, the *nihil,* that grips *Eyeless Eyes,*[52] with lines like "With hard, cruel nerves/Amid the unique struggle between the will and the flesh/I walk exhausted" from Kanbara Tai's 1917 poem "Hirō" (Fatigue),[53] or Hirato Renkichi's "Bird takes flight/Heart and shape both/Dark" from his 1921 poem "Hichō" (Soaring bird).[54] This latter poem in its visual surface embodies the desire for the concrete, the material, that often manifests itself in avant-garde poetry, even to the extent of collage-style illustrations, numbers, technical diagrams, and other paraphernalia crowding the page.

## Poetic Language—the Modernist Lyric

The same desire for the concrete, the real, can be glimpsed in "A Lump of Coal." The lump of coal is an irruption of the real into the world of poetic language: it is more than mere symbol; here Arishima is toying with the notion of anti-art. The notion of anti-art, art or poetry that is real, as real as gunpowder or mutilation as opposed to the unreal rhetorical art of poetic language, hemmed in by convention and history, is fundamental to the modernist revolution ushered in by the fin-de-siècle avant-garde. The dilemma of how to express the reality of life using the most unreal and artificial of constructions—poetic language—came under intense scrutiny at this time.

The usefulness of this aesthetic dilemma as an instrument through which Arishima could explore the several dilemmas besetting him, artistic and nonartistic alike, is apparent. It was linked directly to his writer's block, as the issue of expression provided a means by which he could experiment with different genres and forms in an attempt to rediscover his creative powers. Further, it engaged the larger problem of his role in society: was he to continue to pursue his political activism primarily as a writer or should he take a more active part in social debate? This partially explains why Arishima was so obsessed with the problem of expression in the last literary outpourings before his suicide.

"Kyōfu no mensha" (The veil of fear), the poem directly preceding "A Lump of Coal" in *Eyeless Eyes,* is a clear example of a modernist lyric, the language quite self-conscious in its mixing of metaphors:

**The Veil of Fear**

A handful of courage,
A pinch of desperation,
When they strip off their veils,
Shock
Panic
Intoxicating
Nothing—
Just leap and
A dazzling embrace

. . . . . . . . . . . . . . . .

Ah

Medusa smiles
Like Venus.[55]
   (11 March)

The modernist technique is evident in the first two lines. This is not as obvious in English as it is in Japanese, because the lines *"mō hitonigiri no yūki / hitotsumami no sutebachi"* are quite incongruous in the original. The two concrete expressions relating to amount or degree do not "fit" in Japanese with the abstract nouns they qualify. For the sake of poetic effect, I have used two English idiomatic expressions to translate these opening lines. The second line I have translated almost literally, which indicates that Arishima may have been thinking of the English idiom when he penned the unidiomatic (in Japanese) original. Thus the poem begins with two rather strange metaphors.

The rest of the poem is full of like paradoxes: "Intoxicating" followed by "Nothing." The "Nothing" is, in turn, followed by "A dazzling embrace." And, finally, Medusa, the hideous destructive gorgon, is likened to Venus, the unutterably beautiful goddess of love. The positioning of the poem on the page (if the Chikuma edition of Arishima's collected works reproduces the original exactly) with the occasional dash, a line of dots, and single-word lines left hanging in isolation also strongly suggests the avant-garde "look."

The paradoxes contained in this poem pale beside the striking typography of the poetry contained in an ultramodern journal like *Aka to kuro* (Red and black), which is typical of the avant-garde wave that was to sweep over the contemporary poetry scene. Nonetheless, the resemblance remains. Nakamura Miharu has noted that Arishima assisted *Red and Black* financially and has also outlined the links between Arishima and the dadaist poet Takahashi Shinkichi (1901–1987).[56] Critics have often remarked on the dadaist-like technique in style that Arishima employed in his February 1923 story *Aru seryō kanja* (The charity patient), which, like much of Arishima's fiction during these last years, took as its subject the anarchists to whom Arishima was secretly giving financial support.[57] There is no doubt that Arishima was quite consciously trying to develop a new style that owed much to futurist and expressionist modes of expression.

However, the paradoxes apparent in "The Veil of Fear" are more than mere linguistic experimentation, for the underlying theme is transparently one of a contradictory despair. Once "courage" has been stripped away, like the veil over the face of Medusa, "Nothing" remains. Leaping into the unknown, a leap of passion perhaps, leads only to deception: in this case, the deception of the Medusa posing as Venus: evil masquerading as love. Another reading stresses the note of desperation. If the unnamed subjects of the poem do not leap into the unknown, then they will know nothing. The "dark shadow" of Arishima's last novel *The Conversation of a Dogmatist* warns the character "A" that "an emptiness—a frightening emptiness like death has begun to eat away at your life."[58] This may be the fate awaiting those who do not leap into the unknown futures that passions like love promise.

A most puzzling and at the same time extraordinarily powerful poem is the title poem "Hitomi naki me" (Eyeless eyes). This is the poem that Akita Ujaku described as being full of the "nihilistic ennui of life."[59] An eye without a pupil is an eye that cannot see. This is the contradiction contained at the heart of the poem. "Eyeless Eyes" has great power as a metaphor for anguish, for a self that is totally locked into itself, not in a safe cocoon but, instead, a completely empty sign. The poem uses Buddhist terminology, a little reminiscent of the distinguished poet Yamamoto Tarō's (1925–1988) use of the line "[Sin] resides in the eye and consumes the eye" as part of his celebrated but frightening pastiche of the famous medieval depiction of hell *Ōjōyōshū* (The essentials of salvation)—written in 985 by the priest Genshin (942–1017)—in his book-length 1975 verse collection *Yurishiizu* (Ulysses).[60] Just how this terminology creates the poem can be seen from the following translation:

**Eyeless Eyes (Prologue)**

Let us say it clearly
A thousand great worlds are eyes without pupils.
Open wide, unblinking eyes.
From the beginning to the end of the world,
Like the skin of a squid transparent beneath a glass dish only the white
   of the eye,
Still, unmoving frozen.


One tiny pitiful pupil,
Like a burning blurring meteorite,

Sucked into the grey surface of eyes without pupils.
Visibly
There, whether or not
. . . there no longer.
The pitiful, tiny pupil,
Oh pitiful, tiny pupil,
The tiny pupil smoldering darkly in its delusional self,
Pitiful, tiny pupil . . .
How alone . . . . . . at least cry out? Give voice. Pupil.[61]
    (11 MARCH)

The opening three lines of "Eyeless Eyes" seem to convey a sense of a great emptiness. The image that ends the first stanza is an image of death, a grotesque and repulsive representation. Is Arishima attempting to suggest a Buddhist hell? The strong pictorial quality of this first stanza may seem to point in this direction. The distorted, grotesque quality of the imagery is also, however, a common futurist technique. The second stanza concentrates on a "pitiful, tiny pupil" and a darkly smoldering pupil. Self seems to be not merely locked within, but a delusion. This is not an image of death; rather, it is an image of utter helplessness. The eye is in a state of complete unknowing, absorbed into the "eyeless eyes."

How can a pupil be sucked into an eyeless eye except in a purely pictorial sense? The whole premise of the second stanza is delusional, paradoxical. The poem imitates the limbo between existence and nonexistence. The existence of the narrating voice is outside the world of the "pupil" but not outside the world of the poem. The same speaking, questioning voice also appears in the next poem, "Hand." In the last line of "Eyeless Eyes," this disembodied voice asks the "pupil" for proof of its existence. Or, to put it another way, the voice asks for proof that it can see. Again, this is a question about knowing, not a question about whether the "pupil" is dead or alive.

One way to read this is to see it as Blanchot sees suicide: "not what Kierkegaard calls 'sickness unto death,' but the sickness in which dying does not culminate in death, in which one no longer keeps up hope for death, in which death is no longer to come, but is that which comes no longer."[62] This is the agony of life, not death, the despair that can be expressed but not really known, a despair that may be ultimately a form of self-delusion, in the sense that the idea of self is portrayed as a delusion in the poem. Since one's death cannot be known while one is still alive, so suicide is clearly an expression of a crisis in life. In this sense, suicide belongs not to the domain of death but to the domain of life: part and parcel of the delusion of self, or does this mean the delusion of life?

The paradoxical symbol of the eye without a pupil, the eye that cannot see, embodies this dilemma and metaphorically represents what is a delusion. The pupil not only has metaphoric or symbolic significance, as outlined above, but could also, in the question addressed to it by the narrator, stand for a lonely, questing, and questioning self: the poet's own self. "Eyeless Eyes," the poem and perhaps the collection, ultimately poses a question that has no answer.

# FIVE APPROACHES
# TO POSTWAR
# JAPANESE POETRY

# Chapter 3
# Uttering the Unutterable
## Soh Sakon's Hell Scroll

*I am terrified by this dark thing*
*That sleeps in me;*
*All day I feel its soft, feathery turnings, its malignity.*
—Sylvia Plath, "Elm"

*Put out that Light,*
*Put out that bright Light*
*Let darkness fall.*

*Put out that Day,*
*It is the time for nightfall.*
—Stevie Smith, "The Light of Life"

 Before discussing the long poem or sequence of poems *Moeru haha* (Mother burning, 1968), I need to discuss the status of its author. In 1968 Roland Barthes in a famous article declared that the author is dead.[1] However, Soh Sakon (b. 1919), at the time of writing, was not dead. So the question arises: what is the relationship of Soh Sakon to the work *Mother Burning?*[2] Moreover, given the nature of this intensely personal poem, one might argue that without the notion of the author, *Mother Burning* loses much of its potency; one could assert, in fact, that the experience of the author is the earth in which the fundamental meaning of the poem is rooted.

## The Author-Function

Barthes replaced the author by the reader, a line of reasoning elaborated by proponents of a "reader-response" theory of criticism like Stanley Fish and Wolfgang Iser.[3] However, Barthes' syllogism has not gone unchallenged. Michel Foucault in his essay "What Is an Author?" written in 1969, strives to establish some role for what he describes as the "author-function."[4] In do-

FIGURE 3. Soh Sakon. Courtesy of Soh Sakon

ing so, Foucault seeks to find a way out of the formalist morass, asserting that a "typology [of discourse] . . . cannot be constructed solely from the grammatical features, formal structures, and objects of discourse."[5]

It is worth pausing here to consider this issue in a little more detail. The notion of "author" in general and also in the concrete particularity of the poem *Mother Burning* challenges the formalist dilemma as it has been articulated by structuralist thinkers like Barthes and also certain poststructuralist thinkers, especially those of the Deconstructionist persuasion. This dilemma has been concisely expressed by Jacques Derrida in the following way: "The foundations of the metaphysic of presence have been shaken by means of the concept of a *sign*. But as soon as one attempts to show . . . that there is no transcendental or privileged signified and that at that point the field or play of signification knows no limit, then one ought—but this is exactly what one cannot do—to refuse the very concept and word sign. For the signification 'sign' has always been understood and determined in its meaning as a sign-of, as a signifier pointing back to, a signified, as a signifier different from its signified."[6]

In other words, in Derrida's reckoning, the notion of referential meaning is nullified by an intertextual reading of "sign," which presumes an unlimited field of reference. However, the logical consequence of this line of reasoning, in the specific case of *Mother Burning,* is the contradiction that Derrida recognizes above but cannot resolve: if the word "author" does not actually point back to a real author, one is lost in a solipsistic, closed circle of nonmeaning.

Fredric Jameson outlines this quandary in detail in his book *The Prison-House of Language* (1974), the title of which represents metaphorically the impasse outlined above. It is important to mention here that Jameson sees this as quintessentially a problem of the modernist aesthetic, the focus on language as an end in itself. Jameson notes, "It seems more honest to admit that the notion that everything is language is as indefensible as it is unanswerable."[7] What discursive strategy, then, permits the author to reenter, if only furtively at best, the text?

Jameson provides the seed of such a strategy by remarking that

> the most scandalous aspects of Structuralism . . . as found in both Marxists (Althusser) and in antiMarxists (Foucault) alike—must be understood conceptually as a refusal of the older categories of human nature and of the notion that man (or human consciousness) is an intelligible entity or field of study in himself. From an ethical or psychological point of view . . . it must be pointed out that such a valorization of the Symbolic Order, with its accompanying humiliation of the old-fashioned subject or personal and individual consciousness, is by no means as unproblematical as some of its spokesmen have given us to understand.[8]

Jameson is thus willing to allow the author to reenter the room.

The door is finally wrenched open by another Marxian critic, David Brooks, who has argued that human subjects construct themselves socially by means of language, discourse, and ideology, and in consequence "literary works . . . are . . . produced by individuals with a particular personal history and experience."[9] This conclusion, which validates biography as an aid to literary analysis, may seem obvious, but debates in literary theory over the past two decades or so confirm that this is not necessarily the case. Naturally, my argument does not imply that any projection of the author—as seen with the narrator in *Mother Burning*—is identical with the actual author; it simply makes the claim that the two are inextricably intertwined and that discussion of the poem is enhanced and enriched by taking into account biographical data.

## Mother Burning

The event that acts as a catalyst for *Mother Burning* took place on 25 May 1945, some twenty-three years before the poem was published. This particular day is noteworthy for one reason: it was the day on which there occurred the largest incendiary bombing raid ever carried out over Tokyo in the course of World War II. The assault was made by 564 B-29 Superfortresses, their bombs specifically aimed at the civilian population.[10] The author of this relatively new strategy of targeting civilians, Major General Curtis Le May, described the effects on the Tokyo population of an earlier raid—"scorched and boiled and baked to death."[11] A month or so later, Brigadier General Bonner Fellers described these raids "as one of the most ruthless and barbaric killings of non-combatants in all history."[12]

Soh Sakon has described in an autobiographical essay written in 1972 how the air raid changed his life.

> On the evening of 25 May 1945 the temple outhouse in Samon-chō, Yotsuya, where my mother and I were staying was burnt to the ground by a U.S. Air Force incendiary raid. When we fled, we were left in the middle of a firestorm. We ran through the sea of flames, hands grasped tightly together. We ran anywhere. Our hands slipped apart. I kept on running alone. I left my mother behind. I killed my mother who had given birth to me and raised me.[13]

The personal intersects with the historical, which, in turn, is transformed into a paradox: how to utter the unutterable. This problem has been most directly addressed in recent years by the critic George Steiner (b. 1929). In his famous essay "The Hollow Miracle," published in 1959, he argued that the German language had virtually been killed because of the barbarism wrought on it by the Nazis. He described the process of destruction as "a language being used to run hell, getting the habits of hell into its syntax."[14] In his 1966 essay "Language and the Poet," Steiner meditates on the effect of suffering on language, quoting from Ionesco's *Journal:* "There are no words for the deepest experience. The more I try to explain myself, the less I understand myself. Of course, not everything is unsayable in words, only the living truth."[15] Silence can, therefore, be justified when words are inadequate to express reality. In this context Steiner cites Wittgenstein approvingly, "Whereof one cannot speak, thereof one must be silent."[16]

But discussing the Holocaust and its literary implications in his book *In Bluebeard's Castle* (1971), Steiner argues that hell is made immanent in the horrors of the twentieth century. If hell is now, then where is heaven? Steiner's articulation of the problem echoes Soh's own anguished realization of the same dilemma in *Mother Burning.* Steiner sees the doctrines of heaven and hell as having "vanished into picturesque formality" by the twentieth century.[17] Why, then, is hell alone realized? Steiner writes: "The loss of Hell is the more severe dislocation. . . . To have neither Heaven nor Hell is to be intolerably deprived and alone in a world gone flat. Of the two, Hell proved the easier to re-create. (The pictures had always been more detailed.)"[18] In *Mother Burning,* Soh has anticipated Steiner's solution by describing a many-layered hell, a hell of event, a hell of memory, a hell of being itself.

Steiner's hell is one predominantly arising from the Judeo-Christian tradition. This portrait of hell pictorially derives much of its force from Dante's vision of the same in his *Commedia,* or *La divina commedia* (1307–1321), as it was known later. Dante describes the seventh circle of hell as a river of blood in which violent sinners are boiled. In the eighth circle of hell, fire rains down upon the sinners "as of snow."[19] The parallels with Soh's hell, as I will illustrate, are clear. However, parallels also exist in the Buddhist tradition.

The most famous depiction of a Japanese Buddhist hell in literature is probably Genshin's *Essentials of Salvation,* mentioned in chapter 2. Genshin's description of the second of the various small hells found outside the four portals of hell contains the same trope that Dante used three hundred years

FIGURE 4. Cover of Soh Sakon's collection *Moeru haha* (Mother burning, 1968)

or so later. Genshin describes this hell as "a place rimmed by swords. Inside [its iron walls] eternal flames burn fiercely. Human fire, in comparison, is like snow." He continues, "It rains molten iron, in heavy showers."[20] This particular hell is reserved for those who murder for gain. Later, Genshin describes a great river "within [which] lie iron fishhooks, each one burning with fire. . . . Sinners are hurled into the river and tossed onto the iron fishhooks."[21]

Just as Dante's hell has been made into various visual representations, so the Buddhist hell described by Genshin is also available in various visual formats. One of the best known is the twelfth-century *Jigoku sōshi* (Hell picture book), which has several illustrations taken from sutras describing hell.[22]

Whether, in his narrative mode, Soh was influenced by these representations of hell is moot. What is undeniable is that the many-layered hell created by Soh has significant affinities to both the Christian and Buddhist traditions. Yet Soh's hell is a distinctively twentieth-century hell (arising as it does out of one of the horrific wars of that century). Soh's great masterpiece thus has much in common with other examples of that century's most harrowing yet significant art, such as Picasso's magnificent painting *Guernica,* illustrating the horror of the Spanish Civil War, or *In Parenthesis* (1937), David Jones' (1895–1974) acclaimed book-length poem about World War I. Those affinities and parallels to religious tradition, which will become more evident as my argument unfolds, lie behind the title of this chapter.

*Mother Burning* was published in 1968 by the Yayoi Shobō company in Tokyo and is described by the author on the title page as a "long poem" *(chōhen shi).* In fact the long poem, packed into 313 pages of closely printed text, consists of ninety-six individual poems that are divided up into six sections: "Sono yoru" (That night), "Sakashima ni nozoku bōenkyō no naka no dōwa" (The fairy tale inside the telescope into which you look upside down), "Raireki" (Origins), "Akarui awasa mukishitsu no" (Bright faintness, inorganic), "Inori" (Prayer), and "Sayonara yo sayonara" (Goodbye! Goodbye). In that respect, the poem is not merely a long poem or *"monogatarishi"* (tale poem), as this type of verse came to be called by contemporary critics, but an epic poem.

The first section, "Sono yoru," consisting of fourteen individual poems, describes the night when the narrator set out with his mother to walk to Ueno Station in Tokyo, where his mother was to catch the last train—leaving at 10:30 P.M.—to join the family members who had been relocated to the countryside. This first section sets the tone of the poem, which reads like a narrative, a novel, or a memoir in poetry, as it were. The first poem, titled "Tsuki no hikari" (Moonlight), reads:

### Moonlight: That Night 1

There was nothing else we could do but to walk along
Always carrying our own bags on our backs
It wasn't only because there were not enough carts or trucks
We were always walking dragged forward by the bags we had to bring to the
family since they had been evacuated far away
That night too my mother who was boarding the last
Overnight train leaving Ueno Station at 10:30 P.M. with the family's bags
    on her back
We left my rented one-room outhouse at Shinpukuji, Samon-chō, in Shitaya
    ward
To walk along the train tracks in the main street of Shinano-machi
To the government line Shinano-machi station a little out of breath but
    inconspicuous nonetheless
At 8:30 P.M. the streets were strangely empty
On the asphalt road between the row of houses upon which
A great stillness had descended because of the blackout
A pale darkness arose dim and flowing
Since for some reason the darkness breathed in short sharp breaths
The moon glittered like a silver coin that had accidentally fallen into
    the bottom of a kidney-dish
Pressed down under a thin layer of water and covered by a sheet
Of flat glass its very thickness spreading the light ever more weakly
It glittered but slipped downward as laden down with bags on
Our right shoulders we forced our left feet forward and
Rose again then slipped down again to once more rise again
Just as fish breathe with their gills so
This universe breathes with the moon
For no reason in particular, on the spur of the moment, I began to chatter aloud
Roaring about some nonsense that my mother had no hope of comprehending
Directly in front of my mother's white, newly washed *tabi*
Which thrust strongly forward one after the other from her work pants
My mother who was rocked all the way to Tokyo from Fukushima by night
    train immediately about to return the same

Way by night train must surely have been much more exhausted than me
 but remained silent all the while
A mere two hundred meters away Shinano-machi station somehow felt
 strangely distant[23]

But by poem 4, titled "Honō no kotori: Sono yoru 4" (Flame birds: That
night 4), the raid has begun:

**Flame Birds: That Night 4**

Nothing at all as if rain was falling upon the pool
It fell as if it were perfectly normal
Just as if the space around me had suddenly become a stage
Veiled by a bluish white curtain of metallic light
And I realized that the leaves of reeds in the garden about half a meter wide
 at the end of the verandah in front of me
Were each glowing decorated by flames like a splendid umbrella-shaped
 inflorescence
My mother's silhouette was cut out by a sharp knife abrupt and angular
 against the *fusuma*
And crossing into my swaying self-absorbed shadow carves out a strong
 blackness
*It's started mom let's get a move on, eh*
But outside the side gate was far brighter, far grander
A sacred *sakaki* hedge the height of my waist turned embracing within
A stand of loquat twice my height and numerous Chinese parasol trees,
 making a small path almost a garden
All the leaves, every single one, glittered like candlelit votive dishes
Blazing simultaneously with bright, young whirling lights
Mother and I stood rooted to the spot like two *bunraku* puppets dragged out
From the warehouse for the first time in front of a forest of burning
 candles
*Whistling whistling whistling whistling whistling whistling whistling*
The light metallic whistling that upon reflection must have sounded from
 the opening curtain
Revealed to me with a brilliant splendor once again the chanting of the
 puppet theater

Again, repeatedly making the feathers of the small alumite birds plummet
    downward
When I stopped holding my breath the two of us were already
Enclosed within a burning flower garden of napalm
The astonishing swiftness of the surprise attack must have jolted us into
    action
A few seconds later I pushed aside mother who had run inside to get her
    traveling bags
And flew into my room, no sooner had I carried out a fire dampener
Than I began whipping the tail of my wavering anger like a fireman's
    standard into a frenzied dance
The small flame birds were fluttering down light metal flowers blazing up
    ah now
Only for the sake of the household altar continuing as an altar only for that
In one stroke the theater of the altar transformed everything associated with
    it into a detonator
I don't want to be a performer burning up in it a member of the audience and
I don't want to act according to the instructions of the smug director with his
    obviously stupid script
Whipping into a frenzied dance the tail of my wavering anger the fire
    dampener
Light metal flowers blazing upward small flame birds fluttering down ah
What a commendable model I am as a member of the Home Guard Air Raid
    Wardens Patriotic Association
I began a furious battle to conquer the napalm
Mother who before I knew it was carrying the traveling bags on her back
    standing still behind me[24]

By poem 6, "Valley: That Night," the napalm has begun to fall in earnest:

**Valley: That Night 6**

In terms of time not even two minutes would have passed thrusting
Me, unmoving like a memorial tablet, forward, was the burning wind
    striking my cheek
After moving my head twice as if shaking it in denial I suddenly
Arched my back like a scorched plank and fell toward mother

Mother's hands were clammy her cheek was dry her breath smelled bad
  like peanuts then
Unexpectedly the cogwheels in the machine of my body started to revolve
  frantically
Boring in with the thick rope tips on the fire dampener
I extinguished the flame burning on mother's air-raid hood like an angry
  knight thrusting my
Arm through the crook of mother's elbow I began to stride out like the
  ex-officer neighborhood chief to my mother looking back
*Forget your bags! Give them up!*
I barked angrily at her hauled mother fanned by the fiery wind
We were pushed into the darkness like wild beasts pursued by fire into the
  forest
This six–meter-square space surrounded to the west by the walls of the main
  temple hall to the south by
The front of our outhouse to the east by the cemetery adjacent to the north
  by the hill garden
Resembles the interior of a pool its waves of cold light grotesquely rising
  and falling
Emitted by the napalm flowers ceaselessly descending
Resembles the interior of a pool within which swaying together then apart
Screens made of burning glass rods melt the darkness here and there in
Short only in the four corners of the pool can darkness exist the space
Into which we have been pushed is an alley half a meter wide between
  the main temple hall and outhouse
But the alley is only two meters long immediately turning into a cliff
As if we had unexpectedly come out of a tunnel there is a valley below aah
Valley valley like the scales on a mighty carp tossed into a wooden bowl
  upon the
Dark earth in the farmhouse of my father the fence who
Used it as a side dish to accompany the *sake* for the greedy, shining
Faces of the police chief, taxation chief, fire chief, town councilors and their
  like to drink themselves into a stupor at the evening meal
Like the scales on a carp resembling the many eyelids closed against life
  resembling the underside of those many eyelids
Valley valley in which the lead-colored roof tiles lay quiet and still a wet
  dorsal fin protruding from the shallow waters

Slipping underneath the many scales of the roof tiles
Where are we meant to go now? If I look up the sky is
Dark deep like the inside of a chimney seen from within an oven in a bakery
Straining to see, inside like one or two blue stars beginning to glitter
Standing on a cliff at the bottom of this water tank where the distance in
   which I seem to lose myself shines
I gradually begin to sway as if turning my back upon the valley is turning
   my back upon death
And, more, as if I am the carp who makes its scales quiet
And, more, like the carp waiting to be wrenched out of the water by hand
   and placed on the cutting board
Wriggling about in a shallow dish
Listing toward the valley twisting backward I
Begin to sway even more violently an arm
Hooked through my mother's arm begins to be pulled violently toward her
   every time aah valley
Shooting at random from the depths of the thousand closed eyelids red
   invisible star knives
Quickly pierce to the backs of my eyelids and using the attached threads
Try to beckon me by manipulating and moving me by threads
Apparently away from life toward death aah valley[25]

The narrative continues, and in poem 9, "Kibashigo" (Wooden ladder), the poet and his mother are sprinting to avoid the flames: "Panting / My mother and I were panting / With my panting / My mother panted / With my mother's panting / I panted even more."[26]

With poem 10, "Chiri" (Topography), of "That Night" the sense of foreboding and menace that permeates the poem sequence from the very beginning increases and comes sharply into focus in the last line: "Brightly too too brightly / Here since the very topography was a mass of flame / (forgive me)."[27] In poem 13, "Honō no umi" (A sea of flame), the lines have become short breaths. The rhythms of the verse mimic the thudding tempo of the pair's footsteps, their short staccato breathing: "We ran / At the bottom of the slumbering red sea / A black needle like a sea urchin / Stabbed at our spines so / (Oh violent white electric lance) / We ran . . . Fire snake / Fire awning / Fire train . . . / We ran / (Oh black charcoal spear) / We ran and ran and ran."[28]

In "Hashitte iru" (Running), the last poem of this first section, the breaths, the tempo, the pace have become ragged, broken:

**Running**

Running
Through the sea of fire a road of fire
Stumbling forward like a pier is
Running
On the road of fire
Like a red nail
I am running
Running
Because the flames on the straight road are
Running I am running
Because I can't stop running I am running
Because I am
Running I can't stop running
I'm running
Because I can't stand still I'm running
Beneath my running feet
Before my running feet
Scorching
Burning
Those running are running
Running running
Overtaking those running
Darting between those running
Those running are running
Running
Those

Not running
Are not
Those not running
Are not running
Those running
Run

Run
Those running
Are not running
Are not
Those who
Ran
Are not running
Are not
Those who

Are not

Mother!

Is not

Mother is not
Running ran running
Mother is not

Mother!

Running
Me

Mother!

Running
I
Am running
I cannot
Not run

Slippery slippery
Slippery
The thing that

Slipped through slithered down slid away
That was
That was
That hot thing that
Slipped through slipping through
Slithered down slithering down
Slid away sliding away
It was greasy so greasy so so greasy
Was that
My mother's hand in my own?
My hand in my mother's?
Running

Who
Is it?
Who is it in whose hand?

Running
Looking back
Running
Looking back
Running
Tottering
Hopping on a red-hot plate
Hopping looking back at what's behind

        Mother!
        You
        Have collapsed flat on your back
        On the road of fire
        Raising up
        Your face like a summer orange
        Your right arm aloft
        Like the withered branch of a summer-orange tree
        Thrusting out your right hand
        Stretching out your right hand
        Out toward me

Me
I am hopping on a red-hot plate
A single red nail hopping
Hopping but already
Running
Hopping running
Running hopping

On the road of fire

Mother!
You
flat on your back
Like a summer-orange your face
Burning
Like the withered branch of a summer-orange tree your right hand
Burning
Now
Burning

The road of fire

Running
Can't stop running
Hopping running hopping
Beneath my running feet
Before my running feet
Scorching
Burning
Those running are running
Running hopping
Darting between those running
Overtaking those running
Runners are running
Running
Mother!
Running

Mother!
Road burning
Mother![29]

The poet has let go of his mother's hand, and the hell of flame has been made immanent.

## Documentary Realism and Postwar Poetry

The style of this first section closely approaches what James E. Young in his study of Holocaust literature *Writing and Rewriting the Holocaust* (1990) has described as "documentary realism." He comments: "'Documentary realism' has become the style by which to persuade readers of a work's testamentary character. For the survivor's witness to be credible, it must seem natural and unconstructed."[30] The use of the present tense, particularly in poems 13 and 14 of "That Night," reinforce the sense of immediacy that the poem projects at this point. Nevertheless, the reader is also reminded here and there, subtly yet with a certain menace, that this long poem is an act of memory, of catharsis perhaps, but surely an exorcism of some kind.

Some techniques in this first section echo poems on similar themes written by other modern Japanese poets. Richard H. Minear, commenting on Tōge Sankichi's (1917–1953) *Genbaku shishū,* (Poems of the atomic bomb), first published in 1951, notes the frequent use of repetition, especially visual repetition, and also the extremely short lines—"breathless," as Minear comments.[31] This mode of writing—the thematic focus on the war and the stylistic emphasis on a kind of documentary realism—first made an appearance in postwar poetry in the years immediately following World War II. Until the late fifties, politics was an important theme for many poets, with the war prompting several reevaluations and musings among those poets prominent in the immediate postwar period. However, little of this poetry, written by poets such as Andō Tsuguo (b. 1919), Ayukawa Nobuo (1920–1986), and Tamura Ryūichi (1923–1998), strayed outside the limits of documentary or symbolic verse.[32]

The mainstream of 1950s poetry coalesced around the "Arechi" (Wasteland) group of poets established in September 1947 with the publication of the first issue of the journal *Arechi.* According to one of the founding members, the poet Kuroda Saburō (1912–1980), the group had lost its intensity by 1954, although it still commanded a powerful presence in contemporary poetry circles.[33] Tanikawa Shuntarō commented on the postwar poetry environment in an interview in 1997, noting that "that there was a time when poetry, especially the poets known as the 'Arechi' group, occupied a very powerful position. . . . The distinguished poet and critic Ōoka Makoto later used the phrase 'a festival of sensibility' to sum up the poetry of my [younger] generation. We were opposed to the notion that poetry should be constructed as a critique of society or follow a particular ideology."[34] Thus Tanikawa clearly implies here that the "Arechi" poets were pursuing a distinct social ideology.

The polemical essay "Dedication to X" included in the first Wasteland anthology, published in July 1951, is generally considered to be the manifesto of the group and explains their position in transparent terms. Declaring that the present is a wasteland, the manifesto goes on to say:

> Our escape from destruction, our protest against ruin; it is our will to rebel against our personal fates, the proof of our existence. If you and we have a future, it will emerge from us not despairing of life today. . . . Ignoring peace, asking questions, using the most sensitive organ—the ear—judiciously; and deepening our understanding of our lives, continuing our intellectual quest most patiently—using all the painful endeavors of the spirit, we must face this wasteland of the present. . . . If you can grasp our meaning in this nameless, mass society, in which we are linked so closely, then you will understand all the more."[35]

This manifesto is clearly ideological if not political in its orientation, despite the various statements by group members like Ayukawa Nobuo claiming that they were just a bunch of friends who wrote poetry.[36] Their despair arises from the loss of such prewar ideals as Japanese intellectual independence from the West, as expressed in the wartime slogan "overcoming the modern" (kindai no chōkoku), that is, overcoming the West. The Arechi group is indelibly associated with Ayukawa Nobuo, Tamura Ryūichi, and a number of other poets who wrote verse criticizing the war and Japan's role in it, and also were sharply critical of the role of the United States in postwar Asia. Later the poet and critic Yoshimoto Takaaki (b. 1924) joined the group, and his crusade against the "apostasy" (tenkō) of radical left-wing poets during the 1930s—who had switched their allegiance, under pressure from the authorities, from being idealistic opponents of the regime to becoming spokesmen for the militarists—would have attracted some sympathy from the group.[37]

This criticism of the left Yoshimoto also extended to communist writers, both during and after the war, whom he castigated for their adherence to ideological dogmas.[38] Yoshimoto's criticisms of modernist and avant-garde poets who, after the war's end, deliberately concealed their wartime collaborationist activities with the militarists, in his volume *Jōjō no ronri* (The lyricism of logic, 1959), reveals something of the ideological position of the group by the late 1950s,[39] although Yoshimoto's criticism of postwar leftists may not have been shared by all or even most within the group.

Politics as a theme for poetry was briefly revived once again in the early 1960s, when the renewal of the U.S.-Japan Security Treaty became the focus for mass action and large-scale riots. A new generation of such politically committed poets as Amazawa Taijirō (b. 1936) and Yoshimoto Takaaki donned demonstrators' helmets once again to take to the streets in protest and in the process produced much charged verse. By this time, modernist textual strategies like collage and jazzlike syncopated rhythms had become standard in postwar poetry, so the language of these poets focusing on politics can all be categorized as modernist.

Some of Soh's techniques in the second section of the poem, when the poet traces this tragedy far back to his personal past, are clearly surrealist. While such modernist strategies are commonplace in postwar (and much prewar) Japanese poetry, it is interesting to note that, for example, in Israeli literature on the Shoah, "documentary realism" dominated the work of first-generation Shoah writers, but, for their children, aesthetic fantasies that test the "limits of representation" seem to be more prevalent, as Dvir Abramovich notes, although he is discussing fiction rather than verse.[40]

John Whittier Treat argues in relation to Japanese atomic bomb poets like Tōge and Hara Tamiki (1905–1951) that their verse "hardly strike[s] us as poetry at all." This characteristic derives from "a legitimate distrust of rhetorical figures which might distract from . . . the factuality of the historical event they seek to describe."[41] But Treat also stresses the "documentary fallacy" used by writers such as Hara, that is, the inevitable "triumph of fiction over fact."[42] This technique can also lead, in the words of the atomic bomb poet Kurihara Sadako, to a combination "of Symbolist poetry with a lyricism that cannot be thought of apart from the catastrophe of the atomic bombing."[43] This comment, while specifically directed at the poetry of Tōge, could just as easily apply to Soh in the second section of *Mother Burning*.

## A Vision of Hell

"The Fairy Tale inside the Telescope into Which You Look Upside Down" comprises twelve poems that assemble together a grotesque collage of images of the poet's or, to be more precise, the poet-persona's childhood. The upside-down telescope reverses normal perspective, so readers see childhood from the distant vantage point of an adult. Here the analogy to a narrative scroll, which figures in the title of this chapter, becomes apparent. "Upside down" suggests a kaleidoscope, and, like the distorted grotesquerie of kaleidoscopic representation, the poet's childhood is a nightmarish fairy tale inhabited by child *kappa* (a kind of malevolent water sprite), eggs, fetuses, and fish. The entire fabric is interwoven by gleaming red threads of fire that burn the poet's mother in a horrifying future-to-be; the threads crisscross the narrative bricolage, imposing an almost masochistic burden of guilt over the poet's fantastic portrait of his childhood and adolescence.

Soh's methodology is utterly different from the conventions he employed in "That Night." From the start, lines snake out of control, as if in a Dali painting. In the first poem of the section, "Hi no jinrikisha" (Fire rickshaw), his father's cigarette tip becomes in the darkness of his face "a flame burning a flame floating / Pressing upward creeping upward pressing upward I'm raising my voice screaming."[44] In the fourth poem, "Sukuriin" (Screen)—one of the *kappa* poems—"There is always a massacre at the beginning / The tale will always only begin there."[45] Earlier in the poem: "Of course the *kappa* kills the boy and naturally / The boy becomes the *kappa*. . . ."[46]

At this point, the connection between the *kappa* and the fetus is clearly made.[47] Thus the poet-narrator is transformed into a vengeful fetus, a *kappa*, who will kill his mother. This horrific trope suggests both the Buddhist idea of predestination (karma) and also the Christian doctrine of election—where God has acknowledged or, as some believe, determined the fate (for good or evil) of the individual at or before birth.

The collage technique is vividly demonstrated by the ninth poem in the section, "Shōnenji" (Youth), where the twelfth stanza breaks into the abstract rhetoric of the text with an explosion of flame "Burning burning burning burning burning burning / Things that do not exist are burning things unable to be burnt are burning / Things that cannot not exist are burning / Things that cannot not burn are burning / Burning burning burning burning burning burning."[48]

The eight poems of "Raireki" (History), the relatively short section 3, describe the turbulent history of the narrator's (who I will call "Soh") impoverished family, concentrating on his mother.[49] This section is, in fact, a lament for his mother, who is described in moving tones as a caring, loving person. In a sense, the poems attempt a reconstruction of her memory, the effort at memory overlain by gaps, uncertainties, could-have-beens, and, above all, guilt. The guilt is made explicit in "Haha no isan" (Mother's legacy), which tells of events after her death. The last two poems slowly return to the actual death scene.

Section 4, "Akarui awasa mukishitsu no" (Bright faintness, inorganic), consists of nineteen poems, but no particular narrative or conceptual "structure" links the individual works. Instead, images and ideas recur and develop but neither in collage nor documentary fashion. The word *"mabuta"* (eyelids) appears frequently in the first four poems, which conjure up almost surreal images of the burning of Soh's mother. The brightness of the flames renders the closing of the poet-persona's eyelids meaningless. The next four or five poems contain a scattering of ideas linking images of the mother's bones (having a particular religious significance, as in a reliquary), the poet's icy-cold stonelike nature, and the story of the famous arsonist Yaoya Oshichi (1666?–1683) with a suffocating sense of guilt.[50] The poet continually accuses himself of murder, as in the refrain in "Honō no naka no shiro" (The white in flame) "I left her behind/I left her there to die" (written in *katakana* script for emphasis).[51]

Childhood memories of his mother's tenderness toward him surface again and again as the poems become increasingly brutal. In "Mittsu no yūyake" (Three sunsets), the description of his mother's burning corpse being torn apart by his hands if he attempts to embrace her strikes a sadomasochistic note. The focus on his mother's corpse and the poet's evil reaches a climax in the two poems "Satsujinki" (Ghoul) and "Oni" (Demon), where the poet creates a nightmare fantasy of himself as a vampiric ghoul feasting on his dead mother's flesh, as in this extract from the latter poem: "After twenty-two years from my handmade refrigerator every night/I take you out and place my/worn yellow teeth against your row of teeth and chew on them/As they're burnt black they taste horribly bitter/but on rare occasions when I bite into something soft/A faint sweet nectar comes oozing out."[52]

The final poem in the sequence, "Akarui awasa mukishitsu no" (Bright faintness, inorganic), repeats the harsh ritornello "Atonement is truly impos-

sible / It constitutes an abuse of the logic of the inorganic world."[53] Section
5 "Inori" (Prayer) contains twenty-one poems, and the intensity of its sear-
ing self-analysis justifies, more than any other section, the poet-critic Shibu-
sawa Takasuke's comment that *Mother Burning* "enables readers to see to a de-
gree rare in Japan the depths of the 'existentialist consciousness.'"[54] "Prayer"
begins by returning to the grotesquerie of the previous section with poems
like "Hone o yaku" (Burning the bones), "Midori no soko no hōseki" (The
jewel in the green depth), and "Moeru me" (Burning eyes). "Burning the
Bones" in particular is a harrowing exploration of guilt and horror:

**Burning the Bones**

Why aren't people satisfied unless they burn her once again
The burnt body of my mother
Her body like a scorched lump of dried bonito?
Of course I refuse but because
I could not embrace her cling to her utterly
Dead body her lips pouting like a bonito
I cower under the white bandages in which
The whole of my face is buried like the plaster of paris you put on to make a
    death mask
I hold my breath in the pale darkness that has crept in
Though it is not necessary I close my eyes even more tightly
(Now what is it you don't want to see?
In the light before the dawn having seen during the night not
A selfless heart but a pale iridescent tongue of flame licking burning alive
The person who gave part of herself to me)
I am doing my utmost just to control
The chattering of my teeth
Ah my mother is no more no more only because I tried a
Little longer to remain in this world
The flame inside mother joined the flame outside
In a conflagration beckoning to the flame inside me so
Is that why my teeth are chattering my heart is trembling I'm growing colder
    and colder?

Of course people are not going to
Burn my mother's burnt body once again

Just in order to warm me
If that is their intention then burn me rather than her
Do they intend to burn my mother's burnt body again just
Because I didn't throw myself down before them in supplication?

Mother forgive me this son who has put you
Through being burned twice when for everyone else once is enough
Mother don't forgive me for the act of
Turning you a human being into scorched bonito while you were alive
Mother, no, for exposing you openly before the eyes of
People that you were a bonito hooked beaten fried and
Eaten though you were my mother, no, more to the point even more
   emphatically
Do not on any account forgive me for that for
Not chewing you up as a bonito before the eyes of all
Since
Mother beneath death mask–like bandages where no one can see me
Opening the tip of my mouth in a pout more bonito-like than you
Spitting out a pale phosphorous light
I smacked my lips again and again out of hunger
Hungry maybe for something dark and gamy under the
High blue sky promising a hot summer
Something that I have to spit out as soon as I eat it
Since I wanted to become paralyzed all over my body
Because of my burgeoning hunger shaking with hunger shaking with it

Ah Mother perhaps not left paralyzed in your body numb all over are bones
In order to take out and show me her bones
Do they want to burn once more my mother's scorched body?
I bare my fangs and refuse I am a dog wearing a death mask
Since I could not enjoy my unburnt mother in the flesh
I seize hold of her run my tongue over her burnt bonito body
With her remaining bones in my mouth I snake and twist
Like fallen scorched electric cables round the debris-
Filled streets in the green scum at the bottom of the blazing sun
I wander about anywhere from telegraph pole to telegraph pole fallen
   like wooden grave markers

Mother with your remaining bones in my mouth lifting one leg
Pissing here and there the memories that I have left
It's not a question of forgiving or not forgiving
With death mask in place I am
Unquestionably Mother a dog and so
I refuse once and for all to allow your burnt body to be burnt again[55]

The burning of the bones refers in part to the Buddhist practice of leaving the powdered bones of the dead in an urn in the household altar. Thus, what is described here is an ironic, if not savage, reversal of the practice of honoring the dead through regular ceremonial obeisance. This has the effect of transforming what is normally a ceremonial veneration of the dead into a grisly reminder of both the horror of death by napalm and also the guilt taken on by the narrator. From "Fushigi na warai shika nokoranu taiwa geki" (A performance in dialogue in which only a strange smile survives), the poet engages in an ever more intense self-examination. In "Yurusarenai" (Unforgiven), the self-examination assumes religious overtones with the poet posing the question of whether he must believe that he is saved "only to be delivered unto hell."

**Unforgiven**

The active voice
"Forgive" is impossible
Because God alone
Can forgive
Then only the passive voice "forgiven" is possible
In reality many people are forgiven
But forgiven what?
Only sin can be forgiven
But forgiven by what?
If a forgiving God does not exist
Only Satan can forgive
Mother
I have lived for twenty-two years
Praying that my sin of murdering you be forgiven
These twenty-two years what do they mean?
They cannot mean that I have lived in forgiveness

Mother
I do not seek the forgiveness of Satan
And I will not invent a God to forgive me
Then what shall I do?
I do not seek forgiveness for myself
As I do not wish to become a pig
But I cannot live even for an instant
Without being forgiven
I want to keep on living      I do not want to die
So it is for this reason that I sought forgiveness
Because there was no one else
Mother I sought your forgiveness
But what does it mean for
The murderer to seek forgiveness from his victim?
Please forget that I murdered you
Please don't appear any more before me
Please vanish from my world
That is what I wish
In other words this time
I want to kill you off completely
Haven't I wanted that
In every pore of my body?
Mother
These twenty-two years      I've left my wife abandoned my children
Dreamt of revolution taken women buried myself in European writings
Drowned myself in *sake* gone abroad made speeches written books
I've done all sorts of things
It's an out and out lie to say
I did nothing but try to forget you
I lived quite an easy-going life
Nevertheless I am not at all happy
Far from it my breast was burning
My heart was constantly aching
In no time at all it grew difficult
To cast away my burning breast my aching heart
So it is for these reasons truly for these reasons
Mother

That I sought your forgiveness
It was not only
Because of your fire
That my breast burned and my heart ached
Making my breast burn and my heart ache
Was not only the fires of all types and varieties of people
Who in the same way as you
Had to be turned into fire while still alive
Had to be turned into fire that would not blaze
Mother
The reason why I sought your forgiveness
Was because unless I asked for forgiveness little by little you would
Turn your back to me and go away
And also because from the first
You never blamed me
Mother
When I appeal to you to forgive me
You smile a dry, stupid smile like a pine cone split open
And offer up your breasts to me
Mother
You cannot not forgive me
You cannot comprehend the word forgive or the act itself
The fact that you gave birth to me and raised me
That in return for your breast-feeding
You were struck with an open hand and were cremated while you were
    still alive
That you were wholly a mother and could be nothing else but a mother
These facts alone and more than that with what happened
It is unthinkable that you could be anything other than the one flesh and
    one body with me
Mother Mother of me who is still alive
You cannot forgive me nor can you not forgive me
So it is for this very reason that I
Seek your forgiveness
How absurdly spoilt I am
Mother
To seek forgiveness is to desire salvation

The knowledge that I will not be saved even if I die I will not be saved
Is forced upon me because like it or not you whom I murdered
Continue to burn within me
It is for this very reason I ask you
Just who will save me? And where?
Since I have no God in me
Neither is there God in you
Together we burn one ball of flame
You and I tumbling in space for twenty-two years
Ah must I now believe this?
That this empty green darkness Japan is hell
That being saved means only to be delivered unto hell
By the hand of Satan since there is no one else
Mother[56]

## The Sense of a Vacuum

The above poem can be read as a harrowing examination of survivor guilt and thus is reminiscent of similar verses by such writers as the well-known German poet Paul Celan (1920–1970) and also the atomic bomb poet Shōda Shinoe (1910–1965). Celan himself escaped the fate of being incarcerated in a concentration camp, but his parents did not (being deported in June 1942 to a concentration camp, where they were subsequently murdered by the SS)—Jerry Glenn hypothesizes that Celan suffered "from a burden of personal guilt dating from a specific events which took place during the war."[57]

Israel Chalfen in his biography of Celan's youth (published four years after Glenn's book) states that Celan sought refuge in a friend's house the night before his parents were deported from their home and thus avoided the fate of which he had warned his parents in vain.[58] I presume that this was the specific instance of guilt that Glenn hypothesizes. This guilt emerges in poems like "Espenbaum" (Aspen tree), where Celan writes (in the translation by Michael Hamburger), "Oaken door, who lifted you off your hinges / My gentle mother cannot return,"[59] displaying powerful affinities between Celan's work and that of Soh, especially as seen in "Unforgiven."

Shōda's guilt is most powerfully expressed in her collection *Sange* (Repentance, 1948), but unlike Soh's, it was not a personal guilt. Rather, to quote the poet herself (in the translation of John Treat): "In considering why I had to undergo such a horrible experience [as the atomic bombing], what had to be blamed was not just others but in fact myself, as well. I have had no choice but to examine myself, my odd survival and my subsequent illnesses and repent."[60] This is a religious repentance arising from Buddhist notions of individual responsibility and collective guilt. But many of the same impulses that lie behind Shōda's poetry motivate Soh's verse. The last poem of *Repentance* reads (in John Treat's translation) as follows: "Death presses close / A tribute to the souls / of my brothers and sisters: / A diary of grief."[61] In this respect, Soh's poetry does have predecessors in Japan, although Japanese critics always place atomic bomb poetry in a category of its own.

Later, in the "Prayer" sequence of poems, Soh investigates the possibility of love for someone such as he in "Aishiteiru to iu anata ni" (To you who tells me that you love me) and "Aisuru" (Loving). First he asks whether he can comprehend the nature of love, and then he questions what his love for his mother could mean. In "Ikashite okenai" (Cannot be allowed to live), the poet explores the notion of a God who judges, a notion taken further in "Norotte kudasai" (Curse me), where he enjoins his mother to curse him as "there is no God no Buddha no judge."[62] A series of six short poems concludes this section: cries of despair and resignation.

Section 6, "Sayonara yo sayonara" (Goodbye! Goodbye), the final section of the book-poem, consists of nineteen individual poems. The poetry resembles the first section, "That Night," somewhat, only this last section is more an attempt at exorcising if not the guilt, then at least the pain. The first few poems recount the agonizing images of flame in a not quite "documentary" manner, reflecting the perspective of a child. In these poems, the poet's perspective seems to have receded down the timeline so that the events of that night are seen partially from the viewpoint of a fetus. But at the same time the poems point to the life to come.

In the middle poems, specific incidents from the night are emphasized: "Oshiyaru" (Push away) compares the mother's pushing the poet away, which saves his life, to the poet's pushing away of others later in his life.[63] "Suberi ochiru sonzai" (Existence slipping out) concentrates on the poet's grip slipping out from that of his mother. The following poem, "Yurameku tanagokoro" (Quivering grip), expands on the same notion in a more detailed description of the terrifying sprint the two undertook through the blazing streets.[64] The last line, which has acted as a refrain, recalls poem 14 of "That Night": "Ran panted panting was running running was panting."[65]

The fetus appears once again toward the end of the section in the poem "Taiji ga hashitte ita" (The fetus was running), and here the running poet-persona of the beginning of the book-poem is explicitly identified with a fetus. The last five poems are linked by the general title of "Sayonara yo sayonara" (Goodbye! Goodbye), clearly an attempt to loose the hold these images and memories have had over the past twenty-two years. The title poem, poem 3 in the sequence, states: "I will not say goodbye I cannot say goodbye" and concludes with the line "There is no goodbye goodbye! goodbye!"[66] "Garandō" (Hollow), the fifth poem of the sequence that concludes section six, speaks of "the hollow that is me" and ends on the final note "Mother mother mother," but here it seems sad, as much a genuine farewell as an agonizing cri de coeur.[67]

Soh's attempt to probe the horrors of war in the form of an anamnestic epicedium, a recollected act of mourning, is almost unique in its celebration of, in the critic Sugimoto Haruo's words, "an act of torture pointing to a rupture between logic and beauty, to the absolute contradiction between unconscious action and awakened consciousness."[68] Here, Sugimoto reads the book as almost an autobiography but locates its chief significance in the tension arising from the involuntary process of memory acting on the present. For a less ambiguous comment on the relationship between historical truth and confessional poetry, I could cite James E. Young's comments on the poetry of Sylvia Plath (1932–1963) and apply them to *Mother Burning:* "There is, in fact, a compelling parallel between 'confessional poetry' and the testimonial mode of Holocaust literature: for what is confessional poetry if not that which emphasizes its personal authenticity and link to material over all else?"[69]

A number of other Japanese poets have written about the ordeal of war from the standpoint of personal experience, notably Ayukawa Nobuo in his 1953 "Byōinsen nisshi" (Hospital ship diary) poems and Andō Tsuguo in his 1951 collection *Ran* (Orchids).[70] From the former group of verses, the last lines of Ayukawa's poem "Byōinsenshitsu" (Hospital ship cabin), which reflect a dying soldier's perceptions, reveal the great distance between postwar poetry written on the theme of war and Soh's poem, but these lines also disclose some understandable affinities: "'Someone is looking in' / The keyhole is an unblinking eye . . . / The obstructive silence as wide as the door— / Collapsing tightly down upon my chest / My hot eyes seeking an exit / Exchanging glances with the keyhole staring at me / 'I want to desert!—Sea!—Mother!' / A door without a handle. / A tiny keyhole."[71]

The bombing of Hiroshima and Nagasaki have been the subject of numerous poems by Japanese poets, the most outstanding example being Tōge Sankichi, as mentioned earlier. What then is so striking about Soh's dilemma that it appears to test the very limits of language by daring to utter the unutterable?

The answer lies in the theological or metaphysical dimensions of Soh's ordeal. The reason *Mother Burning* strikes such a common chord with Holocaust narratives, with George Steiner's delineation of the almost existential crises created by the wars of the twentieth century, is its underlying nihilism, the sense of a vacuum or, even worse, of a malignant evil that the poet locates in the place where he had hoped to find God. Such a reaction to suffering is not at all uncommon. In the recent history of the West, a somewhat more optimistic version of this reaction was most famously argued by the thinker Theodor Adorno (1903–1969), who was profoundly affected by the tragedy of Auschwitz and wrote in *Minima Moralia:* "The only philosophy which can be responsibly practised in the face of despair is the attempt to contemplate all things as they would present themselves from the standpoint of redemption."[72]

Perhaps this viewpoint is not that far away from that held by the philosopher Søren Kierkegaard (1813–1855), who wrote in his journal: "In this world of time and sense and also (as Christianity teaches) of sin the idea can only exist in suffering. Only once has the idea existed absolutely, in Christ: therefore his life was unconditioned and absolute suffering."[73] But Soh finds only an empty hell where Kierkegaard can hope for something more. In this long poem, Soh has created a vision of hell, an existentialist vision perhaps, but in the failure of language to articulate even chimerical redemption, one apprehends a despair deeper than words, a despair that points to an emptiness beyond language, an emptiness contiguous with existence itself.

# Chapter 4

# Language as Feminist Discourse
Contemporary Women's Poetry

*Throw away the lights, the definitions*
*And say of what you see in the dark*
—Wallace Stevens, "The Man with the Blue Guitar"

*When in fear I became a woman*
*I first felt your hand.*
*When the shadow of the future first fell across me*
*it was your shadow, my grave and hooded attendant.*
—Judith Wright, "Ishtar"

 This chapter will examine the aesthetic strategies employed by a small group of contemporary women poets in Japan. What is meant by "aesthetic" is the notion adopted by the Russian Formalists, and Roman Jakobson in particular, namely, the language of poetry used autonomously for the sake of the work of art itself with all its textual and thematic reference.[1] The modernist aesthetic espoused or used by these women is expressed in poems that seek, explicitly or otherwise, to envisage meaning in a feminist sense. The meaning of "feminist" in relation to literary strategies will become clearer as the chapter proceeds, but before embarking on an examination of these poets and their works, some basic questions concerning the notion of "feminine" need to be asked.

## The Language of Feminism

The relationship between language and being is a highly complex affair, but that a relationship exists is denied by few modern thinkers. Martin Heidegger (1889–1976), in an essay published in 1959 translated as "The Way to Language," argued the following: "We human beings, in order to be who we are, remain within the essence of language to which we have been granted entry. We can therefore never step outside it in order to look it over circum-spectly from some alternative position. Because of this, we catch a glimpse of the essence of language only to the extent that we ourselves are envisaged by it, remanded to it."[2]

Here Heidegger sees language as a system of being, as a self-representation of experience. Thus the self-representation of experience, conceived by Hei-degger in terms of language, is absolutely vital to any theory of representa-tion or art. The necessary connection of such ideas to any possible formula-tion of feminine experience or the representation of that experience in a "feminine language" is clear: without the logical link between being or ex-perience, self-consciousness, and language, supplied by Heidegger (follow-ing Kant), no theory that connects "feminine language" to being is possible.

Several feminist thinkers have put forward ideas that connect language to being, to representation of the particular or unique feminine experience, in a uniquely "feminine language." The poet Adrienne Rich has written about young women poets, arguing that the language of poetry is alien to female experience, since it has been constructed by men. In her essay "When We Dead Awaken: Writing as Re-vision" published in 1980, Rich writes of the young female poet:

> The girl or woman . . . tries to write because she is peculiarly susceptible to lan-guage. She goes to poetry or fiction looking for *her* way of being in the world, since she too has been putting words and images together; she is looking ea-gerly for guides, maps, possibilities; and over and over again in the words "mas-culine possessive force" of literature she comes up against something that negates everything she is about: she meets the image of Woman in books writ-ten by men.[3]

Rich's solution to this dilemma is to read the work of other women. Thus, implicitly at least, Rich in emphasizing the "community of women" endorses a reductive view of female subjectivity, a view that has its origins in notions of biological essentialism.

Heidegger's view of language, as expressed earlier, is at odds with such an opinion. In the quotation above, Rich claims that language is gender-determined, that books written by men negate the female sense "of being in the world," or, in other words, that language is the slave of its author. How-ever Heidegger's view is more complex. Language, he argues, itself speaks.

In "The Way to Language," Heidegger stresses that we catch a glimpse of the essence of language "only to the extent that we are envisaged by it"; therefore, language has a presence beyond that of the intention of its author in that the author himself (or herself) is shaped, "envisioned" by language. Earlier in the same essay, Heidegger writes, "No matter what other sorts of hearing we engage in, whenever we hear something we find ourselves caught up in a hearing that *lets itself be told,* a hearing that embraces all apprehending and representing."[4] Language is more than an individual's making of it; it embraces meanings that open and extend far beyond an individual determination (whether determined by gender or other means).

In an earlier lecture on language delivered in 1950, Heidegger states, in reference to poetic interpretation: "We . . . still remain confined by the notion of language that has prevailed for thousands of years. According to this idea language is the expression, produced by men, of their feelings and the world view that guides them. Can the spell this idea has cast over language be broken? Why should it be broken? In its essence, language is neither an expression nor an activity of man. Language speaks."[5] Here Heidegger specifically denies that language can be confined to a notion of worldview, a repudiation of the assumption underlying Rich's notion of language, especially if Rich is claiming language as a whole is cast in a masculine mode, rather than simply language produced by males. Heidegger's ideas are similar to those of another modern thinker, Hans-Georg Gadamer, who is at pains to stress the contradictory nature of language.

In his book *Wahrheit und Methode,* first published in 1960 and available since 1986 in English translation under the title *Truth and Method,* Gadamer argues that the hermeneutical experience is open, as it is mediated in language:

> This structure of the hermeneutical experience, which so totally contradicts the idea of scientific methodology [and implicitly biological essentialism], itself depends on the character of language as event. . . . It is not just that the use and development of language is a process which has no single knowing and choosing consciousness standing over it. (Thus it is literally more correct to say that language speaks us, rather than we speak it.) . . . A more important point is the one to which we have constantly referred, namely that what constitutes the hermeneutical event proper is not language as language, whether as grammar or as lexicon; it consists in the coming into language of what has been said in the tradition.[6]

Later Gadamer discusses poetic language, elaborating on the quotation above: "As a successful work and creation the poem is not the ideal but the spirit reawakened from infinite life. . . . It does not describe or signify an entity, but opens up a world of the divine and the human for us. The poetic statement is speculative inasmuch as it does not reflect an existent reality, does not reproduce the appearance of the species in the order of essence, but represents the new appearance of a new world in the imaginary medium of poetic invention."[7]

In the conclusion to this book, Gadamer again emphasizes the open nature of texts—the interplay of reader and text—by speaking of the concept of play. He writes: "the analogue in the present case is neither playing with language nor with the contents of the experience of the world or of tradition that speak to us, but the play of language itself, which addresses us, proposes and withdraws, asks and fulfils itself in the answer."[8]

Gadamer's ideas here seem to resemble some of the pronouncements of that avowed enemy of biological essentialism Hélène Cixous. In her book *La jeune née,* published in 1975, Cixous argues that one cannot talk about "woman" or "man" without getting caught up in an ideological theater that "renders all conceptualisation null and void."[9] Cixous' stress is on language, on women as linguistically structured: thus her dislike of the term *"écriture feminine"* often associated with her. Here she is more conservative than Gadamer, whose view of text is much more open and not, in my reading of *Truth and Method,* gender-determined in any way. Toril Moi in her 1985 study *Sexual/Textual Politics* characterizes Cixous' work as highly contradictory. Cixous herself acknowledges this, writing in 1984: "If I were a philosopher, I could never allow myself to speak in terms of presence, essence etc. . . . or of the meaning of something. I would be capable of carrying on a philosophical discourse, but I do not. . . . I let myself be carried off by the poetic word."[10]

Cixous' projection of libidinal language resembles Luce Irigaray's use of the notion of the speculum, which via Lacanian psychoanalysis reaches back into the imaginary other to imagine women as outside the male specular structure or male gaze. However Irigaray's construction of woman as other using a kind of woman-centered language has been criticized by many as yet another version of essentialism, and she has even been characterized by Monique Plaza as "a patriarchal wolf in sheep's clothing."[11]

Rather than continue this description of various attempts to define or deny the notion of a feminine essential being or of an essentialized feminine language, I shall support the most convincing argument: that of Gadamer who sees texts as essentially open, symbolized in the notion of "play" as quoted above. Gadamer's thinking probably bears, in that respect, a stronger resemblance to Julia Kristeva's theory of intertextuality than to ideas proposed by the other thinkers mentioned earlier.[12]

However, it is important to recognize that the questions raised by the thinkers cited above and the answers that they propose are significant not merely for their intrinsic interest but also because the views of feminist literary critics like Cixous and Kristeva have been used by Japanese women poets in the construction of their poetics, most dramatically by the poet Itō Hiromi, whose work will be discussed later. Thus, some knowledge of these views is an essential step in advancing a reading of the poetry and constructing a conceptual framework in which contemporary Japanese women's poetry can be interpreted.

By using Gadamer's notions of open text and play, one can develop a hermeneutic strategy that permits a reading of texts characterizing the female without invoking a conflict based on an essentialist view of "masculine" or "feminine." As the leading English-language interpreter of Gadamer, Joel C. Weinsheimer, writes of the utility of "play" as it is developed in *Truth and Method:* "Since language is our relation to the world, there is room for play that precludes our being determined by the world as an animal by its environment."[13] Weinsheimer, in his study of *Truth and Method,* expands on the hermeneutic process in its relation to art by annotating and commenting on Gadamer's famous insight: "Alle Begegnung mit der Sprache der Kunst [ist] Begegnung mit einem unabgeschlossenen Geschehen und selbst ein Teil dieses Geschehen" (translated by Weinsheimer and Donald G. Marshall as "all encounter with the language of art is an encounter with an unfinished event and is itself part of this event").[14] This sentence Weinsheimer glosses as follows:

> The sentence beggars translation. Experiencing and interpreting art Gadamer calls *Begegnung:* coming up against something, confronting it, something happening to us, or our happening into something. What we confront in art is *Sprache:* language, discourse, speaking. And to do so is to come up against *Geschehen:* event, happening, an occurrence of *Geschichte* (history) and of *Geschick* (fate), what happens to us. The event that happens to us in an encounter with the language of art is *unabgeschlossen:* unlocked, unclosed, open, disclosed, unconcluded, inconclusive, inclusive (the connotations are negative, double nega-

tive, and positive). What the *unabgeschlossenen Geschehen* is open to and includes is the event that is the language of art. The encounter belongs to the event of language and is caught up in it—for which reason the event is unconcluded. It does not stop happening.[15]

By focusing on language and linguistic strategies in an examination of these texts, a complex array of positions will become evident within the work of a single poet; ambiguity, therefore, is not merely one literary strategy, it is inherent in the language of art and of interpretation.[16]

Before I leave this topic altogether, one other aspect of the notion of female language needs to be mentioned. This is the various linguistic usages in Japanese that mark a distinctive female presence, what can be described as "womanspeak."[17] What is not often realized, however, is that such a set of usages implies a contrary set of distinctive verbal gestures that are unique to men. And such gestures, in fact, exist.[18] But if the Japanese language has a lexicon and syntactical patterns that are gender-marked, is it then impossible to write Japanese without "gendering" the author in some way? The reference to "writing" rather than "speaking" is deliberate, as the spoken voice is normally gender-marked in all languages if only insofar as the listener is concerned. Writing is often addressed to an implied reader, a reader physically removed from the act of writing, whereas listeners are rarely physically removed from the speech act.

It is indeed possible to write in a "neutral" form of Japanese that, ignoring context, contains no clues as to the writer's gender. Such a style of linguistic usage covers several modes of written discourse, and to enumerate them all would require a mini-history of written Japanese. Any, if not all, of these styles could, depending on the reader's perspective, be categorized as patriarchal or phallocentric (by phallocentric what is meant here is the representation of the two sexes by a single, masculine model), but what is usually connoted by these terms are surely patterns of thought rather than expression.[19] Thus the existence of gender-marked expressions in Japanese is largely irrelevant to the issue of women's language discussed above.

## Ishigaki Rin: Feminist Irony

The first postwar woman poet generally acknowledged by readers and critics alike as making a powerful impact on the Japanese consciousness as a distinctly feminist yet modernist writer is Ishigaki Rin. The poet was born in

Akasaka in downtown Tokyo in 1920. From 1934 to 1975 she worked as a
bank clerk and also held a number of positions in the bank employees union.
She first came to notice in a collection of poetry published by the union im-
mediately after the war.[20] Ishigaki is often an acerbic observer of the Japa-
nese domestic scene and the Japanese family. In a poem titled "Tsumi kusa"
(Plucking flowers), which she included in her third collection of verse, *Yasa-
shii kotoba* (Soft words), published in 1984, her reflections on her early life are
recorded in a typically bittersweet key.

**Plucking Flowers**

I plucked wildflowers at Marunouchi in Tokyo.
At the end of the twenties
I was in my mid-teens.

On my way to work
To the bank
The hem of my kimono-skirt flapping
Just a dash up the embankment beside the footpath
Before my eyes an open field.
Clover
Dandelions
Philadelphia fleabane
Wildflowers too poor
To decorate my desk at work.

It's been about fifty years since then
Days came when buildings blazed in the flames of war,
Just like a graph of the economic boom
Tall skyscrapers blossomed.

I retired at the mandatory retirement age,
I don't suppose any firms are left that take
Girls straight from elementary school.
Even women are questioned about their market value
And ranked accordingly.
Women blossom in competition

But the day has finally come when they cannot possibly be wildflowers.

Farewell Marunouchi
Now no open fields anywhere
The thin green stem that I once squeezed
Was my own neck.[21]

The question arises, what is feminist about this text? The poem could be read as a protest against the encroachment of Japanese capitalism on the environment. Japanese capitalism is a subject that Ishigaki has often spoken about in less than flattering terms—as in her poem "Keizai" (The economy), also published in *Yasashii kotoba,* where she reveals the underside to the Japanese miracle.[22] However, the last line, "Are wa watashi jishin no kubi deshita," invests the text with a certain irony, a personal, even sardonic irony.

The irony present in the last line—and it is even more emphatic in Japanese than in English, as *"kubi,"* translated as "neck," also connotes "head" and "throat" in the sense of decapitation or strangulation—works against the tone of nostalgic regret expressed in the last line of the previous stanza, "The day has finally come when they cannot possibly be wildflowers." That this irony can be read as a characteristically feminist gesture is clear in the way in which many other female poets have used irony in precisely the same fashion (I shall demonstrate later that this is a specifically feminine mode of irony). Here I refer to English-language poets such as Sylvia Plath (1932–1963) and Ann Sexton (1928–1974), both of whom use the trope to devastating effect.[23]

Other modern Japanese poets also use this technique, most notably Isaka Yohko (b. 1949), whose verse about schoolteaching abounds in irony, both grotesque and witty.[24] Indeed, Toril Moi takes irony as a fundamental but unacknowledged feminist strategy. She writes, "In the ironic discourse, every position undercuts itself, thus leaving the politically engaged writer in a position where her ironic discourse might just come to deconstruct her own politics."[25]

The assumption behind Moi's identification of irony with a particular mode of woman's writing is that concepts of masculinity and femininity are social constructs, referring to "no real essence" in the world. Thus, when feminine stereotypes are constructed, they deconstruct themselves, and such deconstruction—the feminine mode of irony employed by poets like Ishigaki—is an integral part of a general "rhetorical enterprise" favored by feminist writers.[26] In other words, a deliberate stylistic strategy demonstrates the "insidious effects of thinking by sexual analogy."[27] Since sexuality is not visible at the level of rhetorical strategies (i.e., the text), the specifically feminine mode of irony enables readers to think "outside of (or *elsewhere* than) . . . sexual analogy."[28]

By using the notion of "ironic discourse" in this way, it appears, Moi is working implicitly from Julia Kristeva's adumbration of the "open" text, and such a hermeneutic seems especially apt in the context of Ishigaki's work. In "Plucking Flowers," Ishigaki through the use of irony ridicules the notion of women as mere decorative objects ("flowers") in the conventionally masculine world of white-collar work but also emphasizes the dehumanizing nature of such work by undercutting her own ironic metaphor with an even stronger use of irony to demonstrate how women are "plucked" and "squeezed" of the possibility of even possessing a gendered identity in the competitive environment of late-twentieth-century capitalism, where one's humanity is reduced to the sole category of "market value."

This use of irony where "every position undercuts itself" is manifest in Ishigaki's use of rhetoric, which appears conservative, that is, to be reinforcing gender stereotypes, but, as the nature of such stereotyping is inherently unstable, Ishigaki's ironic deployment of it effectively undercuts any normative value it may point toward. Her strategy is plain in poems like "Watashi no mae ni aru nabe to okama to moeru hi to" (In front of me the pot and rice pot and burning flames), taken from her first collection of poetry of the same name published in 1959 (the poem was written several years earlier), where its use continues to trouble commentators, who are disturbed by the contradictions between the praise of cooking as a traditional element of female culture and the exhortation to study "politics and economics," traditionally perceived as male pursuits.[29]

The first five lines of the sixth stanza of this poem read in translation,

The mysterious irony that made cooking
The task of women
Was not ill fortune I believe
Because of it learning and worldly status
May lag behind but

and the seventh stanza contains the following:

In front of these beloved objects (the pot, rice pot, and so on)
Just like we cook meat and potatoes
With a deep love
Let us study politics and economics and literature[30]

In this poem, through the use of a subtly modulated ironic tone, Ishigaki deconstructs feminine stereotypes by asserting that cooking and studying politics and economics are equally valuable activities; indeed, they are linked in their demands, and their value lies "not for the sake of pride or worldly fame" but as offerings to humanity.[31] Ishigaki unlocks women's work from the straitjacket of gender stereotype while at the same time celebrating its historical significance. In doing so, she enables her readers to see beyond the notion of work as gendered social construct.

One commentator on Ishigaki's work, Suzuki Shiroyasu, sees this poem as deeply feminist, as a reversal or overturning of male logic.[32] But, other commentators, such as the poet Miki Taku, though describing the poem as a masterpiece, largely seem to ignore the ironies it contains.[33] A recent commentator, Tamura Keiji, argues that the poem transcends the ideology of the period in which it was written. He claims that it goes beyond postwar feminist critiques of gender in that humankind is the true subject of the poem.[34]

The double-edged nature of language, partially revealed here, conforms to Julia Kristeva's concept of intertextuality, which, as Kristeva herself notes, implies that "language, and thus sociability, are defined by boundaries admitting of upheaval, dissolution and transformation."[35] In a way, Ishigaki's poetry relies on an essential ambiguity that exploits sexual stereotypes by using them while simultaneously deconstructing them. The possibility of ironic subversion may be implicit in the very nature of language as Kristeva implies, but in any case it is an ambiguity inextricably linked to the representation of female experience, as argued earlier. Numerous examples of this female ambiguity or irony can be found in Ishigaki's work, from her earliest poetry to her more recent collections.

In *Hyōsatsu nado* (Nameplates etc.), Ishigaki's second collection published in 1968, is found the much anthologized "Kurashi" (Living). The poet in the last line again somehow both castigates and ironically empowers the female, but the poet's burden in this poem is a profoundly human burden that touches the sexes in different ways.

Living

I can't survive without eating.
Rice
Vegetables
Meat
Air
Light
Water
Parents
Brothers and sisters too
Teachers
Money too hearts too
I couldn't have survived without eating.
With my belly full
When I wipe my mouth
Scattered about the kitchen
Carrot tails
Chicken bones
My father's guts
My fortieth sunset
For the first time the tears of a wild beast filled my eyes.[36]

The irony in this poem is manifold: instead of dependency, the conventional trope depicting parent-child and student-teacher relationships, there is cannibalism, but an ironic cannibalism where the narrator-persona as dependent, in the various roles of child, sibling, and student, devours those she is dependent on. Thus, a complete reversal of conventional power relationships occurs, which culminates in the spectacle of the child devouring her father. If the narrator-persona is read to be female (as done here), a strategy justified by the overwhelming predominance of female personas in Ishigaki's oeuvre, then the irony is even stronger, as the familiar trope of female dependence is rhetorically deconstructed or, more accurately, destroyed.

However, the implied metaphor of persona as beast undergoes a complete reversal in the last line, where guilt, a uniquely human emotion, is evoked: The parent-devouring beast weeps in the face of the demands created by human dependency. Here the poem goes beyond simple criticism of such notions as gender dependency and egoism to suggest that maturity, the assumption of responsibility, entails an ineluctable burden of guilt.

Hence, to focus on one implied relationship—that of daughter and father—rather than seeing this as just an unequal power relationship, the reader is invited instead to consider it as a continuous loop, where both parties are locked into an unending cycle of dependency, each, by extension, imposing different burdens on the other. Further, like much of Ishigaki's poetry, the inherent complexity of meaning (the tears of the last line, especially insofar as they are related to the forty years of the previous line, signify an essentially ambiguous meaning) generates far more possibilities than touched on above.

In the same collection Ishigaki also includes a deceptively simple poem called "Sentō de" (At the bathhouse). It is deceptive because, as Suzuki Shiroyasu implies, to read it just as a piece of witty social reportage bemoaning poverty (which is to view the women in the bathhouse solely as victims) is to miss the particular humor and irony of a poem that actually manages to suggest a complex relationship between a common ritual of working-class Japanese women and their sexuality.[37] The nature of that relationship is voyeuristic, and it is from the almost unconscious celebration of that fact, the self-conscious sensuous pleasure, visual and otherwise, afforded by the mutual display of naked female bodies, sublimated in the poem to the innocent perspective of a one-yen coin, that the poem gains its complexity and strength.

**At the Bathhouse**

In Tokyo
At the public bathhouse the price went up to nineteen yen and so
When you pay twenty yen at the counter
You get one yen change.

Women have no leeway in their lives
To be able to say that
They don't need one yen
And so they certainly accept the change
They have no place to put it
And drop it among their washing.

Thanks to that
The happy aluminum coins

Soak to their fill in hot water
And are splashed with soap.

One-yen coins have the status of chess pawns
So worthless that they're likely to bob up even now
In the hot water.

What a blessing to be of no value
In monetary terms.

A one-yen coin
Does not distress people in the way a one-thousand-yen note does
Is not as sinful as a ten-thousand-yen note
The one-yen coin in the tub
With healthy naked women.[38]

## Tomioka Taeko: The Poem as Tale

Ishigaki Rin's irony is made more powerful by the plainness of her language. Her language is unadorned and declarative; this style of writing came as something of a revelation to the world of postwar Japanese poetry (although other female poets like Ibaragi Noriko [b. 1926] wrote in a similar vein), as the prewar tradition tended more to the ornate rather than the plain. The poet and novelist Tomioka Taeko continued this tradition of plain writing, but, unlike Ishigaki's, her poetry took a distinctly surrealist turn, attributable, argues the feminist literary historian Asō Naoko, to the influence of her teacher and mentor, the poet Ōno Tōzaburō (b. 1903).[39]

Tomioka was born in 1935 in Osaka and came to prominence as a poet while still a student at Osaka Women's College. Her first book of poetry, *Okaeshi* (Return gift), was published in 1957. With this book, Tomioka established a new mode of writing that was immediately recognized as ushering in a different kind of Japanese poetics, a different kind of diction from that hitherto employed, yet a style of Japanese that gave women poets their own distinctive voice. As Asō Naoko intimates, Tomioka's style was inspired partly by some of the effects that Japanese surrealists strove for, but the writing of Gertrude Stein (1874–1946), whom Tomioka translated, and linguistic experimentation also had a role to play.

In *Return Gift* Tomioka introduced a type of poem that was to become her trademark: the *monogatari shi,* or tale poem. Tomioka's *monogatari shi* seem to tell a story that goes on and on. As Asō Naoko remarks of the first poem in *Return Gift,* "Minouebanashi" (The story of my life), there is no rent, no rip in the language.[40] There is clearly a speaker, a female narrator who speaks of her mother, her father, her lover, and who becomes all things, while possessing a contrary spirit, seeming to conform but not conforming.

But is this the story the poem is telling? Asō Naoko says it is the telling rather than the tale that makes up the plot. Another perceptive commentator on Tomioka's poetry, the poet Amazawa Taijirō, agrees. Amazawa also makes the point that, although Tomioka's poetry progresses in the sense that in *Return Gift* and her other early collections *Karisuma no kashi no ki* (The charismatic oak tree, 1959) and *Monogatari no akuru hi* (The day after the tale, 1960) the second-person narration changes to first-person narration, actually her second-person narrators were all species of first-person narrators.[41] And when Tomioka specifies a person to whom the poem is addressed—using the word *"kimi,"* here denoting "you" in an affectionate way as between lovers or friends—the *"kimi"* seems often to be imaginary, another version of the first-person narrator.

Amazawa sums up the strengths of Tomioka's poetry mainly in terms of the style, the telling. He writes that the great charm of Tomioka's verse lies in the consistent strength of the speaking voice: Tomioka's poetry shuns imagery, metaphor. The voice has great power and speaks on: it seems to continue forever without beginning and without end. Amazawa quotes the following five lines from the last poem in *Return Gift,* titled "Hajimari hajimari" (The beginning the beginning), to prove his point:

| Anta iutara | Talking about you |
|---|---|
| Are mo wakarehen | You don't understand that |
| Kore mo wakarehen | You don't understand this |
| Nanimo wakarehen | You don't understand anything |
| Nanimo arehen | There's nothing to you[42] |

Tomioka often, as here, uses her native Osaka dialect, a quite distinctive dialect, in her "speaking voice" poetry, which, in addition to creating a strong sense of verbal verisimilitude, adds to the appeal. Amazawa's remarks on Tomioka's experiments in tone are a reminder of the stylistic experiments of Gertrude Stein, and this is by no means accidental, given Tomioka's experience in translating Stein.

What is the subject of Tomioka's dialogues—or monologues or imagined dialogues? The answer is just about everything that constitutes quotidian reality, although Tomioka has a clear focus on relationships. Her voice, or rather, narratorial voices, are rich in irony, implication, and non sequiturs. One seems to be caught in the middle of a trunk-line telephone conversation—as with some of John Ashbery's (b. 1927) poems. Nonetheless, Tomioka takes a consistently critical attitude toward social ritual as a whole, especially insofar as it refers to a woman's role. In that sense her poetry is more directly confrontational than Ishigaki's verse. An example of such sentiments is found in the poem "Okaeshi" (Return gift) from *Return Gift*.

**Return Gift**

You two
In front of the woman you love
In front of the man you love
In front of the woman you don't want
In front of the man you don't want
"I love you"
"I loved you"
"I will love you
Forever"

You two
If you come to dislike the woman you love
If you come to dislike the man you love
"I don't love you"
If you come to dislike the woman you want
If you come to dislike the man you want
"I love you"

The man I love
The woman I love
But

The man I dislike
The woman I dislike
Two in love

You two
"I love you"
If you come to dislike one another
"I don't love you"
So
"I don't hate you"

You two
"I love you," you say
How astonishing
You make lots of rules
What gluttons you are
A good daddy
A good mommy
What doting parents
Falling out of love how pleasant an advertisement for the latest drug
Falling out of love how dare you say that
Falling out of love how utterly
Pointless for the two of you
You two
Like never having time to be alone
But anyhow
Don't despair
In any case
You two
Can easily be down in the dumps
You two
Nothing will ever stand in your way
Mmm my man
Mmm my woman
Mmm daddy
Mmm mommy
Fishing and knitting

Lessons and sport
And then
"I love you"

But anyhow
Don't worry
Soon
Soon you two will receive it
You embraced saying, "I love you"
You embraced saying, "I don't love you"
You will receive a hundred times more than
This custom you've so quickly learned
You will receive heaps and heaps
Soon for sure
You two each of you
One person's share for the two of you
More than one person's share for the two of you
More than one person's share for each of you
A return gift of one person's stomachache with no vomit[43]

The use of repetition mocks the entire ritual of courtship as well as conventional expressions of marital affection, although the non sequiturs and contradictions also introduce a strong element of play, a consistent thread in Tomioka's work, into the poem. The institution of marriage, Japanese style, is clearly the target of Tomioka's sardonic speaking voice(s), the satire sharpest in the last line, when the return gift *(okaeshi)* of the title, interpreted here as an ironic reward to the couple, turns out to be abdominal pain.

Asō Naoko characterizes Tomioka's early collections as "revealing a hesitation about the female body, in all its mad anarchistic excess, which is connected both to internal biological sensation and to the flesh."[44] Asō claims that in her early poetry Tomioka's women, by means of their tales of male-female relationships, throw out a challenge to language that depicts women as fertility fetishes or amulets, another rejection of conventional views of the female.[45]

So, in this instance, it may be possible to argue that, using Japanese "womanspeak," Tomioka has created a new, distinctly female speaking voice: a voice for women alone; a voice ambiguous and indefinite, speaking in dialect rather than standard Japanese; a voice standing in stark contrast to an authoritative, univocal narrative whether that be cast in a traditional masculine mode or in a feminine mode. Thus Tomioka effectively deconstructs conventional sexual categories. However, the very complexity and diversity of Tomioka's narratorial voices do not create a generic female self, and thus she avoids the reductive, essentialist trap. As the critic and novelist A. S. Byatt said in 1983 when asked about the idea of a woman's tradition: "What frightens me about [this] . . . is that I'm going to have my interest in literature taken away by women who see literature as a source of interest in women. . . . I'm interested in women anyway. My interest in literature has always been my way out, my escape from the limits of being female."[46]

Unfortunately, however, Tomioka has not escaped this particular trap. In 1991 a leading woman poet, Shiraishi Kazuko (b. 1931), excoriated the misreading of Tomioka's verse in the West, where she has been characterized as a lesbian poet. Shiraishi argued that the English translation of poems from *Onna tomodachi* (Women friends, 1964) resulted in this misjudgment but that only a few of Tomioka's poems could be classified as lesbian verse. Shiraishi praises Tomioka as the first female poet to do what Gertrude Stein did, to defamiliarize the woman's voice by expanding it into all female voices, a cacophony or babble of women.[47]

From *Women Friends* onward Tomioka's poetry, in Asō Naoko's opinion, changes its character, although she is speaking of subject more than style. Asō argues that Tomioka's thematic focus narrows, and death and mourning appear as prominent motifs of her last three collections of verse.[48] The word "last" is used, because with the publication of her *Collected Poems* in 1973, Tomioka ceased to write poetry. Since that time she has become one of Japan's leading novelists. She herself said (in the postscript to *Collected Poems*) that she found poetic form too restrictive to express her ideas and that the move to prose was inevitable.[49] Certainly her poetry, particularly the later poetry, is more accurately described as prose poetry than as free verse.

Tomioka left a powerful legacy for the band of women poets who came after her. Her use of language, her distinctive diction—with its characteristic ambiguity—inspired many women poets to follow in her footsteps, as the seventies and eighties witnessed a flowering of women's verse. Tomioka's remarkable talents are displayed to good advantage in the following poem, "Parafureizu" (Paraphrase, first published in 1967):

Paraphrase

I was peeped at
My friend said
Me
Turning a hedge
I was peeped at
Rubbing my eyes
Cutting my nails
Coming here
I was peeped at
She's just telling a lie
Peeped at—
It has to be a lie
Time for tea![50]

## Itō Hiromi: Poet as Performance Artist

The splintering or diffusion of the female voice or female consciousness found in Tomioka Taeko's writing at the point when the female appears to be realized is raised to even greater heights in the poetry of Itō Hiromi. Indeed, Itō's verse seems to conform to Julia Kristeva's 1981 questioning of the notion of sexual identity: "The very dichotomy man/woman as an opposition between two rival entities may be understood, as belonging to *metaphysics*. What can 'identity,' even 'sexual identity' mean in a new theoretical and scientific space where the very notion of identity is challenged?"[51] A remark even more pertinent to Itō Hiromi's poetic practice appears in Julia Kristeva's book *La révolution du langage poétique* (published in 1974): "If the position of women in the social code is a problem today, it does not at all rest in a mysterious question of feminine *jouissance* . . . but deeply, socially and symbolically in the question of reproduction and the *jouissance* that is articulated therein."[52]

This remark should be kept in mind when examining Itō's poetry on child-bearing and reproduction, if only because it is very likely that Itō has read Kristeva. The scholar Tsuboi Hideto's most impressive study of Itō's poetry, published in three parts between 1989 and 1990, seems to prove that Itō is extremely well-read in feminist texts. He shows not only that Itō has absorbed just about everything published by the French psychoanalytic school of feminism, but that she also has cannibalized (by this I mean that

she deliberately plays with and oc-
casionally caricatures) most of it in
her poetry.[53] Therefore, one should
be aware from the very first that Itō
is a highly self-conscious and well-
read practitioner of the art of feminist
poetry.

Itō was born in Tokyo in 1955
and first came to prominence in the
women's poetry boom of the 1980s.
This "boom" was started by, among
other things, the publication of a Li-
brary of Women Poets (Joseishi no
Genzai Shiriizu) by the Shichōsha
company in Tokyo in 1982. In the
same year Itō's fourth collection of
poetry, Ōme (Ōme [railway line]), ap-
peared, as did the collections of two
other leading women poets of the
1980s: Shiraishi Kōko (b. 1960) and
Isaka Yohko.[54]

FIGURE 5. Itō Hiromi. Courtesy of Itō
Hiromi

A year later, in 1983, two other new, young woman poets, Matsui Keiko
(b. 1948) and Sakakibara Junko, had their first volumes of verse published.
The Shichōsha series introduced all these poets and left a deep impression on
the reading public. Shiraishi Kazuko, the doyenne of Japanese feminist po-
etry, wrote that the 1980s generation brought about a revolution in women's
poetry.[55] However, Itō was less impressed with the series and the subsequent
"boom." In 1983 she wrote a much-quoted article in La mer, a magazine that
published only women poets, which had been established that year by two
veteran feminist poets, Yoshihara Sachiko (b. 1932) and Shinkawa Kazue (b.
1929). In it she stated that "for male readers, Kōko, Yōko, Hiromi, Michiko,
and Junko are all just the generic woman poet," thus expressing her irrita-
tion and deep mistrust of this sudden rage for women's poetry.[56]

Tsuboi begins his study of Itō's two major books of poetry, Teritorii ron 2
(On territory 2, 1985) and Teritorii ron 1 (On territory 1, 1987), her fifth and
sixth books respectively, with a quote from the feminist critic and author Yon-
aha Keiko to the effect that thought and ideology can only be formed via the

existence of the body. Both men and women agree on this, Yonaha states, but
it is only natural that female consciousness and female sensuality are bound
to the female body by virtue of women's unique somatic experience of preg-
nancy and birth.[57]

A poem from Itō's second book of poetry published in 1980 demonstrates,
that, before the publication of *On Territory 2,* Itō had already established a
reputation as a strong, committed feminist poet. The poem titled "Kitto benki
nan darō" (I must be a toilet) had already brought her a certain notoriety.
From the second stanza:

> I rub my crotch against his hard thing
> I touch his tongue and tongue the nape of his neck
> I won't be able to control my cries
> He pushes his fingers into my hair and pulls on a handful
> A moan escapes my lips
> The hard man
> Pulps my breasts searching for their core
> My voice
> Squeaks
> It could be a cry of pain
> Or pleasure
> For me it's always pain
> You always hurt me

The third stanza makes the narrator's point even more clearly:

> What did you say just then?
> What you said was　　you could do it even if you didn't love me
> 　didn't you
> You said, you could manage this tenderest
> Act

In the fourth stanza the ambivalence of the proposition of "narrator as vic-
tim" becomes apparent:

> In "I"'s room "I"
> Had quickly spread out the quilt

With a transparent
Condom, and all
Is this supposed to make me feel good? Well, it
Doesn't, not a bit
When I said this "I"
pulled it out
Despite not feeling real good it still
Filled me up nice and warm though

The last stanza sums up the narrator's dilemma:

Am I a toilet?
Since when
I didn't want to know but
I suspected it then I said it
I asked it I had
To find out once and for all[58]

Already at this early stage in her career, Itō was showing considerable mastery of parody, her ear almost as acute as Tomioka's in mimicking the distinctive rhythms of lower-middle-class "girl-speech" as revealed in the narrator-persona's monologue.

With the publication of "Zendō," or "Peristalsis," a poem appearing about halfway through *Territory 2,* Itō's reputation as the *"shussan shijin,"* or "childbirth poet," was assured. The poem—or, more precisely, prose poem (as the poem is written completely in prose as are virtually all of the poems in this collection)—begins with a documentary-style description of the narrator's pregnancy. At the end of the first paragraph, she writes:

But, at the center, behind my navel, what was connected to my uterus by an umbilical cord was, to the very last, a foreign body, not a fetus at all; this was my continuing perception.

[And in large type the text continues]

In the nineteenth week this foreign body began to move inside my belly. That is, I began to feel that, rather than a foreign body, it was a living creature. From then on, for a period of five months, the living creature kept on moving about inside my belly. For those with no experience of it, I'll explain this way: they were involuntary movements close to my intestines, best expressed in words like squishy, squashing, and so on. That is, every time I felt it move, I wanted to fart. Or perhaps I wanted to poo.[59]

Later in the text, the identification of the fetus with stools or flatulence becomes almost complete. The very next poem in the collection is called "Aa to tamagiru" (A cry of pain and shock). It too is representative of Itō's oeuvre in that it is a collage woven almost entirely from several prose texts. These texts include manuals on childbirth and Caesarean sections, books on *seppuku,* guides to the Lamaze method of childbirth, nineteenth-century novels, scholarly studies of eighteenth-century law, and so on.[60] Itō, according to Tsuboi, is attempting to bury or destroy the original text, whatever that may be— one possibility is that it is a description of an older woman in childbirth— by drowning the reader or the readerly surface in intertext. This, argues Tsuboi, is a radical intervention by the author, who is endeavoring to experience the impossible, namely, the other.[61]

The poem following this astonishing tour-de-force (of technique if nothing else, as the text possesses horrific power) is titled "Mikaijin no seiseikatsu" (The sex life of a barbarian) and is a recorded conversation between an author, who on extratextual grounds can clearly be identified with Itō, and a psychoanalyst who is administering a Rorschach ink-blot test. The extratextual evidence is the analyst's published account of the session, which appeared in a medical journal about the same time that *Territory 2* was published.[62] The Rorschach focus is, first, on female genitals and, second, on diarrhea: the author and the analyst are described in the poem as, to put it mildly, somewhat at odds with each other as to just what genitals and diarrhea signify.[63]

The book ends with possibly the most astonishing poem of all, a double text where two texts are juxtaposed, one at the top of the page, the other at the bottom.[64] The polyphonous nature of the text is made even more transparent when Itō performs the poem at public readings. She plays a tape-recording of her voice declaiming the lower text or poem while simultaneously reading the upper text live.[65] The poem is titled "Kanoko goroshi" (Killing Kanoko). The title refers to the upper text, which plays with notions of abortion and infanticide; the phenomenon of postnatal depression is central to the upper text. The lower text relates the story of the suicide of a friend called

Hiromi. The celebrated poet Ayukawa Nobuo, when reviewing the book, was much impressed by this work but was also rather shocked by the fact that Itō Hiromi's daughter is actually called Kanoko.[66] In the poem the unborn fetus Kanoko and the newly born baby Kanoko are murdered several times over by the mother.

Tsuboi notes that "Killing Kanoko" is based on the psychoanalyst Melanie Klein's (1882–1960) delineation of the peculiar sadism implicit in the notion of the devouring mother (or the "devouring breast," Klein's representation of a child's hostility toward her mother).[67] But, in one sense, the text triumphs over the narrating voice, as Kanoko "eats" the "I." Tsuboi also claims the poem destroys the myth of motherhood by releasing it from idealized conceptions of being a "good mother" and motherhood, which (recall what Julia Kristeva remarked about the same subject) in his words "enslaves gender."[68]

The first six or seven poems in *Teritorii ron 1*, published two years later in 1987, are photographic / poetic collages. Tsuboi labels the book an exercise in pure textuality, as the contributions of the photographer, the notorious Araki Nobuyoshi (b. 1940)—infamous because his exhibitions have been banned several times in Europe on the grounds of pornography—and the layout artist Kikuchi Nobuyoshi are given equal credit with the poet on the front cover, thus obliterating the traditional separation of the poems, as words printed on the page, from the page itself.[69] The poet herself said in an interview about *Territory 1:* "I want to give a sadistic kick to the words born from within me. . . . I see language as just one element in art. I want to make my art purely visual. I want to eliminate the meaning contained in the words, the flow, the story; I am possessed by this masochistic desire."[70]

Among the first group of poems in the book is "Triptych," a collage based mainly on quotations from Francis Bacon and photographs that may be dog vomit or a squashed cat.[71] "Otōsan wa burū" (Dad is blue) is a retelling of Freud's famous Little Hans case, except that the author substitutes a "woman / self" for Little Hans and "father" for Freud's mother, thus totally reversing Freud's discourse.[72] And where in Freud's account the father's "phallus" appears, the author substitutes "poo." Itō also substitutes "I" for "Little Hans," thus combining two of her favorite motifs, "evacuation" and "desire." Grammatical subject and semantic subject are completely disengaged, and, as Tsuboi comments, in these poems the notions of "mother" and "father" are deconstructed utterly, if not destroyed.[73]

The photo part of the text is, to use Tsuboi's term, "noisier" than the written part of the text, as the naked Japanese mother and black child are photographed in various poses deliberately designed to display voyeuristic half glimpses of the mother's and daughter's genitals, as the text itself points out.[74]

Most commentators argue that the masterwork of the collection is "Suyu" (Vinegar and oil), which does work brilliantly as a photo-poem collage. The poem begins by juxtaposing a list of food ingredients against the ambiguous photographic representations of the same ingredients in a catalog of progressively more gooey foods, as seen in lines 15 to 20.

> Gooey onions, gooey beef, gooey rice grains
> sticky kidney beans, chicken, onions
> Pork fat
> Squid, mushrooms
> White squid, shiny mushrooms
> Shiny white squid, stuck-together shiny mushrooms
> Stuck-together shiny white squid, crumbly stuck-together shiny
>     mushrooms[75]

This recitation of cooking ingredients is contrasted with a refrain of two lines that recurs three times throughout this long poem of 104 lines. The refrain reads:

> (Longevity, love, firebreaks, safe births, moles, a pair of tweezers, cripples,
>     child care)
> (Tofu, an obi being untied, sticky syrup, falling from a horse)[76]

This refrain is contrasted later in the poem with a description of the narrator and her lover going out to eat, although the narrator concludes this section of the poem in lines 61 to 70 with

> And I made up my mind not to expect any sushi from the next man
> I want to make love
> I love you
> I really love you
> Love me

Lick me
Suck me
I want to make love[11]

The last sequence of the poem, from line 77 to the end, comprises a ge-
nealogical family history of menstruation. The repetition of the refrain to end
the poem confirms that the refrain is meant to evoke the experience of men-
struation. The comparison of eating to sex is the most obvious of several themes
touched on by the text, but the overall construction of vertigo or nausea,
evoked in the Japanese (the English cannot carry the connotations here) by
the collection of shamanistic articles, almost fetishes, adds the second sense-
dimension of a vertiginous loss of balance (in addition to the visual connota-
tions) to the representation of menstruation.

This is the main reason for the poem's power, as to communicate in
sensuous form the uniquely female experience of menstruation in addition to
locating it within a historical/genealogical and psychic (the synesthetic links
between ingestion, sexuality, and menstruation suggested by the juxtaposi-
tion of photocollage and text) context is surely one of the most difficult tasks
a poet can attempt.

## Fracturing Gender

It might appear that demonstrating the essential "openness" of the texts an-
alyzed above, a hermeneutic strategy based explicitly on a reading of Gadamer,
automatically inhibits the investigation of possible links between them. How-
ever, this is not the case. On the contrary, by showing how all three poets ex-
plore and exploit the complex ambiguities inherent in the nature of language
itself—indeed, that all three poets open "new worlds," as Gadamer puts it—
the essential affinities in approach become easier to apprehend. All three po-
ets focus on female experience but do not, as argued above, attempt to turn
femininity into an essentialized experience. Rather, they point to the funda-
mental limitations inherent in any attempt to confine the female to conven-
tional sexual stereotyping and in fact subvert and ridicule such facile cate-
gorization by a subtle and not-so-subtle use of irony.

Toril Moi characterizes this particular use of irony as part of a "general
rhetorical enterprise that seeks to deconstruct our sexual categories." Thus,
for the three poets discussed above, it is a poetic strategy by which the fem-
inine experience can be explored. Clearly it is not a strategy confined to fe-

male poets, but, as in the cases of the poets whose work is examined here, it applies to the representation of female experience in a crucial way. In this sense, all three poets seek to go beyond what Jan Montefiore describes as the second stage of feminine consciousness (a notion drawn mainly from Julia Kristeva's influential 1981 essay "Women's Time"), "difference feminism," or feminism arising from an essentialist base,[78] to, in Kristeva's words, "bring out the singularity of each woman, and beyond this, her multiplicities, her plural languages, beyond the horizon, beyond sight, beyond faith itself."[79]

Ishigaki Rin's poetry always has a sting in its tail. As demonstrated above, while apparently amenable to readings that simply develop political or social critiques of the roles women play in postwar Japan, Ishigaki's poetry inevitably turns back onto itself, problematizing the narrator-persona herself, investing the reading with an ironic reflexivity that creates new and unexpected possibilities of meaning. That she does so in texts that overtly exploit in part what could be described as traditional female roles (such as cooking) makes her poetry all the more complex. In this respect, she occupies a place in the history of Japanese feminist poetry analogous to Stevie Smith's (1902–1971) verse in the history of postwar British women's poetry: disarmingly easy to follow but with a powerful, even caustic wit that eventually leads the reader to question everything represented in the poem.[80]

Tomioka Takeo's verse is much more enigmatic, but the deconstruction of the narrating subject, foreshadowed by Ishigaki, is developed to an advanced stage in the long tale-poems that have become her trademark. In poems like "Parafureizu"—Tomioka's playful and yet deadly serious juxtaposition of voyeurism, paranoia, and female self-consciousness—it is impossible to distinguish between the two narrating voices. The resulting polyphony is most disturbing, especially when the parodic structure exposes the spaces and gaps in her characteristic conversation/dialogue, so contradictory at times that the whole concept of dialogue becomes questionable. To be sure, any attempt at paraphrase, with any of the three poets, becomes increasingly problematic as the nature of their poetics precludes such a facile understanding of the nature of interpretation. This is why Gadamer's hermeneutic is an appropriate critical tool, as Gadamer openly acknowledges the intractability of the poetic text.

In his afterword to *Truth and Method,* Gadamer notes that "it is in the lyric that language appears in its pure essence, so that all the possibilities of languages and even of the concept, are as it were germinally contained within it."[81] Or, as he expresses it earlier in the same discussion, "a verbal formulation does not merely refer to something that could be verified in other ways; instead it makes something visible in the hour of its meaningfulness."[82] I have sought to imitate something of Gadamer's hermeneutic technique by indicating how the poetry of the three women invites questions but does not answer them directly. Eventually the reader is brought into the questioning process, and presumptions or presuppositions behind not merely the themes brought out in the verse but also the interpretive presuppositions of the reader are rendered transparent by the complex ironies generated by the poem. In the verse of Ishigaki and Tomioka these ironies come increasingly to be focused on the narratorial voice.

Itō Hiromi's poetry often disintegrates the narrative voice. Julia Kristeva, discussing the relationship between the body and the text in her book *Revolution in Poetic Language,* argues that the body is "disarticulated," that it is a process or practice "that has no addressee; no subject."[83] The resultant text "spares nothing; it destroys all constancy to produce another and then destroys that one as well."[84] This description fits perfectly several of Itō's poems, such as "A Cry of Pain and Shock" and "The Sex Life of a Barbarian." The female self is parodied to the point of destruction; in the process, all conceptions of sexual identity, stereotypical or not, are exploded. Itō makes a simulacrum of herself in her poetry and then proceeds to ridicule and destroy even this.

Such texts demand respect because of their technical brilliance and also because of their discursive power. Shiraishi Kazuko claims that this destruction of gender is Itō Hiromi's most impressive poetic achievement; certainly it transcends Montefiore's second stage of feminine consciousness as it is represented in literature.[85] The "Little Hans" parody is perhaps the most powerful example of such a work in Itō's oeuvre to date, but "Suyu," a more traditional work, has received more acclaim.

Although Itō has pushed the boundaries of representation the farthest (in a recent book, she has juxtaposed a large number of quite unglamorous nude photographs of herself against the written text), it may well be premature to assume that she has exhausted all the possibilities of fracturing gender.[86] At the same time, there are numerous women poets of the 1990s generation, Saga Keiko, for instance, who appear to have returned to a quieter, more elliptical representation of womanhood.[87] Nevertheless, the common concerns with irony and narrative voice indicate that the three poets discussed in this chapter have found similar, modernist strategies with which to express the particular dilemmas of their various generations. In this respect these poets are feminist in an explicitly political sense; all are determined to "enact" a decidedly critical and confronting vision of the female in their verse.

# Chapter 5
# Identity in Contemporary Okinawan Poetry
## Ichihara Chikako's Island-Mother

*Past who*
*can recall*
*nothing is*
—Louis Zukofsky, "A"

*. . . all the sea*
*calm and waiting, having*
*come so far*
—Charles Olson, "December 22nd"

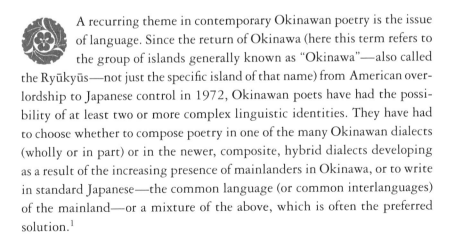 A recurring theme in contemporary Okinawan poetry is the issue of language. Since the return of Okinawa (here this term refers to the group of islands generally known as "Okinawa"—also called the Ryūkyūs—not just the specific island of that name) from American over-lordship to Japanese control in 1972, Okinawan poets have had the possibility of at least two or more complex linguistic identities. They have had to choose whether to compose poetry in one of the many Okinawan dialects (wholly or in part) or in the newer, composite, hybrid dialects developing as a result of the increasing presence of mainlanders in Okinawa, or to write in standard Japanese—the common language (or common interlanguages) of the mainland—or a mixture of the above, which is often the preferred solution.[1]

## The Predicament of Language

The recent history of Okinawa provides an explanation for both its linguistic complexity and its related convoluted ruminations over the issue of identity. After losing its independence in the seventeenth century with the forced annexation of the kingdom of the Ryūkyūs into the Japanese province of

Satsuma—often referred to by Okinawans as the Satsuma invasion—from 1879 Okinawa became part of the Japanese empire. The fact that many Okinawans eventually became fiercely patriotic can be gauged by the huge number of casualties in the Battle of Okinawa, the only land campaign during World War II fought on the homeland Japanese islands. During this campaign, nearly a quarter of the population of the main island of Okinawa died, approximately a quarter of a million deaths. As a result of the war, Okinawa was severed from Japanese control and ruled directly by the United States until its reversion back to Japan.

Consequently, the issue of linguistic expression or poetic expression also begs the larger question of the relationship between linguistic representation and subjective identity. At times, the two concerns may seem identical, but, as discussed in the previous two chapters, the connections between them are intricate and vexed. This chapter will concentrate on two specific issues of identity as aspects of poetic expression: gender and ethnicity. Indeed, the problems of language and identity coincide with these twin themes.

The question of identity is especially complicated in the case of Okinawa on account of the generation gap, which, after the return of Okinawa to Japanese sovereignty, has resulted in a loss of traditional dialect usage among the young. The chief reason is the absorption of Okinawa into the larger mainland cultural domain brought about by the power of the mass media, education, shifting employment patterns, and so forth, after a period of relative isolation during the American interregnum. This has led to the newer, hybrid dialects. Moreover, the youth of Okinawa have grown up as full Japanese citizens, quite a different experience from their parents' generation.

Thus, the question of identity—whether relating to the specific island to which the poet is linked or to Okinawa in general or to connections with the mainland or the larger notion of Japaneseness—does take on different generational dimensions. For the youth of Okinawa, this question is often expressed in terms of the larger contrast between Okinawa and the mainland. This sense of a dual identity in linguistic terms, of being able to choose between at least two distinct styles of expression—between representing oneself as an "Uchinanchū" or as a "Yamatonchū" ("Okinawan" and "Japanese," in Okinawan dialect)—or, more frequently, of being able to shift between the two is a concern that is especially acute for the young, precisely because they have the freedom to choose, a freedom not as easily available to older Okinawans.

This perspective is apparent in the writings of younger Okinawan poets.

In 1992 in an issue of the journal *Shin Okinawa bungaku* (New Okinawa literature) devoted to "The Culture of the Young in Okinawa" (Okinawa no wakamono bunka), a twenty-three-year-old poet called Hirata Daiichi wrote: "'Islander' *(shimanchū)* and 'Japanese' (Yamatonchū). Coming and going between the two, I always had mixed feelings—my poetry was born from this. The theme of my poetry is this 'wavering between two identities,' as it were, and so I've been able to observe the various events that have happened on the islands objectively."[2]

Hirata interprets his position positively: his freedom to choose identities is also a freedom to see both Japanese culture and Okinawan culture from an "objective" point of view, in other words, in some sense, from "outside." But many years earlier, another, older Okinawan poet contemplating a similar question came to radically different conclusions:

> What is created by the combination of the Japanese word "Okinawa" and the [Okinawan] dialect word "Yamatoguchi" [Japanese speech] is something like "Okinawa Yamatoguchi"; we call this "Okinawa Yamatoguchi" [Okinawan Japanese]. It is Japanese language made in Okinawa, so to speak: as a language, it's deformed, it doesn't have much currency. Consequently, on occasion, Okinawan Japanese in normal everyday use is the site of tragedy and, on occasion, the site of bewilderment; sometimes among Okinawans it makes fools out of people.[3]

This poet was the famous Yamanokuchi Baku (1903–1963) writing in his essay "Okinawa Yamatoguchi" (Okinawan Japanese) published in 1976. Here Baku is clearly pessimistic—the differences between the past and the present, and thus the contrasts between different generations, are made starkly apparent. Baku's pessimism relates to the racial or linguistic prejudice against Okinawans and their distinctive dialects harbored by mainland Japanese for much of the past century or so. Thus, language is a key element in defining this problem. The two views quoted above turn out to be emblematic of a larger schism in critical evaluations of contemporary Okinawan poetry.

In 1991, writing in a special issue of *Contemporary Poetry Notebook* devoted to Okinawa, the distinguished Okinawan poet Takara Ben (b. 1949) was pessimistic about the trend toward a "language"-based poetics in recent writing. In his essay "Ryūkyūko de shi o kaku koto" (Writing poetry in the Ryūkyū arc), Takara argues that, after the reversion of Okinawa to Japan, Okinawan poetry was in some sense absorbed back into Japanese poetry, and a sense of separateness and distinctiveness became lost. He also emphasizes the destruction of older paradigms of poetry—the notion (as Yoshimoto Takaaki conceptualized it) of *"sengo shi"* (postwar poetry), the poetry of issues, of politics and ideology. The destruction of this paradigm and its replacement by poetry obsessed with language ("words words words," as the critic Kokai Eiji put it) had plunged Takara into despair.[4]

Naturally, the obsession of contemporary poets with word games has dismayed critics other than Takara, and it is not a phenomenon confined solely to Okinawa. Yoshimoto Takaaki's criticism of contemporary poetry in his famous 1978 book *Zōho sengo shi shiron* (A critique of the history of postwar poetry), which he characterized pejoratively as *"shujiteki na genzai"* (the rhetorical present), echoes that of Takara.[5] However, just as Yoshimoto had his detractors, so has Takara's pessimistic account of language-oriented poetry been counterbalanced by such critics as Ōshiro Sadatoshi. In his 1989 book *Okinawa sengo shishi* (A history of postwar Okinawa poetry), Ōshiro quotes approvingly from poets who, while using language in a deliberately self-conscious way, nevertheless create new, powerful forms of meaning. The poet Matsubara Toshio in the preface to his first collection of verse, *Naha gozen reiji* (Midnight in Naha), published in 1977, writes of language: "These are my reflections on the time when I first began to write poetry. From the latter half of the 1960s until today, what color did my life take on? At the very least, after I consciously walked along the 'path of expression,' I felt that my poetry was closely connected to my actual experience and had expanded while I was pursuing the significance of these links."[6] In the case of Matsubara, the personal did not disappear but was fused with an interest in the poetics of language.

Ōshiro notes that, after the reversion of Okinawa, poets could travel easily to Tokyo, the cultural center of modern Japan, and thus the freedom to choose became a reality. The best-known example of such a poet is Yamanokuchi Baku, who, despite his misgivings concerning Okinawan identity, did indeed relocate to Tokyo.[7] But many other names could be cited. At the same time, poets from the mainland came to live and write in Okinawa, as in the case of the well-known poet Kishimoto Machiko, so the fusion or confusion of language described earlier by Baku became a feature of a particular variety of contemporary Okinawan verse.[8] This mixed language Ōshiro describes as *"konzaishita hyōgen"* (mixed expression).[9]

This is for Ōshiro a positive phenomenon, as it reflects the contemporary

reality of today's high-information, high-tech society, where problems aris-
ing from cultural isolation have largely disappeared. In other words, expres-
sions rooted in a specific place and time have been diffused to the point where
their specificity disappears. The notion of locality has become a universal. This
is especially so for poets who have left Okinawa to travel to the mainland. As
Ōshiro notes: "Those poets who left for the mainland had one characteristic
in common. Even if the center of their life was removed from Okinawa, the
foundation of their respective poetic worlds was vested in a passionate mes-
sage to their homeland, Okinawa. I believe that the vast majority sent to Oki-
nawa poetic language that was more 'words from Yamato [the mainland]' than
'words after having traveled to Yamato.'"[10] Later, he goes on to comment that
"while polishing their individuality, at the same time they captured a sense
of universality in their verse."[11] So for Ōshiro, Takara Ben's pessimism is en-
tirely misplaced.

A poet who, Ōshiro feels, combines both the universality or perhaps the
ambiguity of language with a powerful, local voice is Chinen Eiki. Chinen
falls into this category of poets who were born in Okinawa but immigrated
to the mainland, in Chinen's case to Tokyo. Ōshiro cites Chinen's poem "Shima
e" (To the islands) as an example of a work that evokes Okinawa despite be-
ing written away from Okinawa and that tries to clarify the poet's "individ-
ual fate." An extract from the poem follows:

> To the islands
> Promising rebirth
> I can embrace a giant phantom woman
> Squeezing out the primeval milk to the agony where springs flourish
> In our adoration
> The sun festers on the horizon
> I am forgiven
> I am fondled by hidden words of love from the black mirror that fills all
> Stepping on the shore where I have memories of being born
> Comfort the alien coconuts!
> Burn the fish bones and the shipwrecks
> Till dawn![12]

A noteworthy feature of this poem is the similarity between Chinen's
exoticized vision of his homeland and that of other Okinawan poets who

now reside in the mainland, like Ichihara Chikako (b. 1951) and Iraha Morio (b. 1942).[13]

## Mother as Island, Island as Mother

In the remainder of this chapter, I intend to focus on Ichihara Chikako's second volume of verse, *Umi no tonneru* (The tunnel through the sea), which was published in 1985 and was subsequently awarded the eighth Yamanokuchi Baku Prize. This collection reflects the freedom that Okinawan poets now have—a freedom to choose their identity—as expressed powerfully by Hirata Daiichi. Identity is a most personal matter, and the question of Ichihara's relationship to her birthplace, Ikema Island, is central to an understanding of *The Tunnel through the Sea*. In a postscript, Ichihara explains the background to the collection:

> On the palm of my right hand, there actually appeared a line tracing my impiety in traveling so far away from home. On reflection, my devotion to myself could be said to have begun when I abandoned my ocean homeland and married a strange man from the mountains and plains. It came as a shock that my legal address had shifted to an alien land as a result of my change in family registration due to my marriage. I could not help but feel that this otherwise normal change in circumstances was unreasonable and unfair. It was as if the roots only just linking my underground self to the earth's surface had been severed.
>
> Since I had come to Tokyo as a nineteen year-old, not once had I looked back—I had turned into a rational city girl—but the change of address had awakened a dormant self: I had begun to pant all over, diving down underground to my roots. My speech started to display unmistakable signs of homesickness. My desire to return to mother, my island, the ocean, and Nirai Kanai across the sea could only have been symptoms of a profound longing in my soul.[14]

The notion of "Nirai Kanai," according to the ethnographer Yanagita Kunio (1875–1962), apparently arises from writings of the Okinawan scholar Ifa Fuyu (1876–1947) about the myth of Niruya Kanaya, or Nirai Kanai (rootland). The land of roots, the homeland across the sea where the gods commune and from whence rice came, figures in a myth widely known through the works of Yanagita, especially his book *Kaijō no michi* (The ocean road, 1961), to which Ichihara refers in her volume.[15]

It is also interesting to note that Ichihara's prose poem "Sobo no zurōsu" (Grandmother's drawers), in which she describes her return to Ikema Island from Tokyo many years later as a married woman, notes that "as far as the islanders were concerned, it seems that I was already an outsider."[16] Exile has many consequences—in this respect, perhaps, Ichihara's reconstruction of Ikema in her verse collection is as much an imaginary projection of a childhood dream, nostalgic in both the positive and negative senses, as it is an attempt at realistic description.

FIGURE 6. Ichihara Chikako. Courtesy of Ichihara Chikako

The central trope of the book—the island as mother, mother as island—appears in the very first poem or, rather, poem-epigraph, which reads:

To the cape
That which reaches
That which does not
If there is a perfect mother in the world
It is
The horizon.[17]

The trope of the horizon as mother, indeed the extended trope of the relationship expressed in this poem, defines the two major threads of the collection. The first thread comprises "that which reaches" and "that which does not," links broken and unbroken; the poet's link to home is the link of the sea—the horizon—but this is as much an imaginary link as a real one. Horizons are not simply a matter of the sea and the sky; they can be of any landscape breaking into air. Thus, the notion of horizon is a question of perspective, as much of the mind as of the land. The topography of the mind is defined in Ichihara's case by the notion of exile: the horizon can only be glimpsed from a distance, as Ichihara's persona is also defined by distance.

The second thread relates to motherhood. The sea is Ichihara's mother, an umbilical cord linking the poet to Ikema Island; later in the book the trope of motherhood encompasses the poet-persona herself. The physical body of Ikema, mother earth of the poet-persona, comes to encompass the physical body of the poet-persona, seen in several poems as a nurturing mother, mother of the child of exile.

Both these threads combine in the poems collected in the first third of the collection. In "Minomushi ga yume mita mono" (The bagworm's dream), one can apprehend a process of arrested development. Unlike worms that transform themselves magically into butterflies, the bagworm gradually weaves itself a complex, camouflaged prison. In this poem, the thread of the horizon linking the poet in exile with Ikema is transformed into the thread linking the bagworm with its prison-shell—and note here that the *"mino"* (bag) of the bagworm refers to the straw shoulder-covering traditionally worn by peasant farmers to keep off the rain—as the last two lines of the poem demonstrate:

> The bagworm has stored its completion in a straw raincoat
> Come and look sometime      into this dark hole[18]

The thread of the bagworm to its shell is tenuous, hanging dangerously, threatening to break, as in the fourth stanza:

> The thread sucking the promise of death from the bagworm's maw
> Heavy heavy
> Hanging until the time comes for it to break[19]

The thread becomes a nerve and is contrasted with the threads or arrows of sunlight outside its prison-shell; the contrast of light and dark, heat and cold all construct a strangely sexual metonymy of exile, as the following lines from the second and third stanzas reveal:

> The single sharp nerve
> No longer sucks at the light

The sun shoots its hot arrows upward
The single nerve freezes
Both fast and furious[20]

What is the dream of the bagworm? A dream of darkness? A dream of despair? Is the darkness inside the hole described in the last line of the poem synonymous with the darkness associated with the giant serpent *(daija)* of the first poem (after the epigraph) in the book?

"Tōdai wa daija" (The lighthouse is a giant serpent) is a curious poem, seemingly invested with a form of sexual dimorphism. The giant serpent projects both the male and the female; it harbors a certain sexual ambiguity or, perhaps, potentiality. The phallic lighthouse at the end of the second stanza takes on female dress:

The rigid, perpendicular lie the lighthouse pretended to be was
Too immaculate too tranquil
As if its womb was yet unaware
Of its fate
Standing with its virgin vulva enclosed by heaven's skirts[21]

The darkness at the end of the poem may be the darkness of exile, or it may be a darkness inherent in Ikema itself. Whichever it is, the lighthouse in this poem seems to act in reverse, obscuring rather than clarifying. Or, if it clarifies, then what is revealed is mixed in its revelation:

In the dark
When people shed their falsehoods
They take the shape of misshapen beasts
Utterly black[22]

The sexual imagery of the lighthouse-serpent is succeeded in "Jikanzu" (Magnetic field map), the third poem in the volume, by another ambiguous image of the mother's genitals.

Was
That it?
My mother's pudenda?        When

I scattered iron filings over the paper        and from the back
Applied a magnet
The iron filings' nature
Awoke and assumed an erect stance[23]

## Motherhood as Mythohistory

This erect manifestation of motherhood quickly dissolves into a more famil-
iar emblem of the female in the two poems "U-kei rentō" (U-shaped land-
scape litany) and "U tō danshō" (U Island literary fragments). The logographic
character of the Japanese language informs the poet's use of the letter "U,"
which, combined with the tunnel of the title, provides readers with a graphic
representation of female biology. The first two poems of the four-poem se-
quence "U-Shaped Landscape Litany" focus on the thread of the horizon as
mother, but the last two poems focus more directly on the mystery of birth,
an unadorned evocation of female sexuality. Stanza 4 of "Ikema" (Ikema), the
third poem of the sequence, puts it bluntly:

A U-shaped magnet of
Common graves.
An island of fertile luminous moss        mother's vulva[24]

The last stanza of "Ikema" extends the mother-principle into the realm of
mythohistory, evoking a whole host of associations from history and legend:

The coral reef is
A "giant root"
Spreading out into the ocean floor
The root-land of the world        Ikema![25]

Yanagita Kunio in his groundbreaking book *The Ocean Road*, written on
the theme of the connections in origins and mythology between Okinawa and
the mainland, summarized some of the threads that Ichihara has taken up:
"In the *Omoro* [a sixteenth-century Okinawan song collection], in the land of
roots, the term *'ne no shima'* (island-root) appears frequently. This typically
means the mother country or homeland, and examples exist of it signifying
the main island. Smaller islands have also been called *'ne no kuni'* (root-land)."[26]
He discusses the notion of *"ne no kuni"* in the context of the origin of the word

"Nirai" or "Kanai," which he argues is cognate with *"ne"* (root). Ichihara specifically mentions *The Ocean Road* in "U tō dranshō—Ikemajima oboegaki" (U Island literary fragments—Ikema Island notes), the poem that directly follows "U-Shaped Landscape Litany." In a later poem, "Umi niwa tonneru ga aru" (A tunnel through the sea), she also writes that she first learned of the significance of Nirai and Kanai "after [she] turned twenty."[27]

The last poem of the "U-Shaped Landscape Litany" sequence, called "Ōjako" (Giant clam), is a lament for the despoliation of the poet's birthplace by tourism. But it is also a wonderful celebration of the fecundity and timeless beauty of Mother Nature as symbolized in the generative powers of the giant clam:

On that shore a peculiar magnetism is working so it's an everyday event for people to lose their souls, for women's vulvas to disappear, for men to have their penises removed. On the shore common giant clams and bêche-de-mer live,

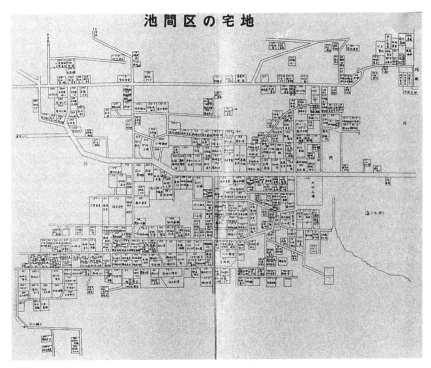

FIGURE 7. Inside cover of Ichihara Chikako's collection *Umi no tonneru* (The tunnel through the sea, 1985): a map of Ikema Island households

they copulate round the clock and thus increase their numbers two or three times. Their numbers grow to such a magnitude that tour companies organize shell-gathering tours.[28]

That same theme is carried into the following poem, "U Island Literary Fragments," which, more than any other poem in the collection, sings the praises of Ikema Island. This is a long, complex prose poem consisting of twenty-three individual poems. The conjunction of island with the female, motherhood, and female genitals is made explicit at the end of the first poem in the sequence:

> The shape of the deep inlet and its magnetic power are exactly as in the female genitalia so that there can be no doubt that the island is female. This fateful island I call U Island.[29]

The fifth poem contains a beautiful trope of sexual congress:

5
    Riding the waves the giant snake, from the mouth of the harbor to the wharf    forcing the many layers of prudent breakwaters    to open one by one and making them flower like layers of overlapping petals on a hard bud penetrates deep into U Island. Will the symmetry of the ripe blossom so easily broken accept the titillation of the murmuring waves in its very heart
    will it then breathe and break with the inevitable high tide? The blossom's scent-bag is overflowing into the harbor.[30]

Poem 7 (and poem 8) signals a solemn evocation of mythohistory, which also evokes the female:

7
    It is difficult to forgive U Island's sins. Sins that have shed much blood from the bottom join of the U. Sins that hide their murderous structure in the back of the bottom join of the U. The sin of handing over to half of humanity this murderous structure. On U Island only after all the sinful blood has been evacuated from their bodies can the elders approach the gods. Day and night the elders pray, asking for forgiveness of their sins.[31]

Poems 10 and 11 contain gentle childhood recollections of Ikema; in poems 14 and 15, imagery of flowers is followed by intimations of the process of birth, which is then confirmed by an anatomical trope:

14

Every time the flashing white beam turned around U Island I hallucinated a corona. The beam brings color to the light as if polishing the green of the petals of the flower that open out      one by one      the twelve points of the compass into the darkness. The flashing white beam allows the black night to blossom into exquisite flower: the wonder the excitement of it! If U Island itself is not a flower what else can it be? Floating all a-glitter in the cosmic mystery enveloped by an instantaneous corona      ah this lonely island in the South Seas!

15

The flashing light that follows me traces me. An umbilical cord that is never cut. In the distance someone tugs      from here I pull it in      I'm always connected to the light source.[32]

The searing pain of exile is revealed in poems 16, 17, and 18:

16

Gravity. What a painful emotional chord. I hide with my eyelids the world's smallest sea. When I open my eyes the sea almost overflows. Ah I can hear them. The small fish breathing painfully huskily through their gills.[33]

18

Gravity. Called by the horizon. In my youth whispered to by what emotions      do I challenge the horizon in a race? Looking at the horizon obliquely      is my shadow even now running along over      the sandy beach? I call out but, like a person in a telescope      my young self is far away.[34]

Poem 22 returns to the conjunction between the island and the female principle:

22

    A hole already reared. A deep sharp incision like scissors. Day by day women mature in the inlet of U Island. Hole! Facing the blue      become a wonderful wound![35]

Finally, this complex poem-garland gathers together all the threads that have been created and weaves them into a many-colored cloth, which fuses the poet-persona, the island, female biology, and primal mystery into a powerful portrayal of the human heart and a sense of place. In this poem Ikema comes alive both as poetic imagining and as personal history; it is one of the peaks of this collection.

The poem that ends this section of the book, indeed, virtually the first half of the book, "Tōkyō e" (Tokyo bound), brings a child's kaleidoscopic panorama of place to a close.

**Tokyo Bound**

To cross the horizon
I needed a passport
I discovered it for the first time on the sea traveling north
The waves sway all together in their thousands their ten thousands
The night sea is black
Other than the pale wave-flowers     there was nothing to be seen
The sea was choppy
Lashed by heavy waves
The ship rocked this way and that continuing on its way
Throwing up
In the washbasin     I thought now I've
Met the horizon head-on
I thought I'm on
My way to the land of *Taira no Masakado,* which I've been reading
   all day
Astride a horse
Shuddering violently     with every wave[36]

The poet-persona is journeying away from Ikema to "the land of *Taira no Masakado.*" Taira no Masakado was a famous tenth-century warrior who rebelled against the government of the day. A historical novel with this title was extremely popular around the time the poem was composed. Thus the poem concludes Ichihara's idyllic realization of her island home, Ikema.

## Island as Shaman

The description of Ikema in this first third of the collection is incontestably female. Another poet from the same island saw Ikema in a slightly different light, while still affirming a female presence.

Iraha Morio's poetry collection *Maboroshi no mikojima* (Phantom island of female shamans), published in 1979, was awarded the second Yamanokuchi Baku Prize. His collection celebrates Ikema Island as a land of female shamans *(miko)* and legends. A comparison between the two poets' recreations of Ikema in their respective collections provides a sharper picture of the poetics at the heart of each poet's craft. The first stanza of Iraha's title poem, "Maboroshi no mikojima" (Phantom island of female shamans), for instance, paints a portrait of an island enshrouded in mist, the mist of legends and gods:

> Phantom island, island of female shamans. It survives as if submersing its body in the center of the far-off southern ocean. Surrounded by a necklace of coral reefs against which white breakers surge to the heavens, enshrouded in the mists of legend, hidden by enigma and mystery, Shamanic Female Isle. From the thirty-first day of the eighth lunar month, for three full days, the gods manifest themselves divinely from the mists of legend. As days pass, the necklace of coral reefs surrounding the isle lift the white breakers to the heavens and all the approaches are sealed off, so even the outline of the island cannot be seen from ships passing nearby.[37]

This view differs in several ways from Ichihara's vision in "U Island Literary Fragments." Gods and female shamans populate Iraha's Ikema much more prominently than they do Ichihara's. Moreover, in Iraha's poem "Iinu Puu" (Northern Inlet), the female anatomy of U Island is nowhere in evidence. Indeed, as seen from the first stanza, a different anatomical metaphor altogether is employed.

> Surrounded by sea on all sides, Shamanic Female Isle is a horseshoe-shaped atoll alone in the ocean. This inlet, which appeared to have been gouged out by a mighty giants's left hand, was called "Iinu Puu" (Northern Inlet). If you

proceed to the north from the anus of the island, which opens out into the south, then you arrive at the northernmost point called "Iibata," which almost divides the island into two halves.[38]

The scholar Nakahodo Masanori comments on Iraha's journey as a poet in his book *Okinawa bungaku ron no hōhō* (The methodology of Okinawan literary studies), published in 1987: "We can say that the distinguishing feature of Iraha's work was the floating sensation provoked by his estrangement from the outside world, which gave birth to his vision, and this was expressed as automatic writing in his prose poetry. However, he soon became absorbed, body and soul, in the world of myth through his discovery of 'Shamanic Female Isle,' where he opened up his own unique territory."[39]

Both Ichihara and Iraha, then, are inspired by a similar impulse, but the results differ significantly. While Iraha views Ikema as an island populated by female deities and female mediums, he does not actually envision the island as a whole as female.

## Mother and Child

What lies at the heart of Ichihara's poetics? A concern with female biology stands out prominently. This concern is made transparent by the anthropomorphizing of Ikema Island in the poems of the first part of *The Tunnel through the Sea.* In the next section, Ichihara's feminine concerns focus on the poet-persona herself. The second thread of motherhood here takes on a personal dimension as poem after poem explores the mystery, the pleasures, and the complexities of female experience. In this section of the book, flower imagery largely replaces the images of the sea that have dominated until now.

After the first poem, "Kobushi no naka no umi" (The ocean in the fist), a poem of motherhood and exile, the first of the flower poems, titled "Shigatsu sakura uroko no koro" (April cherry blossom scales season) appears. In this poem the mother's wonder at her newborn child, a wonder that signals the beginnings of love, is beautifully captured in the image of the *"sakura fubuki"* (cherry blossom snowstorm). This image of cascading cherry blossom petals seems to come from dance, whether traditional Japanese dance *(Nihon buyō)* or traditional Okinawan dance *(Okinawa buyō),* with the image so formal and pictorial, and yet oddly appropriate in its suggestion of the child as object. The two lines at the end of the first stanza and the two lines at the beginning of the second stanza characterize perfectly this sense of aesthetic completion implicit in a mother remembering her new-born child.

Now         lost in ecstatic memory
My whole body         stained pink by a snowstorm of cherry blossoms

Scales         scales         cherry blossom scales
To the heavens the heavens         for millions of years hence         do they
    return dancing white?[40]

Julia Kristeva has often reflected on the mother-child relationship and its implications for semiotics and aesthetics. The following passage from her important 1979 essay "Le temps des femmes" (Women's time), translated by Alice Jardine and Harry Blake, contains reflections that are remarkably similar in intent to Ichihara's poetic reflections in "April Cherry Blossom Scales Season": "The arrival of the child . . . leads the mother into the labyrinths of an experience that, without the child, she would only rarely encounter: love for an other. Not for herself, nor for an identical being, and still less for another person with whom 'I' fuse (love or sexual passion). But the slow, difficult and delightful apprenticeship in attentiveness, gentleness, forgetting oneself."[41]

Kristeva, in her 1974 book *Revolution in Poetic Language,* links birth and the subsequent process of separation to autoerotism. Before considering this last phase of the second thread of motherhood in Ichihara's collection, I will examine one more poem in this middle section that is also strongly suggestive of Freudian and post-Freudian notions of motherhood. "Kuchiai (oraritei)" (Mouthlove [orality]) seems to draw its very name from Freudian conceptualizations of the sexual nature of the mothering experience.

**Mouthlove (Orality)**

You suck at my breast
You stare

I hug you with both arms
I return your stare entranced

The meeting between you and me was
Brought about by a mysterious flood of water

A break        on a journey tugging at an eternal waterway
Riding on a fateful lotus-boat        from far far away        to somewhere far
    away

Making        a short short detour on the journey
Trying to fix me in your memory
To become one with me you stare
And then        we gaze at one another

This a ceremony of the journey of life
The milk-white sacred water I give to you
Penetrates deeply into the folds of your sleep
Joining your and my
Time
This        our wisdom        lest the journey of life grows too lonely
Now and again
On the flood of water we gently float two boats
Thanking
Vast existence that joined us on the shores of this early summer

Now and again
From far far away        on our journey to somewhere far far away        in the
    small space
Forlornly we shake some petals

Everything begins        everything continues on
Creating ripples
In the flow of time deeply rooted in existence
Behind lukewarm yawns
That disentangle themselves from the folds of your sleep
Finally we met
A gentle        mysterious sadness
In the blossom light on the transient waters of life        we fold onto each
    other[42]

The notion of the child as a source of sensual and sexual pleasure as well
as an object (thus implying a mother-child separation of ego and object) is

implicit in the opening stanza of the poem. It is important here that the poet-persona—or, better, mother-persona—locates the maternal experience on water. Consequently, the earlier thread of connection to the poet's island home is picked up once more. The journey within the womb and that outside are both marine journeys, as seen from the fourth stanza. This lovely, elegaic poem ends with a quite enchanting trope of the unity of the flesh after a temporary separation, a trope celebrating or perhaps lamenting birth for its inevitable intimations of death.

One is reminded of Julia Kristeva's parallel enunciation in her long chapter on maternity in her 1983 book *Histoires d'amour* (Tales of love): "a woman as mother would be, instead, a strange fold that changes culture into nature, the speaking into biology."[43]

## Feminine Poetics

It would be possible to construct a playful dialogue, indeed a poetic dialectic, between Ichihara and Kristeva. This possibility, it seems to me, points to likely sources for the uses of the feminine, and in particular feminine biology, in *The Tunnel through the Sea.* For the decade in which this volume was published was also the period when the "boom" in women's poetry began in Japan.

Several commentators have pointed to the 1980s as being the decade of women's poetry. A number of events brought about this explosion in women's writing and publishing. Kunimine Teruko in her review of women's poetry serialized in *Contemporary Poetry Notebook* from March 1993 to January 1994 points to 1983 as a key year. The poetry journal *Modern Poetry Journal: La mer* (the publication's full title) started publication that year.

The first award of a new poetry prize from Shichōsha (which was the original publisher of *La mer*) went to the Osaka woman poet Hirata Toshiko (b. 1955) which caused the *Mainichi* newspaper to exclaim "Not another woman!"[44] The reason for the *Mainichi*'s indignation was that four out of the five previous recipients of the *Contemporary Poetry Notebook* poetry prize had been women. Similarly, the prestigious Mr. H poetry prize winners for 1982 and 1983 were both women. But, as Kunimine points out, no woman had been awarded the prestigious Mr. H prize for the ten years before 1992.[45]

Consequently, the women's poetry "boom" progressed at a rapid pace. In 1984, Suzuki Yuriika (b. 1941) was awarded the inaugural *La mer* poetry prize and also the Mr. H prize for her first volume of verse, *MOBILE Ai* (Mobile love, 1984). Her second volume of poetry, *Umi no baiorin ga kikoeru* (I can hear the violin of the sea, 1985), was awarded another poetry prize. Hirata Toshiko's successor in 1984 in the award of the Shichōsha poetry prize was another new woman poet, Nakamoto Michiyo (b. 1949). *La mer* quickly became a success: seven thousand copies were printed of the first issue alone.[46]

Moreover, the birth of *La mer* was accompanied by a hugely successful new series of selected woman poets, the *Library of Women Poets,* which had commenced publication the year before, in 1982. A number of young poets were published in this series, which rode on a wave of journalistic acclaim and attracted many new readers to poetry.[47] Some of these poets were partly inspired by ideas associated with feminist thinkers like Julia Kristeva. It is no accident that similar notions surface in the work of Ichihara Chikako. Perhaps the most pertinent of these is autoerotism.

The autoerotic elements in the poems collected in the middle and final sections of *The Tunnel through the Sea* center on female physiology. "Chūrippu" (Tulip) and "Ano hi oiwai da to iwarete" (That day that you call a celebration) both treat menstruation. Of the two, "Tulip" is the more playful in its subtle hints at transformation. Describing the change from a girl to a woman, it also hints at something more, as seen in what may be a parodic allusion to Nishiwaki Junzaburō's well-known poem "Tenki" (The weather) from the "Le monde ancien" section of his celebrated collection *Ambarvalia* (1933).[48] The theme of Ichihara's poem becomes evident about halfway through "Tulip."

> When        and in what way
> Beneath me
> Will it take root in the flow of women from antiquity
> And join with me?
> Ah        one of this year's tulips        a new crimson flood
> Originally in me!

The last two lines provide the possible reference to Nishiwaki's poem.

> As if an irritating curtain-closer
> Seemed to whisper something about a birthday directly behind me[49]

The fact that in Nishiwaki's verse the birthday is, as Nishiwaki writes, "the birthday of a god," may provide a link to the earlier thread of the homeland in

Iraha and Ichihara.[50] Or it may be a positive affirmation of womanhood, an appropriate coda to the process of transformation signaled in the woman-flower at the beginning of the poem. In any case, it is an elegant and joyous example of play that takes its pleasure from the celebration of female biology. Kristeva, in her semiotic analysis of the separation of child from mother in *Revolution in Poetic Language,* argues along similar lines, claiming that "[fantasies] shift the metonymy of desire, which acts within the place of the Other, onto a jouissance that divests the object and turns back toward the autoerotic body."[51]

"Rasen" (Spiral), the final poem of the middle section, is transparently a celebration of aesthetic and sexual play:

### Spiral

Hokusai's arabesque
Explodes into spray
Beats against a pillow
A naked snail
Emerges
Looks up alive
In the sea
You conceive an apparition
A bell
Rings
A bell rings
In the sea you put the receiver to your ear
There is no one there
Only the dark shadow of the apparition hangs spirals
Quickens
. . . . . . . .

Hello
Hello
Hello

. . . . . . . . . .

Distant places are awe-inspiring aren't they
The light source standing far in front of the spiraling telephone cord
Is the lighthouse!
The serpent-god!
Look      the apparition has grown into a beautiful coil

Born in light
The cape is awe-inspiring isn't it.

Into the body of a god        go forth!
When the blood for the sacrifice comes armed with magnetism
It smells of sharp iron
Tugging at a fragrant tideway        go forth to the moon!
Painted gold by the cape
Revolve around the globe!
The spiral that cannot be cut
In the darkness that deepens every evening
The cape is awe-inspiring isn't it.
Morning        you through the pale blue mist
Touched a railing of waves
Came back swaying and
Into a single woman
Slipped slippery[52]

## Ovulation as Autobiography

The final section of the book is a melange composed of memoirs of childhood, poems of nature, further explorations of female physiology, and some language poems that attempt the kind of conceptual displacement made famous by Isaka Yohko in her 1979 collection *Chōrei* (Morning assembly).[53] It is the third of these strands that I will attempt to unravel below.

The theme of menstruation occurs prominently in two poems: "Yūyake" (Evening glow) and the five-poem sequence "Kawa ni tsuite no memowaaru" (River memoirs). In "Evening Glow" the setting sun acts as a poetic symbol: both color and shape, and also the spreading subsidence of dusk in shape and light, are emblematic of ovulation.

Dusk        all is the egg of the sun
A red egg bending arms and legs within an O
Something overflowing        brightly
It swells
This is a dangerous way
To reproduce[54]

This is a conceptually harder conceit than Ichihara's early figurations of menstruation. The ovulatory process is now dangerous, the gentle flower imagery of the previous poems has been given a more direct, more declarative tone. The same shift occurs in the following poem, "River Memoirs," where the first poem in the five-poem sequence, "Ketsuryū" (Bloodflow), uses a bizarre metaphor that likens ovulation to the flickering of a neon sign.

**Bloodflow**

I am a neon sign
At night        I stand erect
The apparatus by which my blood patterns itself bulks itself up is
Exposed under my skin
For all to see.
What am I advertising?
Flickering on and off I send out an incarnation that cannot be caught
At double time I embellish words
In order to ovulate
I came to town.
Exceeding the absolute temperature of the human body
In this region of much commotion.[55]

The sense of the grotesque, the conceptual sleight of hand that throws the reader off balance and introduces ambiguity into any attempt at "rewording" the meaning in plain terms is of a piece with like-minded poetry from such writers as Isaka Yohko. The poem is at the same time a flamboyant display of female physicality and an ironic subversion of such display: if, like a neon sign, the poet-persona advertises her fertile condition to all and sundry, is not the invitation also a threat? In this poem, Ichihara's poetic debt to her Tokyo contemporaries is easier to find than any specifically Okinawan sense of self or language.

The three prose poems in the set that concludes the book all give detailed explanations of the poet's relationship with Ikema Island and thus illuminate the autobiographical threads that criss-cross throughout the earlier poems. The last of the three prose poems is called "Umi no kabe" (The wall of sea), and it is the only poem in the book to make extensive use of Ikema dialect. The thread of the horizon is woven onto that of the *"tamasu"* (spirit), and this thread is further sourced to the poet-persona's own roots, as the last stanza demonstrates.

> Horizon!
> Spiritual home!
> Great barrier blocking the way to one's roots!
> Figurative masterpiece that the waves make!
>
> The wall of sea![56]

In this final poem, the poet comes clean about her two contradictory identities, as native daughter of Ikema and as a contemporary Tokyo poet—or are these identities merely two among many? Ichihara acknowledges the influence of the doyenne of Japanese women's poetry, Shiraishi Kazuko, on the poetic design of the collection, but she also reveals the debt she owes to her grandmother, whose "soul" (*tamasu*) lies at the center of Ichihara's poetics. Thus one comes full circle, returning to the freedom that is characteristic of the youth of Okinawa.

Again, for Ichihara, as a younger Okinawan poet, the choice is manifold: is Ikema her home, or is there a larger conception of identity encompassing both Okinawa and Japan? Further, the use of her native dialect foregrounds the role of language in dramatizing that choice. Hence, as the circle is completed, and the poet links the congeries of identities that she inhabits in the image of a wall of water, a wave that connects all the points on her aquatic meridian, this may be an appropriate way to end this chapter, as islands too are circular. As T. S. Eliot said, speaking in the idiom of a different poetics:

> Home is where one starts from. As we grow older
> The world becomes stranger, the pattern more complicated
> . . . . . . . . . . . . . . . . . . . . . . . . . . . . . . . . . . . . .
> . . . . . . . . . . . . . . . . In my end is my beginning.[57]

## Chapter 6

# Language as Postmodern Expression

### The Poetry of Asabuki Ryōji

*. . . it coheres all right*
*even if my notes do not cohere.*
—Ezra Pound, "Cantos CXVI"

*it's whats called a*
*post-ephemeral object*
*always a day late, their error lay of course*
*in looking for an object*
—Edward Dorn, "Literate Projector"

 Before I examine Asabuki Ryōji's (b. 1952) acclaimed collection *Opus* (1987), it is necessary to investigate the nature of the post- or late modernist aesthetic. It is otiose in the light of this work to suggest that Asabuki would not be aware of the current debate raging around the notion of postmodernism. Is *Opus* a postmodernist work—that is to say, a late development of modernism—and if it is, how does one evaluate it?[1]

## Postmodernism Defined

Fredric Jameson allows both positive and negative appraisals of the postmodernist aesthetic. He argues that Jürgen Habermas provides a dramatic insight: "We are indebted to Jürgen for . . . the affirmation of the supreme value of the modern and the repudiation of the theory and the practice of postmodernism. For Habermas . . . the vice of postmodernism consists very centrally in its politically reactionary function, as the attempt everywhere to discredit a modernist impulse Habermas himself associates with the bourgeois Enlightenment and with the latter's still universalizing and Utopian spirit."[2] Jameson himself seems to adopt an ambiguous position regarding postmodernism (echoing Jean-François Lyotard), arguing, "We are *within* the culture of postmodernism to the point where its facile repudiation is as impossible as any equally facile celebration of it is complacent and corrupt."[3]

Jameson had previously argued that history might well dispense with the categorization of postmodernism by assigning it to a late development of modernism, which, in turn, Jameson notes may well be regarded as "continuity with romanticism."[4] This is the position argued in chapter 1 and the basic assumption behind my use of the notion of postmodernism in this chapter. However, holding a position or accepting a definition does not mean there is no need to investigate this category of literary history and literary production more critically.

The Marxian critic Terry Eagleton is unambiguous in his condemnation of postmodernism: "The aesthetics of postmodernism is a dark parody of . . . anti-representationalism: if art no longer reflects, it is not because it seeks to change the world rather than mimic it, but because there is in truth nothing there to be reflected, no reality which is not itself already image, spectacle, simulacrum, gratuitous fiction."[5] Eagleton contrasts the "mystical positivism" of postmodernism (which is represented at its worst in the "banal anarchist rhetoric" of Gilles Deleuze and Félix Guattari's *Anti-Oedipus: Capitalism and Schizophrenia* [1983]) with classical high modernism, which "dramatizes in its very internal structures a crucial contradiction in the ideology of the subject . . . the subject of late capitalism, in other words, is neither the self-regulating synthetic agent posited by classical humanist ideology, nor merely a decentered network of desire, but a contradictory amalgam of the two."[6]

Vital issues here are the notions of "play" and of "subject," and these issues are crucial to *Opus* too. "Play" has been appropriated by theoreticians of postmodernism as central to its aesthetic. Terry Eagleton, in *The Ideology of the Aesthetic* (1990) caricatures the position thus: "In post-structuralist theory [art] will become the trace or aporia or ineffable flicker of difference which eludes all formalization, that giddy moment of failure, slippage or *jouissance* where you might just glimpse, in some necessarily empty, unspeakable way, something beyond the prison house of metaphysics."[7]

Jameson also emphasizes "play"—or, as he puts it, "the play of figuration"—as a means of overcoming the aesthetic dilemma of representing individual experience when this experience cannot access the "new and enormous global realities" of late capitalism.[8] One of Jameson's configurations of play is irony, which he sees as a key rhetorical technique—thus implicitly allowing him to offer a positive reading of such definitive modernist authors as Henry James and Proust.[9] Whether play is read in this concrete way as a discrete rhetorical trope or as something much larger is crucial to discussion of the postmodern aesthetic.

In Japan, Asada Akira has been one of the chief proponents of the view that puts great emphasis on play, argues Marilyn Ivy, who claims Asada's argument in *Kōzō to chikara* (Structure and power, 1983) "is a defense of knowledge as 'play' *(tawamure, yūgi)*, a game suitable for the generation that has been labeled apathetic and superficial. . . . Knowledge is that which appears in the interstices of dualistic choice, a line of escape to the outside, a chance encounter . . . Nietzschean 'gay science,' modulated through Deleuze and Guattari."[10]

Ivy argues that, for Asada, the postmodern aesthetic, and indeed history itself, is "marked by chance, play, escape" as against the "hierarchy of the modern," a formulation that seems to stand for late capitalism.[11] By any measure, such logic is vulnerable to the critique already outlined by Eagleton, where an art of "play" is entirely complicit with a society that enables its production. No real critique of society or art can emerge from such a position.

To this point I have scrutinized caricatures rather than examined texts that seriously advocate notions of "play." Jacques Derrida in 1966 at Johns Hopkins University, at what David Lodge describes as a "historic moment,"[12] read a paper titled "Structure, Sign, and Play in the Human Sciences" (translated by Alan Bass). In it he argued:

Play is the disruption of presence. The presence of an element is always a signifying and substitutive reference inscribed in a system of differences and the movement of a chain. Play is always play of absence and presence, but if it is to be thought radically, play must be conceived of before the alternative of presence and absence. Being must be conceived as presence or absence on the basis of the possibility of play and not the other way around. . . . There are thus two interpretations of interpretation, of structure, of sign, of play. The one seeks to decipher, dreams of deciphering a truth or an origin which escapes play and the order of the sign, and which lives the necessity of interpretation as an exile. The other . . . affirms play and tries to pass beyond man and humanism.[13]

My view is that in some sense this is an articulation of the same kind of logic that Jameson has constructed about irony as rhetorical trope. Derrida is attempting to break out from the prison-house of language, to escape signifying practices that structure expression in preconceived social or philosophic formulations. Thus the play between and of texts creates an infinite set of references that, paradoxically, may have the effect of destroying reference as a meaningful rhetorical or literary strategy: this process is known as "deconstruction." It resembles the Frankfurt School's assault on capitalism, which turns on the notion of ideology as an abstract reference to the governing system.[14] But Derrida is primarily a philosopher, not a literary critic, and therefore, in the quotation above, he seeks to ground play in patterns of human behavior other than aesthetics or social science.

Michel Foucault restates succinctly the fundamental conundrum of the "prison-house of language," an image first put forth by Nietzsche. In his influential study Les mots et les choses (The order of things, 1966), Foucault discusses how the discovery of philology in the modern world, the "linguistic swerve," has turned back from representations composed in language to a focus on language itself: "What [modern consciousness] reveals is . . . the fact that we are already governed . . . and paralyzed by language."[15] How does this dilemma manifest itself in literature?

Foucault argues that, as a result, "literature becomes progressively more differentiated from the discourse of ideas, and encloses itself within a radical intransitivity. . . . It breaks with the whole definition of genres as forms adapted to an order of representations, and becomes merely a manifestation of a language which has no other law than that of affirming . . . its own precipitous existence."[16] Or, to put it more bluntly, literature "[curves] back in a perpetual return upon itself."[17]

Thus Foucault describes the essence of the modernist revolution in literature, the linguistic turn back to writing itself: what the critics quoted above refer to (in terms of literary expression) as postmodernism. This type of literature, the literature of language, postmodernist literature, represents a kind of ideal for Foucault. He does not evaluate this mode of writing negatively as does Eagleton. On the contrary, Foucault asserts that this is not narcissism within literature, but rather such writing "makes us believe that something new is about to begin."[18] This kind of literature—representative of the postclassical consciousness that spawned it—may well herald a new type of culture. What manner of culture Foucault does not presume to know. As he writes in his conclusion: "They are at most questions to which it is not possible to reply."[19] Might one see "play" as an integral aspect of this new literature?

In chapter 4, I cited Hans-Georg Gadamer on how play in literature "asks and fulfills itself in the answer."[20] Gadamer elaborates by comparing the function of play in reading a text to the classic aesthetic exemplum of the process of apprehending beauty in a text: "When we understand a text, what is meaningful in it captivates us just as the beautiful captivates us. It has asserted itself and captivates us before we can come to ourselves and be in a position to test the claim to meaning that it makes. What we encounter in the experience of the beautiful and in understanding the meaning of tradition really has something of the truth of play about it."[21]

A paraphrase of this notion in respect to the poetry of Asabuki would go as follows: the poetic text works upon us by the complex process of understanding—which also incorporates lacunae, gaps, and disrupted logic—that occurs as we read and reread the text, as the text plays with our cognizing of its contents and logic. As both Derrida and Foucault recognize, this process is characteristic of a literature of play, indeed it is absolutely essential to such a literature and to the poetry of the postmodern condition as articulated by Asabuki and like-minded authors. If one can accept the premise that Japanese modernist poetry is a literature constructed on the notion of the linguistic turn, as articulated by Jameson and Foucault, that it is a typical example of the literature of the late twentieth century as it has developed in advanced capitalist states, then one can see why play is such a crucial ingredient in creating an anatomy or strategy of reading for this mode of writing.

Postmodern literature takes as a given the disintegration of the self or the subject (by no means identical, but they are conflated here for the sake of discussion) described by Foucault in *Les mots et les choses*. It takes as its axiomatic premise the disjunction between words and things (the literal translation of Foucault's title). This is why such writing is full of self-knowing gaps and non sequiturs and why phonetic correspondence is prior to or at least as important as semantic equivalence (defined in terms of the similarity of sign associations) in determining meaning.

This study of *Opus* does not provide definite answers to a number of the questions posed by the postmodernist abyss outlined by Derrida and Foucault, nor, for example, does its "subject" correspond exactly to the definition offered up by Eagleton in his exposition of classical modernism. But an examination of *Opus* will make these categories more clear and thus aid attempts at interpretation. Before beginning that examination, however, let me pause to consider some possible precursors to Asabuki in the Western and Japanese literary tradition.

## Postmodern Poetics

In the West a group of poets actually claim to have carried out some of the programmatics outlined by poststructuralist and deconstructionist thinkers. *The L=A=N=G=U=A=G=E Book* (1984), edited by two of the poets involved, Bruce Andrews and Charles Bernstein, contains a comprehensive statement of postmodernist poetics. One of the key sources of inspiration is Ludwig Wittgenstein. In his collage of quotations "Tying and Untying," Ray Dipalma cites an important Wittgensteinean hypothesis: "When I think in language, there aren't meanings going through my head in addition to the verbal expressions: the language is itself the vehicle of thought."[22]

Bruce Andrews in his essay "Text and Content" elaborates on this notion:

The vertical axis (downwards, as a ladder tempting us) need not structure the reading—for it does not structure the text. This is what I would mean by calling it non-referentially organized writing, as a subset of language-centered writing. . . . Meaning is not produced by the sign, but by the contents we bring to the potentials of language. . . . A more playful anarchy, a Möbius free-for-all is created. Texts are themselves *signifieds,* not mere signifiers. TEXT: it requires no hermeneusis for it is itself one—of itself. . . . Referentiality is diminished by organizing the language around other features or axes, around features which make present to us words' lack of transparency, their physicality, their refusal to be motivated along schematic lines by frames exterior to themselves. Refusing to 'point,' or to be arranged according to a 'pointing system,' they risk the charge of being pointless. . . . References are not foregrounded. The body of work is not organized around the referential axis.[23]

These notions were explored in practice by the L=A=N=G=U=A=G=E poets and resulted in a variety of poetry practices, in some instances having very little in common except perhaps for what Charles Bernstein (one of the group's leading poet-theoreticians) refers to as a "syntactical exploration of consciousness."[24] "Such poetry," he asserts, "emphasizes its medium as being constructed, rule governed, everywhere circumscribed by grammar and syntax."[25]

The poet Steve McCaffery demonstrates how such poetry works in practice with his analysis of the work of Michael Palmer, one of the leading L=A=N=G=U=A=G=E poets:

> Michael Palmer writes a splendid poetry of displacement, of shifts, and nomadic drifts of text through zones of page. The operative semantic is copulative, a linking (purely syntagmatically) of isolated units still preserving their molecular independency. . . . Reference is rendered intransitive and instigates the arbitrary flow of linguistic signs. Referrals without the finality of references, ectoskeletal structures carrying deliberately interior deformations. Frequently logic is placed in context with a syntax resulting in the gravity of utterance being withheld. . . . Everything happens on the level of the signifier: semic discharge across a surface and the surface is that discharge. . . . Palmer's most radical displacement is the break with transivity itself. For language has become the subject of language and we enter, as readers, the ambiguous zone of texts without absolute speakers.[26]

The two poetic texts below reveal, beyond doubt, "the ambiguous zone of texts without absolute speakers." First, the opening fifteen lines from Michael Palmer's "Notes for Echo Lake 4":

Who did he talk to
Did she trust what she saw
Who does the talking
Whose words formed awkward curves
Did the lion finally talk
Did the sleeping lion talk
Did you trust a north window
What made the dog bark
What causes a grey dog to bark
What does the juggler tell us
What does the juggler's redness tell us
Is she standing in an image
Were they lost in the forest
Were they walking through a forest
Has anything been forgotten[27]

And from Australia, witness Philip Hammial's poem "Sally":

> On which foot
> is she fast approaching? And how straight
> is her path? And where the proof that what
> She'll take from me is so reciprocal
> as to be indistinguishable, as speech
> from sound, wine
> from blood? An exchange,
> simple, perhaps divine, but what guarantee
> that from this trundling will emerge, celestially
> gowned, wand in hand, a sister, a twin who'll lift
> my skirts, who'll probe me for the music
> I must possess & then, sung, sated, flesh
> of my flesh, will not, on
> the other, on my lame
> foot flee?[28]

French linguistic influences are manifest in the nonreferential aesthetic: not merely the poststructuralist writers cited earlier, but also structuralists like Claude Lévi-Strauss. In a conversation with Georges Charbonnier in 1959, Lévi-Strauss spoke of poetry in the following way: "The poet stands in the same relation to language as the painter to the object. Language is his raw material and it is this raw material that he sets out to signify—not exactly the ideas or concepts that we may try to transmit in speech, but those more massive linguistic objects that are constituted by fragments or sections of speech. . . . Or again, the poet may proceed by a process of disintegration, as Rimbaud does. Poetry therefore seems to exist between two conflicting formulae: linguistic integration and semantic disintegration."[29]

These remarks, it may be argued, stem as much from Ferdinand de Saussure's *Cours de linguistique générale* (1915) as from symbolist or (in its later incarnation) surrealist poetry. It goes without saying that Japanese poets and poet-translators from Ueda Bin (1874-1916) onward have been acutely aware of the French tradition—it is almost a cliché to remark that modern Japanese poetry is largely built on the French romantic and symbolist heritage— and Asabuki Ryōji, quite apart from his profession (he is a professor of French), is no exception to this rule.

Another technique mastered by Asabuki in both *Opus* and his succeeding volume *Misshitsuron/Le traité de la chambre close* (Closed room treatise, 1989) is what Marjorie Perloff describes as "the most interesting side of the Pound legacy: namely, the poet's canto structure."[30] The one-hundred-poem *Opus*, which could easily be read as one long poem, exemplifies what Perloff describes as a "move beyond the isolated lyric poem *(poema)* valorized by New Critics like Stanley Burnshaw . . . toward a larger, more capacious poetic form *(poesis)* that could once again accommodate various levels of discourse."[31] The name of Ezra Pound is significant here, since it might be argued that the first long poem Pound had a hand in composing was T. S. Eliot's "The Waste Land" (recall the dedication "For Ezra Pound / il miglior fabbro"), which proved pivotal in the development of Nishiwaki Junzaburō, perhaps the first Japanese master of the long poem.

Nishiwaki studied at New College, Oxford University, at exactly the same time that Eliot (with Pound's editorial assistance) was working on the "The Waste Land."[32] No critic doubts the impact of Eliot on Nishiwaki, who has been described by Donald Keene as having "probably exercised the greatest influence of any Japanese poet on the post-1945 generation."[33] Nishiwaki increasingly came to favor the long poem and, in two such long poems, *No Traveler Returns (Tabibito kaerazu)* and *Ushinawareta toki* (Time lost, 1960),[34] established a modernist foundation on which poets of Asabuki's generation could build. There have been more precursors since then.[35] Irisawa Yasuo's *Waga Izumo, Waga chinkon* (My Izumo, my requiem, 1968), Shiraishi Kazuko's *Seinaru inja no kisetsu* (Season of the sacred lecher, 1970), and Yoshimasu Gōzō's *Neppu, a Thousand Steps* (Devil's wind, a thousand steps, 1979) are but some of the most notable of the long poems produced in volume form in recent years.[36]

Not all critics are receptive to the "self-referential" or "nonreferential" poem. I have already considered criticism of postmodernism by such thinkers as Terry Eagleton and Jürgen Habermas. The poet and critic Yoshimoto Takaaki in his influential *Zōho sengo shi shiron* (A historical study of postwar poetry, revised edition 1983) argued strongly against such poetry, describing it derisively as mere "rhetoric" without substance or soul. In the section of his study titled "Shūjiteki no genzai" (The rhetorical present), he claimed: "Postwar poetry has become significantly estranged from contemporary poets and poetry in respect of mainstream concerns. . . . To single out poets' individual characteristics from the ground of their sensibility and the solipsism of their thought has become meaningless. What differentiates one poet from another is language, rhetorical bias *(shūjiteki kodawari)."*[37]

Yoshimoto traces rhetorical influence back to the progenitor of Japanese modernism: Nishiwaki Junzaburō. He argues: "Poetic rhetoric has become distanced from all certainty *(setsujitsusa)."*[38] He stresses the importance of phonemic association, rather than literal "meaning," for contemporary poets: "The 'phoneme' is simply subordinated to 'consciousness'; the connection with 'meaning' is a secondary consideration."[39] Yoshimoto picks out the poetry of Hiraide Takashi (b. 1950), a contemporary and in some ways a mentor of Asabuki, as particularly notorious in this regard.[40]

A number of poets reacted to Yoshimoto's critique; one of the most vehement counterattacks came from the poet Inagawa Masato (b. 1949), a contemporary of both Hiraide and Asabuki.[41] In his essay "'Wareware' to wa dareka?: Aruiwa 'genzai' to iu ryōiki" (Who are "we"? Or, the territory of the "present") published in the 1990 edition of his selected poems, Asabuki delivered a potent counterblow to Yoshimoto's polemics. Inagawa satirized and derided Yoshimoto's concerns—the notion of the "present," which Yoshimoto famously explored in his 1984 book *Masu imēji ron* (On mass images), Inagawa subjects to withering criticism—by arguing that, in effect, Yoshimoto was denying the legitimate concerns of contemporary poets by refusing to recognize their presence and failing to grapple with the issues that they raise.[42]

There is also a disguised argument over the notion of poetry as ideology (putatively held by Yoshimoto) and poetry as an exploration of language, although Inagawa does not want to concede that contemporary poetry does not deal with ideas. The overall effect of this counterpolemic is to emphasize the low regard contemporary poets hold for Yoshimoto's criticisms, although such an assertion could actually be taken as an indication to the contrary.

Hiraide put an even stronger counterargument in a 1985 essay called "Danshō 31" (31 fragments), where he presents thirty-one utterances almost as poetic manifestos or principles. The twenty-eighth and twenty-ninth utterances make an emphatic case:

> The system of power that works of poetry possess is directly expressed in the dynamics of the tension between subjectivity and the world. In that sense, a poem is a social act. Thus, the dynamics of the poem in this sense can be categorized as political critique.

Instead, to the degree that political and social concerns do not make up the subject matter of poetry, the dynamics of subjectivity that structure poetry today embody various types of political and social dynamic as they are.[43]

Here Hiraide rewrites the old argument that form rather than content represents the main thematic strength of poetry for the late twentieth century. His contention is that subjectivity as literary expression structures perception of social and political reality, and thus can act as a powerful critique of that reality. The emphasis is on language as the chief vehicle of meaning, since it is subjectivity in action. The connections to *Opus* are apparent: language is the main marker of subjectivity that in Asabuki's book occupies a decentered space. Hence, both as theory and as practice, Yoshimoto's criticism of "language"-oriented poetry has had little effect, it would seem, on poets who continue to write in this mode. Asabuki is a case in point.

## *Opus* as Language Field

*Opus* was published in 1987 by the Shichōsha company, and the following year it was awarded the prestigious Rekitei poetry award. The hundred poems in the book are numbered consecutively from 00 to 99 and, it will be argued here, can be considered as a discrete whole. The length of the poems varies from as little as two to as long as eighty lines.

The only way to proceed through the poem sequence is by tracing words, lines, and the occasional notion or character as they reoccur in this palimpsest of a poem; a useful analogy may be to tracing leitmotifs through Wagnerian music-dramas. The first two lines of "00" establish the mood from the beginning: "I will begin here by erasing one name / Is it a person's name? Or the name of a tale?"[44] The repetition of lines can be seen clearly in "01" and "02," where the last line of the former poem is repeated as the last line of the latter verse. Let me trace one or two interweavings out of many.

The verb "to erase" in "00" is "*masshō suru,*" already quoted in the first line of that poem. The notion "erase" is elaborated or cross-referenced five lines later with the verb "peel" *(muku)* in the expression "peel the skin." This is later developed into "splits open" *(hajikeru),* "wipe clean" *(issō suru),* "negate" *(nakusu),* and then "erase" in the last line. The subjects of these verbs are all different, but the verbal gesture or direction is remarkably consistent. Poem "02" accelerates the disrobing of language, as seen from the following translations of the first three poems:

00

I will begin here by erasing one name
Is it a person's name? Or the name of a tale?


The summer tree
I send my sight along the separate branches one by one
For my morning fruit
Peel the skin with my thin fingernail
Stew the fruit in sugar
Lacuna
The sound of a book being beaten, dust rising
Trembling in the light


The summer tree
The pipe of air may be sent along each branch separately, water flowing
    backward providing the makeup, swamp-eye never drying, a lake-body
    sitting up, forever desiring endless extravagance, but no traces of the castle
    remain, like a black bull strolling at his leisure up a hill reeking of aniseed
    and peppermint, this walk must proceed!


The regular sound of an electron
Splits open
Acrylic blue, this is a part of the sea floating in the giant brain
Brain with your swamp eyes awake!
In your exorcised form
In the morning will you wipe it all clean?
The morning preserves the long continuation of night in itself
Retraces the writings of the night twisted as they may be
Looks cool
Ripens the fruit, shakes the zelkova, laurel, magnolia no wild roses no wild
    strawberries but it stews up a compote of fruit, cleans its teeth, the bees
    start to buzz, the soldier ants do not cease their marching


The summer tree
Latent in its liquid
I will answer for its sinister motives

Even if I return
For the time being I will negate the morning's greeting
I will begin here by erasing one name

01

How many nights did the rain continue? it's been ages since your last service, said the woman smiling eyes downcast, with a studied motion she exposed her breast, allowed an erect nipple to peep out, when I grasped her breast in my right hand and squeezed she trembled slightly, this woman who arrived wearing a fox's mask, her eyelids pale, or, was it makeup? I sucked her eyelids which appeared cerise aquamarine smelling of rouge and powder, as if we had been making love for years my lips moved from behind her ears to below her waist, how many days did I spend cataloging her smells, was I in a stupor, the smell of the rain, the wet bedding, and the smell of my wet fingers, this deserted dwelling become a waterway! the woman communicated her heat her liquids front and back, her eyebrows lengthening, the bridge of her nose shrinking, until I could stand it no longer, back become a half-moon lake! Late into the night the woman retained the rain, she remained hard, without communicating the heart of my heat, I push my face between her legs, I continue to catalog the smell of glucose flowing unbearably, what am I trying to prolong?

02

Peeling water folds
Withholding sexual water-veins
What am I trying to prolong?[45]

In the first two poems the connotations are overtly sexual. But this only scratches the surface of a whole fretwork of associations, cross-references, sound correspondences, and repetitions. To use a term popularized by the L=A=N=G=U=A=G=E poets, one can only begin to trace the birth of a "language (or poem) field."[46]

Again in "05" the sixth line reads, "One membrane of hydrogen is peeled (*mekurareru*) like an eardrum."[47] Seven lines later, "They peel a thin skin-colored membrane."[48] The association of "membrane" (*maku*) and "peel" is established, and "peel" is repeated twice more in the poem. While all this is happening, "lakes," "water-veins," and "hydrogen"(water element) begin to effect a poetic mitosis. In "06" the second line of the three line poem reads, "Diving through layer upon layer of water folds."[49] By "07," in line eight, "erase" reappears, and it reappears again three lines later; this time the web of connections is lengthened to include "transparent" and "symmetry." The notion of "layering" is layered even more explicitly in "08" with the first appearance of *"kosō"* (ancient layers). For the next three poems, *"ito no kuzu"* (ravelings) assumes the role of metonymic trope, but by "12," "erase" *(kezuru)*, is back with a vengeance, being mentioned almost every second line in this fifteen-line poem. And the last line of "15," "Something newly elongated," directly echoes "01" *("hikinobasareru"* as compared to *"hikinobasō to shite iru"* in "01").[50] By "15" the field is full, bristling with lakes, membranes, peelings, and erasures.

The reader may object that without reference to larger meaning-fragments, such a field tracing is incomprehensible. But the point is that the field alone, in all its complexity and variety, reveals or, better still, constitutes meaning. The field is, as Yoshimoto Takaaki noted, a phoneme complex as much as anything else. Poem "04" demonstrates this plainly in its first four lines: *"Taikei to iu koto ni shite okōka, kasuka ni nejikurete wa hane ka / esu (nejikurete wa hanekaesu?), kasuka ni yodonde wa uchikae / su (yodonde wa uchikaesu?), ōkina nami, ōkina kimi no nami / kimichi, ōkina kimi no michimichiru michi, shiomichiru jikan, sama."*[51] A version in English might read as follows: "Shall we make it a system, it twists slightly and bounces back (twists slightly and bounces back?), pauses a little and rolls back (pauses and rolls back?) a huge wave, your huge tree-lined street, your big filled to the brim street."

The homophonic ambiguity of the text is emphasized by the fact that it is written entirely in *hiragana*. As the lines thicken and elongate, so the ambiguity (and deliberately obscure "open" punning) becomes even more prominent. This is not to say that individual poems within Asabuki's crazy patchwork quilt do not operate, on one level at least, as distinct poems that can be scanned to produce something resembling a conventional reading.

## Semantic Vectors

An examination of some larger meaning-fragments that cohere in a conventional way, or appear to, demonstrate equally effectively the postmodernist nature of Asabuki's exercise. If one draws a quite arbitrary line after poem "35" and thus examines poems "15" to "35," one of the most consistent threads that make up the text is the conjunction of sex and language. Poem "15" begins with a "presence," a speaking subject, but the nature of the lesson is made abundantly clear by lines 16 and 17: "I open my legs / I thrust out my pelvis under a naked light bulb." Two lines later the word *"kuda"* (tube, pipe) is introduced into the poem. This word is one of the many lexical reference points that act as knots to center a "vector" or an "axis" on this grid of one hundred poems. The last line performs a similar role; moreover, the "subject" of "15" is sexually ambiguous. These points are clearly demonstrated in the following translation:

15

Teach me mouth to mouth
What cannot be taught mouth to mouth
Since I am not thinking of anything in this shameful position
I have made my heart empty so
With your hard lips
With your hangnailed fingers
Trace
Certain shapes and no-shapes
Just the winter landscape reflected in my eyes
Carve it
On my rotting organ
Mouth to mouth
Not just empty love-play
Not just empty pain
Teach me the unteachable what should not be taught
I open my legs
I thrust out my pelvis under a naked light bulb
Worrying about the fluff on my jumper
Because I will become forever a shameful vessel
Because I will remain a tube of glue
I want you to trace
Mouth to mouth
With your cracked lips
I want you to send into the back of my head
A new madness
That you will never know

That I do not know
Something newly elongated[52]

In poem "17," the gender seems male (the stanza is italicized in the original):

17

*/ For a long time I kept thinking about you*
*about your rusted mouth, about your*
*organs used only for sex-play like your*
*rusted tube, I was in this closed room, in*
*this double closed room, enduring burial*
*in the air, without any fingers to lead, to*
*be led, thinking and thinking about the*
*indeterminate perimeter of a border about*
*to be closed, with my eyeless*
*eyes burning with the energy of a moray eel I*
*will keep on pursuing your body so*
*difficult to tolerate, with its protruding lip,*
*suspicious, empty /* [53]

The link between "naming" and sexuality is made more explicit in the next poem, "18." The sixth, seventh, and eighth lines read: "For example, a clitoris protruding like my finger, hangnails and all, a vagina collapsed like my cilia-dry throat, names of formless organs like these. Blind as I am, I detest names of these difficult-to-tolerate, unformed organs."[54] Poem "19" begins like a conventional lyric: "Lover on the lawn of our sexual love / Numerous sheep jump about, slowly."[55] Some eleven lines later, in the middle of the poem, the heat is turned up: "So from my mania my passion for young girls I choose you with your strong smells / I seduce you, I undress you and put you into bed / In the bedclothes of my mania, but I do not let you sleep, since I cannot rape you / It becomes irritated, such is my mania / Holding a hard nipple in my mouth irritated like a seaslug."[56]

However, from this point the paratactic impulse reveals a poem not erotic in the conventional sense but in a linguistic sense:[57] "Our eight limbs like this simply go mad, our / Gold, is gold that does not melt in passion / Since it is a distorted mirror that sways in the night it reflects nothing / Nothing / One sheep two sheep, so we do not share in the night, since we do not share / My mania alone does not consume, becomes / A constellation on the rooftop of the insomniac Imperial Hotel / Ravelings of empty desire leaking from a box that has simply become a constellation, one sheep two sheep . . ."[58]

## Erasing / Writing

The poet's passion is for words, not for the narrative presence, the "lover" who is addressed in the first line. Poem "19" quoted above ends in a simultaneous celebration of both a disintegrative and an associative moment. There is no "story" there. The following poem, "20," restates the poet's technique:

20

/ Sometimes I copied, sometimes I rewrote, I erased names, sometimes a person's name, sometimes a shapeless dream fragment from a single tale (naturally nobody's in particular), sometimes I transcribed whole texts perfectly, I became a student, at that time between the lines of modernity accumulating erasure, I thought of a single transparent tree that will tower, no doubt, above the future collected works of an aged poet, I will plant trees between my lines too, the breaking of the gas bubbles will reduce the oxygen, in summer, while I put my impossible-to-read letters in order, I sometimes rewrote whole texts as they were, into my tree, into my modern transparent giant tree / I keep on classifying, starting first from the smell of the woman I loved, I didn't love, into the particulars of her fat, into the gelatine sea, I keep on classifying, where did her hair grow from? Where did her body hair end? The flexibility of her arms, her upper arm, the length of her nipples, the diameter of her areoles, their nodules, her skin with my various wickednesses engraved upon it, her stomach that planted a bad seed, I will classify them all, one by one for example your seaweed stomach, seafood / a cross between a journal and letters (naturally not addressed to anyone) I copy wastepaper, I made it an exercise every morning to rewrite it, in order to cross out names, names of people, and being a person /[59]

The poet himself has characterized his method of writing as an exploration of sound. In his essay "Chinmoku / Hakushi ni tsuite" (Silence / On blank paper), published in the 1992 edition of his selected poetry, Asabuki begins with a criticism of the viewpoint that sees poetry as purely concerned with meaning expressed as word-image; practically no one imagines that poetry might be expressed as a kind of music. He then takes up the notion of indeterminate sound that he finds in the work of the American composer John Cage (b. 1912). This he associates with Cage's conceptualization of silence. He declares: "We are continually enclosed in a myriad of background noises, and so, we cannot even experience silence, let alone sound."[60] He proceeds to analyze Cage's work with specific reference to Mallarmé's writings on tabula rasa. He argues: "Poetry, that is to say, language, is nothingness itself. . . . A tabula rasa presents before the poet's very eyes the darkness of this nothingness."[61]

Here the poet is reading Mallarmé's poetry as an exploration of words in the form of a kind of music. He notes: "This tabula rasa is the repeated prayer of countless silent words: the words of silence humming."[62] Nevertheless, Asabuki states: "For the present, it is necessary to declare that silence does not exist. . . . We are overloaded with noise."[63] And, returning implicitly to his own poetry, he notes: "Whether we know it or not . . . innumerable sounds exist here all the time. We must grow sensitive to this type of disordered sound . . .

attend to the variety and complexity of sound. . . . Noise exists not merely without but within."

His conclusion to the essay can serve as a powerful statement of his own aesthetic: "We must listen to the diversity of disordered sound with our eardrums; still more, we must listen with our bodies. The texts we weave are always here; we live noise."[64] This association of bodily sensation and the unconscious rhythms of sound association make up the organizing principle of Asabuki's work. Also clear from this account is the explicitly modernist or postmodernist (depending on one's viewpoint) nature of Asabuki's poetics.

FIGURE 8. Asabuki Ryōji. Courtesy of Asabuki Ryōji

Returning to *Opus* and a clear demonstration of these poetics, poems "23," "24," and "25" scan a matrix of associations centering on the notions of "erasing" and "writing," each written with a single narrating subject, an "I" *(watashi)*. Poem "27" begins with "you" *(anata):* "You called it in play a 'Land of Birds' / This prison of love,"[65] then mixes erotic juxtapositions with transparencies, rivers, waters, and sheep, finally concluding: "In order to close this thing swelling up into my sexual love / In order to close this thing overflowing from the shape of my sexual love."[66]

As if in deliberate balance, poem "28" talks more of the frustrations of language than of sexual love. The last three lines claim: "I do not have the mouth to imitate human speech / I want to take leave of my white immersed brain, my heart full / I will become the edge of a cloud."[67] Poem "29" blends a run of puns and alliterative onomatopoeia with hard, clear images. Poems "30," "31," and "32" are all short poems, none longer than four lines, that celebrate the paradox of language:

30

Angels raise a clamor, trumpets in the blue sky where
Angels fly, small cumulonimbi flicked by angels
Nameless words, silent bodies being exchanged
While angels ring bells, scatter stars and roar with laughter

31

Two cloud-shaped women who loved a mad old poet
One traces a yellow madness
The other traces the lovemaking of description
Somewhere else is another one

32

Chirpchirpwonderfulclamorclamorcryclamoringdisappearingstarlings[68]

Poem "33" is a more intricate mesh of phonemic/semic interchange. The last line reads in Japanese: *"Kikantekikubun wa shōkyoshite shimaitai, itaiitai to hanpuku suru yubi mo,"* which comes into English very poorly and with significant losses in a near-literal gloss: "I want to eliminate divisions between organs, my finger repeating it hurts hurts."[69] Poem "34" is once again a rich mixture of the erotic and the play of presence and absence. Poem "35" is full of birds, numbers, and stars and concludes with a Molly Bloom–like monologue.

From the above (the remainder of the poem does not differ in any essential from the process described), one can argue all kinds of contradictory propositions—there is no progression (argument, sequence, presence, subject, object, or narrative), or the poem explodes outward in an ever more complex and intricate network of concatenation, melodic relationships, multiple planes, displacements, transformations, referential self-encodings—and find that all the contraries meet, all the paradoxes become ever more paradoxical.

And lest we readers lose ourselves in the play, the pleasure of the text, and then fall prey to notions like the inevitable and selfless autonomy of automatic writing (an extreme expression of ideas held by some "language" advocates), we should remember Craig Watson's "Statement":

> I'm trying now to deal with a poetics that actively conditions my self/environment and serves as a tuning process and as a means of mediating personal experiences. Obviously such an internalized approach disavows allegiance to any code of poetic behaviour and repudiates any sort of cultural standards. . . . This urge seems to lie within the rooted and individual beginnings of the activity, centered on a meditative, self-encoded embrace of those issues and inclinations I find within my own humanness. The intention therefore becomes the opening of experience toward a continual address of the self."[70]

Surely Asabuki would quarrel with little (and agree with much) of the viewpoint held by Watson.

Asabuki's long sequence winds in and out, sometimes repeating patterns but mostly augmenting them until it resembles nothing so much as a giant kaleidoscope of language. There is little point in attempting to characterize or capture the entire network of associations that make up the work—the task is surely Sisyphean. As each succeeding poem both enriches and adds to the meaning-worm, so readers grasp the ambition of Asabuki's project, which perhaps not unintentionally resembles the process of gene patterning, where nothing, no scrap of information, is ever discarded, no matter how irrelevant. In the poet's own words, from poem "93," "It's a prism / This is a / p /

rism,"[71] or, as poem "95" states, "Countless words caught in a small ray of sunlight."[72]

Poem "96" returns to the motif of classification. The second stanza begins thus:

> I classify,
> Tales, into those that have endings and those that don't, names,
> into those that I can remember and those that I can't, into
> whisperings in the ear, into names that always tremble pleasurably
> on my lips and those that don't,[73]

The poem continues to elaborate this theme, playing with Claude Lévi-Strauss' notions of raw and cooked as a system of classification, linking these motifs to more abstract and philosophical ideas like notions of discourse advocated by Foucault and Derrida. As the second last stanza states: "I classify . . . discourse, into that which is here and that which isn't." The last stanza expands on the implications of discourse: "I classify . . . that which is me and that which is you, or,".[74]

The poem refuses to end. The last lines of this monumentally decentered text, where referentiality fuses into itself and idealist notions of language contradict themselves constantly (as signifiers signify not only words but things and more), conclude: "There is nothing / Closed."[75]

# Chapter 7
# The Limits of Language
## The Poetry of Tanikawa Shuntarō

*meine Trauer, ich seh's,*
*läuft zu dir über.*
—Paul Celan, *Zeitgehöft*

*It was an old theme even for me:*
*Language cannot do everything—*
—Adrienne Rich, "Cartographies of Silence"

In 1997, the poet Tanikawa Shuntarō (b. 1931) decided to abandon poetry. Some five or so years later, he relented and, in a partial retreat from this decision, began to publish verse again, but only as short, three-line poems.[1] This hiatus in Tanikawa's career and his subsequent resumption of verse composition is an event of no small significance, as Tanikawa is generally acknowledged to be Japan's most famous living poet. The last three volumes Tanikawa wrote before the hiatus, like the entire corpus of the poet's oeuvre, are concerned—one could use the word "obsessed"—with language. In this respect, Tanikawa's struggle with the theme of language is typical of modernist poets of his generation and demonstrates one of the central fixations of modernism itself.

## The Limits of Poetry

In the July 1993 edition of *Contemporary Poetry Notebook,* the poet Shimizu Akira wrote that, in his view, Tanikawa deserved the Nobel Prize in Literature.[2] This was a special issue of the journal devoted to Tanikawa's 1993 volume *Seken shirazu* (The naif ), which was later awarded the first Hagiwara Sakutarō Prize; virtually all of the thirty or so articles that dealt with *The Naif* expressed similar praise for this collection and for the historic position it occupied in the history of postwar Japanese poetry. The fact that most of the poems in Tanikawa's book were originally published in the *Contemporary Po-*

*etry Notebook* may seem to account for the special issue—and perhaps for some of the praise—but in reality this is probably not the case. This volume has been almost universally acclaimed as a masterpiece and a turning point in Tanikawa's career. At more or less the same time, Tanikawa published two other major original volumes of poetry before his abandonment of verse: *Mōtsaruto wo kiku hito* (A man who listens to Mozart, 1995) and *Masshiro de iru yori mo* (Rather than being pure white, 1995), and these three collections form the primary subject of this chapter.

How did people know that they were the last books of verse Tanikawa intended to write, that they signaled a major break in his brilliant career as a poet? Tanikawa himself in 1997 in a conversation with the scholar Takachi Jun'ichirō remarked: "I want to keep myself away from poetry and not to write poems any more, unless it is unremittably required writing."[3] To put the point beyond dispute, Tanikawa repeated the same sentiments in an interview in November 1997, saying: "Now I have forbidden myself poetry. I can't write poetry any more. I believe if I were to go on writing poetry, it could be bad for me. Poetry has invaded my real life, so I want to reclaim an ordinary life for myself."[4] Tanikawa also mentioned in the same interview that editions of his selected and collected poems would continue to appear and also that many poems he had written before his decision to abandon poetry were still to be published. Perhaps an example of such a volume is his 1996 book *Yasashisa wa ai ja nai* (Tenderness is not love), a collaboration with the photographer Araki Nobuyoshi.

Nevertheless, that a poet as prolific as Tanikawa, with fifty or so collections of poetry and more than four hundred other books to his name, should have decided to abandon poetry, even if only for five years, prompts a deeper inquiry into his decision than might be satisfied by his public utterances (even if those public pronouncements probably do go to the heart of the matter). The poems that ended this hiatus were published between May and July 2002 in the *Contemporary Poetry Notebook*. These verses were later collected in a single volume (with English translations attached) and published under the English title *Minimal* in October 2002.[5]

However, I will not examine *Minimal* here. The focus of this chapter will be on the poetry that was written in the period leading up to the hiatus, and the emphasis will be more on the struggle with language than directly with biographical concerns, although, when appropriate, the connections between the poet and his poetry will come under scrutiny. Before embarking on a de-

FIGURE 9. Tanikawa Shuntarō (photo by Miyauchi Masaru). Courtesy of Tanikawa Shuntarō

tailed analysis of the three books written in the 1990s, immediately before his break from verse, and the theme of language that distinguished them, let me first retrace the genesis of this hiatus and its ending in an attempt to explore the issue of how poetry came to impose limits on the poet himself.

The year before his decision to give up poetry was a particularly traumatic one for Tanikawa. In 1996, the poet was divorced from his third wife, the artist Sano Yōko, to whom he had dedicated a volume of love poetry in 1991 (which was awarded a major poetry prize).[6] As a result of the divorce, according to Takachi Jun'ichirō, Tanikawa fell into a deep depression.[7] It is not hard to imagine that the poet's personal trauma during 1996 played some role in his decision the following year to end his career as a poet, which until that time had spanned over forty years, covering almost the entire history of postwar Japan. The fact that five years later he ended this pause in his career also strengthens the implication that it was in some way related to personal issues. In the postscript to *Minimal,* Tanikawa reviewed his hiatus and also commented on how he came to rescind his decision:

Several years ago I believed that I wanted to distance myself from poetry for a time. This was not because I was suffering from writer's block, on the contrary, I found it was all too easy to compose poetry; it could be said that I had come to see reality only through poetry and consequently experienced a strong reaction against this. It was like an occupational disease picked up as a result of writing poetry for such a long time. Yet, now and again, when I was asked, I wrote poetry. . . . I had the opportunity to travel to China. From this relaxed journey, unexpectedly, a number of short poems *(tanshi)* resulted. Was it because I unconsciously felt some sympathy for that tone found in haiku and some Chinese verse, a quality utterly removed from any kind of verbosity? After I returned to Japan, whenever the mood took me, I continued to compose these short three line verses I had discovered on my Chinese pilgrimage, and for some reason or other I gave the name "minimal" to them.[8]

Finally, it is fascinating to note that the poet Morinaka Takaaki argued in an article published in 1995 that the one consistent theme of Tanikawa's poetry, a theme evident in his first collection published in 1952 and found equally prominently in his later collections, is a profound distrust of language. Morinaka, discussing *The Naif,* characterizes this distrust as an "opaque membrane blocking the poet's ego from the world"; such a distrust is common to contemporary poetry, but Tanikawa's sustained and intense embrace of it is exceptional, and that it should lead for a time ultimately to silence may not seem so great a paradox.[9]

## The Naif

*The Naif* is a highly praised collection not merely for the aesthetic merit of the individual poems, but also for its significance in Tanikawa's overall oeuvre. In *Tabi* (Journeys, 1968), Tanikawa's most celebrated collection before *The Naif,* the poet wrote the famous lines "I've posed as a poet / But I'm not."[10] It is arguable that this antagonism to writing reaches its climax in *The Naif,* as seen in the first poem "Chichi no shi" (My father's death), which is translated in full:

### My Father's Death

My father died aged ninety-four years and four months.
The day before he died he went to a barber shop.
In bed at midnight he got rid of the entire contents of his stomach.
Summonsed at dawn by the person attending him, his mouth was open with
   the false teeth removed and his face had turned into a nō mask of an old
   man, he was already dead. His face was cold but his hands and feet were
   still warm.
Nothing had come out of his nose or mouth or the hole in his backside, his
   body was so clean that nothing needed wiping.
They said if he died at home it would be an unnatural death and so I called an
   ambulance. During the trip and even after we arrived at the hospital, they
   administered oxygen and a heart massage.

It was ridiculous so I asked them to stop.

They took the body home from the hospital.

My son and the son of the woman who I was living with cleaned up the room.

Three people came from the medical examiner's office. On the death certificate, the time of death was put several hours in advance of the actual time of death.

People gathered.

Telegrams of condolence came one after another.

Successive baskets of flowers arrived.

My wife, from whom I was separated, arrived. Upstairs I argued with a woman.

I got busier and busier, and less and less able to comprehend what was going on.

At night, a man came running in from the entrance, bawling like a child.

"The professor's dead, the professor's dead and gone!" he yelled.

The man, who had come from Suwa, said, weeping, "Are there trains still running? I suppose not. I'm going home," and left.

Something called a votive offering arrived from the emperor and empress.

The notation "30,000 yen" was rubber-stamped on the envelope.

The First-Class Order of the Sacred Treasure arrived from the emperor. Three ribbons were enclosed, the miniature decoration was like a small, dried-up slice of lemon. Father often used to rub the dry, cracked skin of his legs with a slice of lemon.

A Junior Third Court Rank arrived from the prime minister.

Nothing was attached to this but a mass of mail-order catalogs arrived selling picture frames for patents of decoration and diplomas of posthumous court rank.

Father was a handsome man and so I thought the decorations would have looked good on him.

The funeral director told us that the highest form of funeral was the "Funeral Feast."

I felt father was so emaciated that we could only make soup out of him.

*

While you are asleep, Death,
With its silent, swift hand
Sweeps away all the detail of life but
For us who talk away the small time

Until the flowers placed as offerings on the altar fade
There is no end to foolish chatter

Death is the unknown
In the unknown there is no detail
This resembles poetry
Both Death and poetry tend to abridge life but
Those who are left alive rejoice in puzzling detail
Rather than abridgment

*

The chief mourner's speech

16 October 1989, Kita Kamakura Tōkeiji Temple

The photographs of my father Tetsuzō and my mother Takiko displayed on the altar, ever since my mother's death five years ago, father had kept close by his side. Not only the photographs, but her bones too, father did not let them out of hand's reach. Whether this was an act of love or just plain idleness is something that I, their son, am not sure of. In any case, today will be a departure from the usual practice. Having received permission from the priest, I have arranged for the bones of both father and mother to be placed on the altar. Mother's funeral, this was father's idea, was conducted very privately, and so, today, those of you who knew mother can make your farewells to her as well as to my father.

Looking from my perspective as his son, all his life, father was a man who adhered to his own precepts, perhaps that was why he was lonely, but I believe he lived out his allotted years fortunately and happily. I wish to thank you all for taking the time to come here today to send off my father.

*

I was in the bathroom in our old house in Suginami before we had it renovated, washing an old, rusty metal ashtray, when my father came in, he must have been in his sixties, wearing his overcoat over his black kimono. He remarked that the washing basket that he had made out of brick in the same shape as the previous one had turned out fine. I washed my hands and wiped them with a towel hanging from the towel rack in the far corner of the bathroom, the thought struck me that I'd have to move the towel rack closer to the washbasin. When I asked father if there was anything wrong, he answered that he was fine. How I felt then about father was exactly the same as how I felt a month ago. The moment the scene suddenly changed to a long shot of my aunt's old house viewed from her garden, I realized that father had died, and, in a dream, my chest swelled, and I burst into tears. Even when I awoke, I wasn't sure if I had truly wept or not.[11]

This poem has been much praised by all the critics cited in the special edition of *Contemporary Poetry Notebook* devoted to *The Naif*. However, most commentators find the poem troubling, in that if a kind of self-critical irony is one of the most sustained threads among the many found in the work, then what exactly does this signify? The poet and critic Kitagawa Tōru focuses on the notion of "performance" in his attempts to characterize the prevailing narrative voice: Tanikawa is painting a portrait of the artist that explicitly contradicts the artifice inherent in the nature of poetry, indeed inherent in all writing. The infusion into the poem of large chunks of prose—the chief mourner's speech (whether this was actually the requiem address Tanikawa gave at his father's funeral is irrelevant, claims Kitagawa)—is a rhetorical strategy designed to strip this immensely moving lament for the poet's father of sentimentality, of its very rhetorical qualities. Yet, it is patently nonsensical to view Tanikawa's requiem as anything but a most powerful work of art, a poem.[12]

By construing the poet's narrative art as predominantly ironic, Kitagawa seeks to fuse the personal, biographical elements in the poem with the struggle with language that he discerns as the keynote of this collection, thus arguing for a harsher, more self-critical voice (on both the thematic and rhetorical levels) than seen in any previous Tanikawa collection. This voice strikes Kitagawa and most other commentators on this poem as signaling Tanikawa's achievement of an even deeper level of artistic excellence than before. But the clear contradiction between the mastery of a rhetoric of confession or self-construction and the intense antagonism toward the notion of rhetoric itself, expressed perfectly in the last line of the poem, which manages simultaneously to be both ironic and ambiguous, leads many critics to a profound distrust of any statement of poetics implicit in the poem.

In order to comment on this poem, the poet and novelist Nejime Shōichi (b. 1948) tells an anecdote about the poet that somehow suggests the poet's public persona is so consciously constructed that Tanikawa's irony is a kind of evasion.[13] The critic Yokogi Tokuhisa warns against any attempt to construct a critique of *The Naif* based on irony, as irony emerges as a rhetorical technique rather than as self-critique. Hence several critics are drawn to the question: What is there to hide?[14]

## Death as Theme

The aesthetic struggle to situate self in relation to language in poems of self-revelation is a familiar theme for readers of modern poetry in English. The American poet Robert Lowell's (1917–1977) journey from elegiac irony in "For Sale," his poem about his mother from *Life Studies* (1959), to the chaos of his marriage expressed in *The Dolphin* (1973) charts a journey common to many English-language poets of the period. The Australian poet Robert Gray's (b. 1945) lament for his father, "Poem to My Father" from *Grass Script* (1979), expresses in harsh caricature the paradoxical freedom that the death of a parent can bring, something that Tanikawa touches on but much more reticently in "My Father's Death."[15]

Another Australian poet, Les Murray (b. 1938), in his 1983 volume *The People's Otherworld,* composed "Three Poems in Memory of My Mother" with a narrative voice less ironic than that of Tanikawa but just as constructed. The American poet John Berryman's (1914–1972) "Dream Song 145," from his 1964 volume *The Dream Songs,* leaves his narrator, Henry, pondering the suicide of his father and thus, as narrative technique, uses the rhetoric of dream to contemplate ironically a father's suicide.[16]

However, none of the Western poets cited above confronts the dilemma of language in relation to death as directly as does Tanikawa. Perhaps this is because Tanikawa is writing later than most of the English-language poets mentioned above. The Australian poet John Forbes (1950–1998) in his 1988 volume *The Stunned Mullet and Other Poems* wrote a humorous poem about death—"Death, an Ode"—which derives its wit from conscious play on a variety of metaphorical and metonymic expressions or reminders of death. Despite the shared consciousness of language, however, such a light-handed treatment of the subject could also be read, perhaps ironically, as a kind of evasion.[17]

A more stimulating comparison might be with the American poet John Ashbery's 1992 volume *Flow Chart,* which, while in many ways the ultimate expression of metaphor as rhetoric, reads as a dark, elegiac meditation on death, or, at least, ends. If one were to conduct a systematic review of recent English-language poetry on the death of a parent or on death as event, no doubt, hundreds of more pertinent examples would appear. However, the conjunction of poetry, poetry as the language of rhetoric, and death seems not that common in the West, although the topic of death and poets is much more so, as, for instance, in the Australian poet Bruce Beaver's (b. 1928) poem "XVI" in his 1978 volume *Death's Directives*.[18]

Very few of the critiques collected in *The Naif* special edition of *Contemporary Poetry Notebook* compare "My Father's Death" with poems about poetry and death by other contemporary Japanese poets. Indeed, there are practically no comparisons to other poets made at all. The personal, autobiographical nature of the collection apparently played a role in persuading critics to view *The Naif* more in terms of Tanikawa's personal evolution as a poet than as an interesting group of poems written on broadly similar themes.

If one were to nominate one distinguished Japanese poet, an older contemporary of Tanikawa, who could be described as obsessed by the theme of death and, occasionally, by how language is inadequate to express such a theme, then the name of Soh Sakon would immediately spring to mind. However, as Soh's verse on death is directly related to World War II, his affinities would be closer to Holocaust poets like Paul Celan, and, besides, Soh is by no means alone among Japanese poets in focusing on death and the war, as noted earlier.[19]

Tanikawa's affinities with his Japanese (and Western) contemporaries, as illustrated in *The Naif,* relate more to the central theme of language and how it intersects with the construction of self. Again, the central issue is the adequacy (or inadequacy) of language to represent meaning.

## From Estrangement to Ambiguity

In some ways, the second poem in *The Naif,* the title poem "Seken shirazu" (The naif), reveals the connection between language and representation even more transparently than "My Father's Death." Kitagawa Tōru notes that the first three poems in the book read as if they are a linked verse sequence. I will translate the second and third poems. First, "The Naif," which reads as follows:

**The Naif**

The tips of my toes seem disturbingly far away
My five toes like five complete and utter strangers
Draw together distantly
Beside my bed a telephone connects me to the outside world but

There is no one I want to talk to
Ever since I can remember, somehow or other I've always been busy
My father and mother did not teach me how to engage in small talk

These forty years I've continued to write just relying upon line spaces
It's odd that
When I'm asked, "Who are you exactly?" to answer "a poet" most sets my
    mind at rest
Was I a poet when I abandoned those women?
Am I a poet eating my favorite roast sweet potatoes?
Am I a poet, I wonder, with my hair thinning?
There are millions of middle-aged men like this, poets or not

I am a naive child
As this child
Merely chasing after the butterfly of fine words
So innocent that he is not even aware of having hurt others
So the man

Poetry is
Comedy[20]

The self-critical tone is particularly evident in "The Naif," with the register of the poem shifting from bathos to sarcasm, from estrangement to ambiguity. This poem, more than "My Father's Death," prompts many commentators to question what exactly the narrative voice is trying to say. Are readers meant to suspend disbelief and take flat assertions at face value, or does the constant undercutting of meaning render even irony ambiguous? Morinaka's characterization of "The Naif" as a struggle between language and subjectivity is useful for emphasizing the ambiguous notion of the subject or, to use an older term, narrative voice.[21]

The nub of the difficulty that various critics have with Tanikawa's use of narrative voice bears a marked resemblance to the American critic Wayne Booth's difficulty reading D. H. Lawrence, namely, a problem distinguishing the implied author from the narrator in the work of art. Related to this difficulty is another of Booth's useful distinctions: the "implied reader."[22] Who exactly is the reader constructed by "The Naif"—another version of the im-

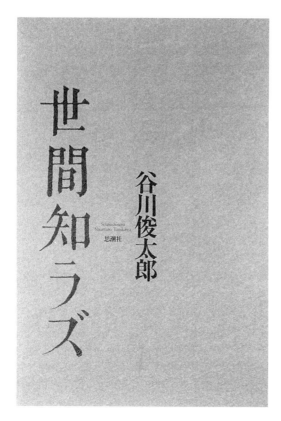

FIGURE 10. Cover of Tanikawa Shuntarō's collection *Seken shirazu* (The naif, 1993)

plied author perhaps? If so, then the poem appears locked into a continuous loop, which, as the much-quoted line "Poetry is Comedy" implies, has clear narcissistic tendencies. It may be objected, however, that this is precisely the object of the (aesthetic) enterprise. The poem that follows may clarify matters somewhat. A complete translation of "Masakari" (Broadax), the last poem in this "linked verse" sequence, follows:

### Broadax

I woke just after nine, drank some coffee
Sat down in front of my word processor
In the house in front some trees remain
A bird is singing but I don't know its name
Is the reason why I don't try to remember the names of trees, animals,
   and stars
Because I am gazing at the world with the eyes of a passerby?

Out of the blue the word "broadax" floated into my head
Occasionally a poem starts in this way
But I have never used the tool called a "broadax"
I have never even touched one with my hands
I only vaguely recall that when I was a child
"Kintarō," the Boys Festival doll, carried one on his shoulder
Despite this I open a dictionary and look up the word "broadax"

If, as Wordsworth said, poetry
Takes its origin from an emotion recollected in tranquillity
Then my broadax has no connection to tranquillity or emotion
It's just a prop loud with imaginative power

Poetry is the surface of life with the bitterness scooped out
A just divorced woman told me in bed

When I turn off the switch the words before my eyes vanish in an instant
Will this poem also vanish for me?[23]

Paradoxically, poetry, in this poem, may seem to be making a comeback, if only in response to the challenge implied in the remark made by the divorced woman in bed. The question that the poet asks at the end may be the most direct answer that can be given to the anodyne, dismissive view of art expressed by the woman's words. The narrator (here perhaps rather close to implied author) is affirming the fact that his own presence is constituted solely by words, by the artifact of language.

## Debates on Poetics

In an interview-dialogue with Tanikawa in the July 1993 *Contemporary Poetry Notebook* special issue, the poet Tsujii Takashi (b. 1927) alluded to various exchanges between Tanikawa and two leading poet-critics, Hiraide Takashi and Inagawa Masato, discussed briefly in chapter 6.[24] Both Hiraide and Inagawa are considerably younger than Tanikawa but share with him a fascination with language. However their viewpoints differ considerably from that held by the older poet. In some respects—their fascination with rhetoric as rhetoric, their preference for prose poetry—they resemble that group of older American poets (one generation removed) who began to appear in the $L=A=N=G=U=A=G=E$ magazine around 1978, whose poetic work was considered in chapter 6. While it is not necessary to give a detailed account of these exchanges, tracing a few points on the line that these exchanges followed will provide insight into the intellectual context behind the debate over language and the poetics that derives from it.

A dialogue between Inagawa and Tanikawa appeared in the July 1991 issue of *Contemporary Poetry Notebook*. This exchange was organized by the journal after differences between the two poets emerged over selecting poetry for an anthology of modern verse. First, the two poets disagree over the notion of "an ordinary reader." Inagawa asserts that no consensus exists among modern poets as to whether such a creature actually exists, in contradiction to Tanikawa's claim that ordinary readers are the people for whom he writes. This difference widens into a debate over the nature of contemporary verse—Tanikawa wishes to draw a sharp line between poetry and other genres of writing like prose poetry, while Inagawa sees a convergence of multimedia and writing so that distinctions are irrelevant.

The debate between the two is wide-ranging, covering domestic politics and the Gulf War among other topics. Finally, fundamental differences surface over the relationship between poetry and reality, indeed, over the nature of reality itself. Tanikawa continues to insist on an absolute barrier between everyday life and poetry. Inagawa says that Tanikawa is unique among contemporary Japanese poets in belonging to a school of writing that makes such distinctions, as life is only knowable through language. When, to Tanikawa's astonishment, Inagawa puts the argument that poetry is more "real" than life itself, there is a connection to a second point on this line.[25] I should add that I have only cited a few items of debate from an extremely broad and extensive discussion.

The second point is an article published in the next (August 1991) issue of *Contemporary Poetry Notebook* by Hiraide Takashi titled "Gengoteki yuibutsu-shugi ni tsuite—shijin ni yoru jissen" (On linguistic materialism—the practice of poets). The phrase "linguistic materialism" Hiraide takes from Paul Valéry, and it is his contention that this is an old doctrine, much misunderstood but central to the practice of poetry. Hiraide quotes a long extract from the dialogue between Tanikawa and Inagawa in the July issue of the journal and then describes Tanikawa's "antagonism" *(kikkō)* toward prose poetry as being more or less the same idea as that with which the younger generation of poets were obsessed.[26] He tries to contextualize Inagawa and Tanikawa as two poets simply working in different areas.

Tanikawa's surprise at Inagawa's blunt assertion about poetry and reality, Hiraide remarks, is more than matched by Inagawa's at the contrast in viewpoint revealed in the interview. Hiraide glosses Inagawa's statement as another way of expounding the doctrine of poetic materialism, which is merely the notion that all ideas are expressed in words. Connecting such a commonplace truth to the assertions that "life is fiction" or that the language school

FIGURE 11. Hiraide Takashi. Courtesy of Hiraide Takashi

of writing insists that reality is only visible in language is wrong. Finally, Hiraide criticizes Tanikawa for making the statement (in the interview) that he wished to draw closer in his poetry to people who live ordinary lives, remarking that this comment sounds like something a little prince would say.[27]

Two things emerge here: one is Hiraide's off-hand description of Tanikawa's views as either immature or pretentious (depending on how one views princes); the second is the repetition of the term "language school" (*gengoha*). This leads to the third point on the line, which now closes to become a circle, returning to the interview in the special Tanikawa 1993 issue of *Contemporary Poetry Notebook* between Tanikawa and Tsujii. From the points I've traced it is possible to interpret the full meaning of Tsujii's question to Tanikawa "Is the title *The Naif* an antithetical rejoinder to Hiraide Takashi and Inagawa Masato?" as referring to the debate summarized above.

Tanikawa's answer, that the title derived from self-criticism not the debate, is characteristically ambiguous. Tanikawa continues, "Since Hiraide and the other fellow said something to that effect earlier, I came to the realization that I was indeed naïve. . . . After the interview, I was troubled by the division between a 'linguistic school' and a 'school of [ordinary] life,' but because I used the words 'contemporary life,' Hiraide mocked me with the title of 'Le petit prince' of the stars."[28]

Here is a conceptual framework, a debate over poetics, into which it is possible the place the concerns with subjectivity, reality, poetry, and sincerity that distinguish the three poems translated earlier. Thus, the source of some of the ambiguities, which in the view of many commentators enhance and strengthen the power of Tanikawa's text, may be traced, at least in part, to the decade of the 1980s and early 1990s and the intense debate over language that characterized it. In this connection, it is important to note that the first three poems of *The Naif* first appeared in the January and June 1990 issues of *Contemporary Poetry Notebook;* in fact, virtually all of the poems in the book were published in the magazine during the period from 1990 to 1993.

I do not mean to argue that the book originates purely in a debate over poetics; on the contrary, the thematic structure is manifestly related to personal, autobiographical concerns, and, as the critic Morinaka Takaaki has noted, affinities with Tanikawa's 1968 collection *Journeys* are undeniable. However, the arguments over poetics that have occurred frequently over the past three decades or so in Japan (especially during the last two decades) and that focus on language, as traced (in part) above, create a conceptual context that underlines and accentuates some of the rhetoric in this much-lauded book. These debates also generate contradictions and ambiguities in Tanikawa's poetic practice that demand deeper investigation.

## Poetry as Autobiography

Another interpretative context for *The Naif* is provided by the publication of *A Man Who Listens to Mozart* and *Rather Than Being Pure White* in 1995. Tanikawa wrote most of the poems in the former volume at the same time he was writing the poems collected in *The Naif,* and the same is generally true of the latter volume.[29] Although these two volumes may be written for a different audience than *The Naif*—a readership less knowledgeable about poetry and poetics, especially in the case of *Rather Than Being Pure White,* as the editor Suzuki Keisuke intimates—nevertheless, the self-critical, almost sarcastic tone and, in a number of instances, the same doubts about poetry or language resurface equally strongly in these two collections.[30]

Neither volume has garnered anything like the praise accorded *The Naif,* probably because of the expectations regarding readership. Another reason for their comparative neglect may be that familiarity with Tanikawa's new narrative voice has lessened the impact made by the revelatory poetry found in *Rather Than Being Pure White*. The focus on self as poet and poetry as vocation occur in "Soyokaze, hakuba, darushimā" (Gentle breeze, graveyard, dulcimer), the sole poem that I will translate from *A Man Who Listens to Mozart*:

### Gentle Breeze, Graveyard, Dulcimer

The night a noisy friend returned late, I thought I'd write something on
   the dining table
And remembered something that happened one morning over thirty years ago
On a different table in a different house, I wrote something
With the title "Farewell" addressed to a woman I'd become friends with over
   the summer
I wrote and wrote endlessly as if I was writing a letter full of regrets
At that time too music came wafting from a radio
Even now I dimly remember that melody

Then that was fine
Since I was young
But now I wonder if it is all right to write "something" like this?
Without reading Marx or Dostoevsky
Listening to Mozart I've grown old
The ability to sympathize with the pain of others got left out of me
Living life to the full, I pleased myself

I talked much laughed often but really loved serenity
A gentle breeze a graveyard a dulcimer a smile white paper
Myself who will leave this world sometime
But I wonder if it's all right just to believe in a poetry next to silence
   and in andante?
Pressured by the noise of the fierce desire and passion concealed in ordinary
   prose and drama

Or is it already too late?
Can I only be a poet? Since that morning over thirty years ago
Just perfect[31]

The slightly self-indulgent air that Nejime Shōichi hints at in his critique of *The Naif* resurfaces in this poem. The ambiguity of the last line—"Just perfect" (*"mukizu,"* which could also be translated as "without blemish")—works to cast doubt on this self-characterization, whether of the poet-persona's vocation or of the poet-persona's character, and of the implied author's vocation or character as well. Yet, it also implies that such a characterization, whether of vocation or character, could indeed be "just perfect," thus adding a narcissistic dimension to the narrator's (or poet-persona's) question. Such a question, as well as being self-critical, could also be sarcastic, acting to strengthen both the critical aspect—if sarcastic, then the tone shifts to one of self-loathing—and also the narcissistic aspect, which would then enable the line to be read as hyperbole.

The main body of the poem is clearly self-critical, the second and third stanzas amounting to a reexamination of the poet-persona's life. In this, the poem shares a common theme with "The Naif," and the thematic as well as chronological links between the two collections become apparent.

The poem "Anpan" (Sweet bean bun) from *Rather Than Being Pure White* recalls "My Father's Death" but focuses on the personal relationship with the poet's father rather than on language.

### Sweet Bean Bun

My father scorned buns stuffed with sweet bean paste but
He respected foie gras
And all his life he loved garlic
I feel he also loved mother but

Mother said father had a mean nature.
During the war hiding it from me, his son
He ate a dried sweet potato without sharing it
And for that reason she had once decided to divorce him, I was told.

Father was impressed by Miyazawa Kenji's poem "I Will Not Be Defeated
  by the Rain"
"Everyday four cups of brown rice / I eat miso and a few vegetables"
Was it because perhaps he knew
That he could not live on a diet such as that?

At the age of ninety-one he went to Barcelona
He cursed Gandhi vehemently
He praised Iberian Airlines
Because they served caviar for lunch

After he died he received a decoration
No one betrayed him to the authorities
For eating a salamander in defiance of the law
Incidentally, father was a philosopher

I am writing this now with a sweet bean bun in one hand[32]

The bittersweet recollections of the poet's father in "My Father's Death" are complicated by the questioning of the narrator's voice, which acts to undercut any single, "autobiographical" reading of the relationship between the poet-persona and his father. In "Sweet Bean Bun," however, such complications are absent, and, as a result, the thematic focus is clearer and the attitude of the narrator much less ambiguous. This poem displays one of Tanikawa's great gifts as a poet: his ability to paint a rich, many-hued portrait of a complex human relationship in language so simple that it seems devoid of artifice.

The absolute mastery that Tanikawa reveals in his creation of a poetic diction that mimics everyday language is perfectly demonstrated by this poem. The unspoken pauses and ellipses (usually by rhetorical questions, but sometimes by assertion, as in the last line of the fifth stanza) add considerably to the semantic burden of almost every line. The poet's skill at condensing and concentrating meaning in declarative utterances is equally apparent. The total effect of this linguistic concentration is to imply a great deal more than the laconic observations of the narrator appear to say. However, this technique is nowhere near as disturbing or fundamentally dislocatory (creating a clear, conscious gap between thematic intention and rhetorical act) as that used by Tanikawa in "My Father's Death."

## The Inadequacy of Poetry

Takachi Jun'ichirō links some of Tanikawa's recent poetry, especially in the book *The Naif*, to a tendency to deride poetry itself as an artistic act and as a vocation.[33] It is possible to discern this tendency in all three books under examination. In "Kokū" (Into empty space), from *The Naif,* Tanikawa writes the following about poetry: "It may be just an entirely individual moment of pleasure / Where is the necessity to record that?" In the very next poem in the book, "Risōteki na shi no shohotekina setsumei" (An elementary explanation of an ideal poem), the poet writes: "It can only be written in words but a poem is not the words themselves / I've felt to turn it into words is to debase it."[34] Here Tanikawa is expressing more than a conventional lament for the inadequacy of poetry to represent reality. The sentiment expressed in the opening two lines of the above poem "I'm called a poet by the world but / Normally I'm utterly estranged from poetry" is echoed by the last line "Called a poet," which uses ellipsis to suggest strong disgust at such a description.[35] The poem "Panjii" (Pansy) from *Rather Than Being Pure White* is a powerful reiteration of this disgust.

**Pansy**

You want poetry
You are starving for poetry, the woman said
And then gave me a pansy that had started to wilt

"This is a quotation from the universe"
The woman said without the slightest trace of embarrassment
It was better than receiving a few lines from a bad poem typed on her
    word processor

But I am not starving for poetry in particular
And having said that, I'm not hungry either

She doesn't appear to be looking at me
She doesn't appear to be able to smell anything
Despite her pretty face

Don't you see that what I need now more than poetry is affection
I said in my heart
In the universe not even a sliver of affection exists
That's why the stars look so pretty[36]

In this poem, the disgust is linked to a personal crisis in the life of the narrator, and the bathos of the opening line of the last stanza is more than balanced by the cynicism of the last line. This cynicism is not simply the back wash of a lovers' tiff but a cynicism about the nature of art. The stars appear so pretty because of their falsity; they conventionally represent beauty or hope, but, in the end, they are indifferent, distant suns. The attribution of affective qualities to stars is purely metaphoric, a convenient falsehood or fiction.

This fiction is causally linked to the coldness and cruelty of the void: that is, the paradoxical and deliberate metaphorical untruth of the cruel reality of the universe endows the stars with beauty. Metaphor—or, metaphorically, art—is not merely a lie but has to be so to exist as art. This viewpoint can and has been expressed by poets in far less cynical language, and the connection the poet-persona characterizes as causal has often been seen as purely contingent or accidental. That Tanikawa chose not to allow his persona to see it this way strengthens the antipathy toward poetry expressed in the rest of the poem.

This is not a new theme in Tanikawa's poetry. The lines quoted earlier from *Journeys* (1968) "I've posed as a poet / But I'm not" are an earlier manifestation of precisely the same kind of impulse. Actors are often compared to translators, but a more pertinent comparison might be to poets. To have to take on a succession of different personas, indeed to create them, has led notoriously to psychological problems in the careers of many actors as they struggle to define a self distinct from those they adopt for a living. It seems that Tanikawa has often struggled, intellectually, in verse, with precisely this dilemma. And crises of confidence about vocation are also common among members of the acting profession, as can be seen in their autobiographies.

It might be thought that this is a particularly contemporary phenomenon, a trauma afflicting twentieth-century poets more than those in earlier centuries, but an examination of Lord Byron's life and poetry will quickly dispel such thoughts. Tanikawa has pursued this theme (among many others, it must be said) consistently in his verse over the last three decades, but the theme appears to have gained even more prominence over the last few years, as is evident from these three collections. Also, there is no denying that the conflict between intention and expression—in effect, a fundamental mistrust of language itself—is basic to modernist writing as a whole. Tanikawa is very much the heir of the modernist heritage in postwar Japanese poetry, although he may well not characterize his position thus, as he often casts himself in opposition to whatever the prevailing trend is in poetry circles.

One final observation concerns Tanikawa's skill at puns and wordplay. I have refrained from drawing attention to this rather obvious pun until now, although most commentators on the three collections do not share this reticence. The pun is on the word *"shi"*: a homonym for the two words "poetry" and "death." This pun runs through all three books but only really surfaces in the minds of readers, as the poet, characteristically, avoids the explicit exploitation of such an obvious pun. Morinaka Takaaki, discussing *The Naif,* points to the almost complete disjunction between intention and expression in the poetry collected in this book. In his view, the relationship between them—the fundamental relationship between the word and the world—is undefined despite the apparent coherence of theme.

So, while "silence" is paradoxically affirmed by *Journeys,* this particular avenue of retreat or of reaffirmation of the vocation of poetry is absent from *The Naif.* What mention there is of silence, whether word or idea, is ironic.[37] What is left is a grotesque pun, and in "Pansy," the chilling image of the stars shorn of all beauty, of all meaning. In this absence of meaning, only the poet's sarcasm remains. Or is that blank, blunt assertion about the stars, and implicitly about the power of art, meant to be taken as the literal truth, or as literal a truth as poetry can convey?

# Epilogue

*Asunder by another*
*witless witness*
who just happens
*to wander by.*
—Philip Hammial, "Eight Flounces"


*still writing,*
*writed, written,*
*interrupted, begun.*
—Michael Palmer, "Six Hermetic Songs"

The Japanese poets discussed in this volume have used a number of literary and aesthetic techniques to create their particular poetic worlds, but all share a common legacy of modernism, if not post-modernism—seen as a late development of the Modern movement. Japanese histories of modern poetry tend to begin in the late nineteenth century and generally argue that modernist poetry emerged as a distinct genre of verse in the 1920s. The most recent book-length history of modern Japanese poetry to be published in Japanese with which I am familiar is Shimaoka Shin's 1998 volume, which has a separate chapter devoted to modernist poetry. Shimaoka locates the birth of modernism essentially in the 1920s and sees modernism as a distinct genre of writing imported from the West. He distinguishes between modernist writing and avant-garde verse, which he dates to 1914 and sees also as an importation of a Western mode of poetry.[1]

Chiba Sen'ichi, the distinguished historian of modern poetry, also sees modernist writing as an importation from the West. However, his schema is a comparatively sophisticated one, as he is probing the nature of literary borrowing itself. Nevertheless, he also dates modernist writing in Japan for the most part to the first two decades of the twentieth century.[2] This is the preferred approach of historians of Japanese avant-garde verse like Kikuchi Yasuo, Nakano Kaichi, and Komata Yūsuke.[3] Books by these writers on avant-garde poetry all begin with the decade of the twenties. Itō Shinkichi, a leading modern poet and critic, in his reminiscences of "poetic anarchism" also dates the beginnings of avant-garde poetry to this period.[4]

The approach of this study is quite different from the existing approaches that constitute the mainstream of Japanese literary history as it is practiced in Japan. Of the handful of studies of modern Japanese poetry published in English, none to my knowledge proposes an approach to literary history significantly different from their Japanese counterparts. However, the study of modernism in the West in most cases, as seen in chapter 1, begins from the middle of the nineteenth century, if not before. Since translations of Western verse of this period appeared in increasing quantity in the last two decades of the nineteenth century in Japan, some knowledge of Western modernist verse would have been available in Japan from this time.

Tracing the exact direction these translations took and the influence they exercised on the evolution of Japanese modern poetry is an ongoing area of research undertaken by many scholars in Japan, including those mentioned above. Yet few of the researchers working on modern poetry in Japan have attempted to characterize the various verse experiments stimulated by translations of modernist Western poetry in the late nineteenth and the first decade of the twentieth century as modernism in practice. This is what I have attempted to do in chapter 1, if only as the first step toward such a tracing.

The most dramatic manifestation of modernist Japanese poetry arising out of the nineteenth century are the verse experiments conducted amongst the Myōjō circle of poets led by Yosano Tekkan and Akiko. The examples of modernist poetry created by Yosano Akiko and her husband were essentially derived from late Western romantic verse and its child, symbolism. I therefore have commenced with their writing.

Arishima Takeo is more famous for his prose than his poetry. Nevertheless, his book of modernist verse (typical of such volumes at the time) holds much interest for investigators examining the connections between verse and biography, and between modernist writers and radical politics. It also provides the means to survey broad trends in modernist verse that were developing in the first two decades of the twentieth century. Because this period coincides with the traditional Japanese literary periodization of modernism in Japan, there are numerous studies of literature in Japanese that treat the first three or four decades of the twentieth century in detail. The majority of studies of modern Japanese poetry in English also focus on these decades. There is no particular need to repeat their research findings here.

Therefore, this study skips to the 1960s to examine Soh Sakon, whose work, like that of Arishima Takeo, has not been examined in English before. By the 1960s virtually all Japanese modern poetry could be described as modernist, having had nearly half a century to absorb the lessons and legacy of modernism itself. Soh's verse is no different from the majority of his literary compatriots in being essentially written in the modernist mode. What is notable about Soh's verse is his theme, which is almost entirely concerned with the legacy left by World War II, in his case, a very personal legacy. However, Soh's language does resemble that of other writers in Japan and elsewhere who experimented with various styles of writing to express the horrors of war. The connection between the virtually inexpressible cruelties of war—the atrocities that result—and modernist modes of expression is well known and has often been the subject of analysis.[5] George Steiner is one of the most distinguished commentators of our time on this problem, with his writings about literature dealing with the Shoah, and so his perspective is especially useful.

The first three decades following the war were also the time when a new generation of women writers came onto the scene who probably exercised a greater influence on contemporary verse than any previous generation of women poets. From the thematic and linguistic analysis provided in chapter 4, it is clear that most of these women are working in a modernist mode, but a mode that has been altered under the influence of contemporary Western literary and philosophical discourses like feminism. This factor chiefly distinguishes their verse from the verse of the previous generation of women poets, whose work was accomplished in the years that straddle the prewar and postwar eras.

The emphasis in chapter 4 is on Western influences, but there is no doubt that influence from fellow Japanese modernist poets has been equally or more important. Such influence can be traced, in part, through a careful scrutiny of debates over poetics and poetry published in contemporary poetry journals during these decades like *Contemporary Poetry Notebook, La mer* or *Yuriika* (Eureka); another significant factor is the personal contacts detailed in the various public meetings and events listed in these journals. For the most part, Japanese writers (and poets are no exception) are notoriously clannish, with close social connections with each other, developed from their mutual associations in formal groupings centered on coterie or cooperative magazines and their various poetic apprenticeships.

Even Tanikawa Shuntarō, who in several interviews has stressed how much his poetry differs from the dominant "Wasteland" school discussed in chapter 3, has noted his own poetic connections to the group of poets based around *Kai* (Oar) magazine.[6] Inevitably, these connections lead to shared viewpoints and positions, irrespective of individual differences in poetic style. This is one of the reasons why debates over poetics are important; they enable scholars and readers to tease out these shared viewpoints.

The reversion of Okinawa to Japanese control from American occupation in 1972 signaled a great watershed for Okinawan writing generally. The poets investigated in chapter 5 were affected not only by this momentous historical event, but also by the tradition of modernist poetry to which they considered themselves to be heirs. The combination of a search for Okinawan linguistic identity and for a sense of the modern created a special emphasis on the diction that they used in their verse, thus serving as a useful reminder of the role of language as the key determinant of modernist poetry strategies.

The poetry of Ichihara Chikako and Iraha Morio also draws attention to the prominent role that women play in traditional Okinawan society, which, in some areas, is quite different from that of women on the Japanese mainland, as evidenced by the images relating to female shamanism in the verse of both poets. By their time, the impact of late modernist or postmodernist verse was being felt in Japan. Just as in the beginnings of modernism, so in this late manifestation of modernist vitality the emphasis was on language.

It is natural therefore to pursue this last stage of poetic experimentation by considering the case of Asabuki Ryōji, one of the most prominent of that generation of contemporary poets who have been actively involved in linguistic experimentation. But his experiments do not focus solely on the written word. It is important to note that Asabuki, like many of his contemporaries (such as Tanikawa), crosses media borders, using video and computer-generated poetic collages (including sound as well as image) to construct his poetic oeuvre. The mass of Japanese poetry sites on the Internet, which include many leading Japanese contemporary poets often with web pages showcasing their work, is evidence of the trend in Japan, as elsewhere, to use multimedia in composing poetry, although this changes the nature of poetry from a literary artifact to a more fluid art form. Unfortunately, this aspect of Asabuki's work lies outside the boundaries of this study, which concentrates on written poetry.

Tanikawa Shuntarō is by far the best-known poet of his generation, and although he is from the generation before the dominant school of contemporary poetry, nevertheless, his writing has anticipated much of their linguistic experimentation. It has served as an inspiration for younger poets as well as representing a viewpoint that the following generation often agrees to oppose. Thus the last chapter examines in some detail Tanikawa's major three books of the 1990s, while contextualizing the contemporary debate over postmodernist poetics by focusing on a series of important exchanges carried out between Tanikawa and his opponents in the pages of the *Contemporary Poetry Notebook* journal during the 1990s. These debates are the theoretical well from which twenty-first-century poets in Japan will draw their inspiration and much of the justification for their experiments and adventures in verse. Hence the legacy of modernism, the dominant literary movement of the twentieth century, endures in these verse experiments that postmodernist poets are embarking upon.

Broadly speaking, in the West, by the nineteenth century, poetry had been displaced by prose, specifically by the novel, as the major genre of writing. In Japan the same displacement occurred in the mid- to late nineteenth century (here I am categorizing Edo period drama as performance rather than literature). In the twentieth century, in turn, the novel has been displaced by cinema as the major artistic genre. Nevertheless, free-verse poets have continued to write both in the West and in Japan during the twentieth century and, free from the dictates of the mass market, have produced art that is almost entirely engaged with intellectual and aesthetic concerns.

Tanikawa is one of the few poets writing in Japan, outside those engaged primarily in performance poetry, who has a small but significant commercial market for his verse—although, it must be said, since the late 1990s Tanikawa too is primarily a performance poet, reading his poetry to music as part of performances by his son's band. Most of the other modern contemporary poets discussed in this book write "art poetry" or "conceptual poetry," which is the major mode of contemporary verse today. Naturally, debates continue about the proper role and function of poetry, whether exclusively as a pure form of art—a claim that has been made consistently about poetry since the beginning of the twentieth century (not to mention earlier centuries)—or as an art form that has commercial or popular pretensions.

Some participants in the debate, such as the critic Yoshimoto Takaaki, even argue that copywriters and songwriters like Nakajima Miyuki (b. 1952)

are now the main practitioners of commercial poetry, a claim strongly dis-
puted by contemporary poets like Inagawa Masato, who are reluctant to grant
the status of poetry to such writings.[7] Similar claims are made about practi-
tioners of popular verse, whose work is arguably better described as song than
as formal poetry, like Mado Michio (b. 1909).[8] The same debate can be
glimpsed in the West, with, for example, the argument that Bob Dylan's song
lyrics or rap (in the case of Nakajima, the singer songwriter Jewel might be
a better analogue) are as important for contemporary American poetry as John
Ashbery or Michael Palmer. It is fascinating that the modernist mode is ca-
pable of embracing both kinds of poetry, even if at the end of the century the
battle seems to be favoring the proponents of poetry as pure art.

Traditional genres of Japanese verse have not escaped the influence of mod-
ernism either, but, apart from the experiments of the Myōjō group, that par-
ticular story remains to be told in English.[9] It is interesting that some con-
temporary poets, and this was noticeable early in the twentieth century as
well, are working occasionally in a mode of expression that resembles the two
major genres of traditional verse, haiku and *tanka.* Both genres of traditional
verse, but especially *tanka,* have maintained a mass market, as can be seen in
the poetry of Tawara Machi (b. 1962), known as "the [Yosano] Akiko of the
[modern] Shōwa era." Some practitioners of traditional genres of verse do not
aspire, except in the most abstract sense, to art but, rather, view their work
as fulfilling a social, or in some cases private, function or purpose, but the
majority of professionals engaged in traditional verse see themselves as artists
first and as "artisans" or teachers second.

The recent commercial success of professional poets working in traditional
genres proves that there is also space for modern verse—even some kinds of
"art poetry" as opposed to more popular varieties—to be commercial and to
gain a comparable market, if that is the intention of the poets. Tanikawa's
career demonstrates that this is possible. It is true that a number of contem-
porary performance poets (dating from the time of Terayama Shūji or even
earlier) see some of their work as "action" or art that is limited spatially and
temporally, and therefore a conscious decision is made not to preserve it (un-
less it is sound- or videotaped), outside any working notes that the artist may
choose to keep. Some of Itō Hiromi's most significant poems, like "Killing
Kanoko," are performance pieces, and written transcriptions of these works
inevitably lack an important aesthetic dimension. Nevertheless, the concep-
tual conventions of modernism are now largely understood by most Japanese

as they have been absorbed into artistic expression generally, whether poetry, prose, painting, cinema, or television.[10] In this sense, the twenty-first century will truly be an age of postmodernism, but what precise modes of expression art, and especially poetry, will adopt in the future is still a matter of conjecture.

# Notes

Japanese names are in the Japanese order of surname first followed by personal name except for texts written in English, which follow the English convention.

## Introduction

Charles Tomlinson translates from Paz' "Renga": "Orange, apple, breast, sphere, all inherits at last the emptiness of the *stupa*. Earth powders away" in Octavio Paz, Edoardo Sanguinetti, and Charles Tomlinson, *Renga*, p. 56. The quotation from John Forbes appears in *Damaged Glamour,* p. 11.

1. There exists a pioneering anthology, *Southern Exposure: Modern Japanese Literature from Okinawa,* edited by Michael Molasky and Steve Rabson, but very few poems are included among the translations.

2. See Fredric Jameson, *Postmodernism or, the Cultural Logic of Late Capitalism,* pp. 44–45, 317, for an expression of this view.

3. All translations are those of the author unless otherwise stated.

4. For details, see Donald Keene, *Dawn to the West;* vol. 2, pp. 194–204, and also the special issue of *Literature East and West: Toward a Modern Japanese Poetry.*

5. Only a tiny handful of studies exist of Arishima's poetry in Japanese. See the journal *Arishima Takeo kenkyū* (Arishima Takeo studies), which commenced publication in 1997, for the two or three studies of Arishima's verse that are generally available: namely, in issues 1 (1997), 3 (2000), and 4 (2001).

6. For some previous studies of modern Japanese poetry in English, see, for example, the following excellent books: Yukihito Hijiya, *Ishikawa Takuboku;* James Morita, *Kaneko Mitsuharu;* A. V. Heinrich, *Fragments of Rainbows: The Life and Poetry of Saitō Mokichi;* Makoto Ueda, *Modern Japanese Poets and the Nature of Literature;* Keene, *Dawn to the West,* vol. 2; Janine Beichman, *Masaoka Shiki* and *Embracing the Firebird: Yosano Akiko and the Birth of the Female Voice in Modern Japanese Poetry;* Miriam Silverberg, *Changing Song: The Marxist Manifestoes of Nakano Shigeharu;* Margaret Benton Fukasawa, *Kitahara Hakushū;* Hosea Hirata, *The Poetry and Poetics of Nishiwaki Junzaburō;* John Solt, *Shredding the Tapestry of Meaning: The Poetry and Poetics of Kitasono Katue;* and Miryam Sas, *Fault Lines: Cultural Memory and Japanese Surrealism.*

7. Shimaoka Shin, *Shi to wa nanika*, p. 279.

8. Kaneko Mitsuharu et al., [*Zenshishū taisei*] *gendai Nihon shijin zenshū; Nihon shijin zenshū*, ed. Katsumoto Seiichirō et al.; *Nihon no shiika*, ed. Itō Shinkichi et al.; *Gendai shi bunko*, ed. Oda Kyūrō; and *Nihon gendai shi bunko*, ed. Kokai Eiji.

9. The fruits of that research in the form of scholarly publications will be referred to throughout this study, but the most direct result of this work is the two volumes of translations of postwar poetry that I have produced: Leith Morton, trans., *Mt Fuji: Selected Poems 1945–1986 by Kusano Shinpei;* and Leith Morton, ed. and trans., *An Anthology of Contemporary Japanese Poetry.*

10. For Ōgai, see Seki Ryōichi, "Kindai shiika no akebono," pp. 330–331. For Tanikawa, see his *Kotoba asobi uta* and Leith Morton, "An Interview with Tanikawa Shuntarō," pp. 27–28. For Umemoto, Inaba, and Matsumoto, see Shimaoka, *Shi to wa nanika*, pp. 305–306.

11. Shimaoka, *Shi to wa nanika*, p. 306.

12. Steve McCaffery, *Prior to Meaning*, p. 162.

13. For a more detailed explanation of my translating technique, see Leith Morton, "Translating Japanese Poetry."

14. Takahashi Seori, "Shiteki gengo no genzai," pp. 337–339.

15. Quoted in Shimaoka, *Shi to wa nanika*, p. 275.

16. Ibid., pp. 276–277.

17. Takahashi Seori, "Shiteki gengo no genzai," pp. 337–339.

18. Miryam Sas in *Fault Lines* discusses Takiguchi's theoretical manifestos on pp. 103–120. Another poet who wrote in this vein is Kitasono Katsue; see Solt, *Shredding the Tapestry of Meaning*, pp. 251–294 for details.

19. Kokai Eiji, *Nihon sengo shi no tenbō*, pp. 3–25.

## Chapter 1: The Birth of the Modern

"Love's Body" appears in John Forbes, *Stalin's Holidays*, p. 15; "Where We Live," in Harry Clifton, *Night Train through the Brenner*, p. 25.

1. Toshiko Ellis, "Nihon modanizumu no saiteigi—1930 nendai sekai no bunmyaku."

2. This view can be found in Dennis Keene, *Yokomitsu Riichi*, pp. 58–85.

3. Marshall Berman, *All That Is Solid Melts into Air*, pp. 35–45 passim, pp. 88–91; Malcolm Bradbury and James McFarlane, *Modernism*, pp. 20–46.

4. Earl Miner, "Inventions of Literary Modernity," p. 13.

5. Karatani Kōjin, *Nihon kindai bungaku no kigen*, p. 25; see also the translation edited by Brett de Bary: Karatani, *Origins of Japanese Literature*, p. 23.

6. Mizutani Akio, *Nihon kindai bungeishi no kōsai*, p. 4 and pp. 1–6, respectively.

7. Suzuki Sadami, *Nihon no bungaku gainen*, pp. 268, 270.

8. Ibid., pp. 261–268.

9. Ibid., pp. 282–296.

10. Ibid., pp. 313–336.

11. Chiba Sen'ichi, *Modanizumu no hikakubungakuteki kenkyū,* pp. 67–92.

12. An earlier version of some of these ideas is argued in Leith Morton, "The Aesthetics of Modernism." Also, see chapter 1 of Leith Morton, *Modern Japanese Culture.*

13. Shimamura quoted in Ken Henshall, "A Call for a Reconsideration of the Japanese Concept of Naturalism," p. 418. On the French and German versions of naturalism, see Henshall, "Naturalism," pp. 401–421.

14. Quoted in Henshall, "Naturalism," p. 416.

15. See Leith Morton, "The Concept of Romantic Love in the *Taiyō* Magazine, 1895–1905"; Leith Morton, "Courtly Love in France and Japan"; and Leith Morton, "Sōgō Zasshi 'Taiyō' to 'Jogaku zasshi' ni mirareru ren'ai kan."

16. Miner, "Inventions of Literary Modernity," pp. 13–14.

17. Camille Paglia, *Sexual Personae,* pp. 445–446. For an analysis, see Leith Morton, "Akiko, Tomiko and Hiroshi."

18. Paglia, *Sexual Personae,* p. 453.

19. Ibid., p. 455.

20. Leith Morton, "The Clash of Traditions," pp. 104–143; Haga Tōru, *Midaregami no keifu,* pp. 20–40. Isoda Kōichi, *{Kindai Nihon bungeishishi} rokumeikan no keifu,* pp. 131–163.

21. See Kawai Suimei's 1911 article "Midaregami jidai," p. 170.

22. On *tanka* reform, see Keene, *Dawn to the West,* vol. 2, pp. 8–54; and Morton, "Clash of Traditions," pp. 104–109.

23. Yano Hōjin, *Tekkan Akiko to sono jidai,* p. 113; Itō Sei, *Nihon bundanshi,* vol. 6, p. 78.

24. Ishimoto Ryūichi, "Shizenshugi undō no ryūkō," p. 207.

25. Watanabe Sumiko, *Yosano Akiko,* p. 75.

26. For a reception history of *Midaregami,* see Leith Morton, "The Canonization of Yosano Akiko's *Midaregami.*"

27. See, for instance, Isoda, *Rokumeikan no keifu,* pp. 156–157.

28. Wada Hirofumi, "Isseiki o koeta Nihon no shishi," p. 5.

29. Shimaoka Shin, *Shi to wa nanika,* p. 42.

30. Suzuki Sadami, *Modan toshi no hyōgen,* pp. 153–154.

31. Watanabe, *Yosano Akiko,* p. 79.

32. Iwasaki Yukinori, "Myōjō no katsuyaku to romanshugi," pp. 88–89.

33. For details of his and Akiko's early life together, see Janine Beichman, "Yosano Akiko"; Edwin A. Cranston, "Young Akiko"; and Morton, "Clash of Traditions."

34. *Myōjō,* no. 6 (September 1900), p. 68.

35. Ibid.

36. Itsumi Kumi, ed., *Murasaki zenshaku,* p. 117.

37. Ibid., p. 236.

38. Uda Notarō, ed., *Yosano Tekkan Akiko shū,* vol. 51 of *Meiji bungaku zenshū,* p. 77.

39. Itsumi, *Murasaki,* p. 268.

40. Ibid.

41. Bradbury and McFarlane, *Modernism,* pp. 40–47.

42. Ōta Seikyū, "Shintaishi no shigeki to waka kakushin," p. 53; Itsumi, *Murasaki,* p. 195.

43. Ōta, "Shintaishi," p. 53; Itsumi, *Murasaki,* pp. 276–277.

44. Tekkan quoted in Itsumi, *Murasaki,* p. 195.

45. Ueda Hiroshi, "Tekkan to Akiko," p. 102.

46. Itsumi, *Murasaki,* p. 146.

47. Quoted in Paglia, *Sexual Personae,* p. 471.

48. Numerous translations of poetry from *Tangled Hair* exist. Two older translated volumes are Yosano Akiko, *Tangled Hair,* trans. Shio Sakanishi; and *Tangled Hair,* trans. Sanford Goldstein and Seishi Shinoda. A recent sample is provided in *River of Stars,* trans. Sam Hamill and Keiko Matsui Gibson.

49. Quoted in Itsumi Kumi, ed., *Shin midaregami zenshaku,* p. 203.

50. Itsumi, *Shin midaregami,* p. 204.

51. Ibid., pp. 204–205.

52. Ibid., p. 205.

53. Ibid., p. 205.

54. Ibid., p. 344.

55. Ibid., p. 308.

56. Ibid., p. 267.

57. Ibid., p. 6.

58. See Morton, "Clash of Traditions," pp. 112–120. Isoda, *Rokumeikan no keifu,* pp. 148–150.

59. See further Morton, "Akiko, Tomiko and Hiroshi."

60. Itsumi, *Shin midaregami,* p. 308.

61. Quoted in Bradbury and McFarlane, *Modernism,* p. 43.

62. Quoted in ibid., p. 31.

63. See the translation by Kenneth G. Henshall, *The Quilt and Other Stories by Tayami Katai,* pp. 35–97.

64. Dennis Washburn, *The Dilemma of the Modern in Japanese Fiction,* pp. 142–143.

65. See Morton, "'Taiyō' to 'Jogaku Zasshi,'" pp. 319–326 for details. Also see Rebecca L. Copeland, *Lost Leaves,* especially pp. 7–126; and Michael Brownstein, "*Jogaku Zasshi* and the Founding of *Bungakukai.*"

66. Denis De Rougemont, *Love in the Western World.*

67. Irving Singer, *The Nature of Love,* vol. 2: *Courtly and Romantic,* p. 299.

68. Ibid.

69. Nakamaru Nobuaki, "'Monogatari' o tsumugu onna tachi—'shizenshugi' shōsetsu no ichidanmen," pp. 22–23.

70. Ibid., p. 23.

71. Ibid., p. 29.

72. Saeki Junko, "'Ren'ai' no zenkindai kindai datsukindai," pp 167–181, esp. pp. 174–178.

73. Saeki Junko, *"Iro" to "ai" no hikaku bunka,* esp. chapter 8.

74. Takumi Hideo, "Meiji 30 nendai ni okeru bungaku to bijutsu kakawari ni tsuite," pp. 62–65.

75. Ibid., p. 63.

76. Itsumi, *Murasaki,* p. 228.

77. Ibid., p. 290.

78. Uda, *Tekkan Akiko shū,* p. 119.

79. Itsumi, *Murasaki,* p. 232.

80. Ibid., pp. 227–228.

81. Ibid., p. 92.

82. Ibid., p. 144.

83. Ibid., p. 241.

84. Ibid., p. 272.

85. Itsumi, *Shin midaregami,* p. 232.

86. Itsumi, *Murasaki,* p. 219.

87. Itsumi, *Shin midaregami,* p. 300.

88. Ibid., p. 300.

89. Itsumi, *Murasaki,* p. 174.

90. Itsumi, *Shin midaregami,* p. 78.

91. Quoted in Itsumi, *Shin midaregami,* p. 220.

92. Ibid., p. 208.

93. Ibid., p. 313.

94. Ibid., p. 314.

95. Itsumi interprets the poem as referring to Tekkan's wife Takino (*Murasaki,* p. 88), but Ueda argues it refers to Akiko ("Tekkan to Akiko" p. 106).

96. Itsumi, *Murasaki,* p. 88.

97. Ibid., p. 287.

98. For translations of Shiki, in addition to Beichman, *Masaoka Shiki,* see Ruth S. McCreery, *Shiki and Matsuyama.* For translations of Takuboku, in addition to Hijiya, *Ishikawa Takuboku,* see Ishikawa Takuboku, *Takuboku: Poems to Eat,* trans. Carl Sesar.

99. Morton, "Clash of Traditions."

100. Suzuki Sadami, *"Seimei" de yomu Nihon kindai,* pp. 186–192. Writing from the perspective of "vitalism," Suzuki argues that poets like Kambara Ariake (1875–1952) and Kitahara Hakushū explored sexuality in a new and radical way. He links this exploration to the romantic movement (pp. 98–99). Similarly, Isoda in *Rokumeikan no keifu* also argues that the legacy of the Myōjō school is various, citing several later *shi* poets (pp. 156–157).

## Chapter 2: The Expression of Despair

"No wind, no stars. Night." Quoted in Georg Trakl, *Selected Poems,* p. 88. The second epigraph is from John Ashbery, *Flow Chart,* p. 30.

1. Quoted in Maurice Blanchot (trans. Ann Smock), *The Space of Literature,* p. 97.

2. For details concerning their relationship, consult Leith Morton, *Divided Self,* pp. 206–211. The only other English-language book on Arishima is Paul Anderer, *Other Worlds.*

3. Blanchot, *Space of Literature,* p. 103.

4. Arishima Takeo, *Arishima Takeo zenshū,* vol. 6, p. 178.

5. *Arishima zenshū,* vol. 14, p. 667.

6. Ibid.

7. Ibid., vol. 14, p. 669.

8. Ibid., vol. 5, p. 530.

9. Akita Ujaku, "Buronzu no te," p. 878; Endō Yū, "Arishima Takeo no shi," p. 61.

10. Wayne Booth, *The Company We Keep,* pp. 128, 438–457.

11. *Arishima zenshū,* vol. 6, p. 183.

12. Ibid.

13. Ibid., supplementary vol. *(Bekkan),* p. 878.

14. Ibid., *Bekkan,* p. 877.

15. Ibid., vol. 6, p. 181. Parenthetical dates for poems from *Eyeless Eyes* refer to the year 1923.

16. Egashira's article is found in the supplementary essays attached to *Arishima zenshū,* vol. 6.

17. *Arishima zenshū,* vol. 14, p. 243.

18. Ibid.

19. Ibid., vol. 6, pp. 176–177.

20. Ibid., vol. 6, p. 178.

21. For translations of Nishiwaki, see Nishiwaki Junzaburō, *Gen'ei: Selected Poems of Nishiwaki Junzaburō, 1894–1982,* trans. Yasuko Claremont; and Hirata, *The Poetry and Poetics of Nishiwaki Junzaburō.* On the "phantom man," see Yasuko Claremont, "A Turning Point in Nishiwaki Junzaburō's Poetic Career," pp. 29–32.

22. Arishima's view of the self and the links between this view and European thinkers like Schopenhauer and Nietzsche are most transparently revealed in his 1920 treatise *Oshiminaku ai wa ubau* (Love, the generous plunderer). See Morton, *Divided Self*, pp. 174–178, for details.

23. Quoted in Kaneko Mitsuharu and Momota Sōji, eds., *Zenshishū taisei gendai Nihon shijin zenshū*, vol. 11, p. 147. For a complete translation of Hagiwara's poems, see Hagiwara Sakutarō, *Rats' Nests*, trans. Robert Epp.

24. *Arishima zenshū*, vol. 6, p. 179.

25. Ibid., vol. 6, p. 181–182.

26. See Morton, *Divided Self*, p. 61.

27. *Arishima zenshū*, vol. 8, p. 198.

28. Ibid., vol. 8, p. 200.

29. Ibid., vol. 9, p. 17.

30. Ibid., vol. 8, p. 193.

31. Ibid., vol. 9, p. 152.

32. Ibid., vol. 9, p. 157.

33. Ibid.

34. For details of these crises overwhelming Arishima, see Morton, *Divided Self*, pp. 179–211.

35. Chiba Sen'ichi, *Gendai bungaku no hikakubungakuteki kenkyū—modanizumu no shiteki dōtai*. See also Chiba *Modanizumu no hikakubungakuteki kenkyū*.

36. Marjorie Perloff, *The Futurist Moment*, pp. 18–20.

37. Chiba, *Gendai bungaku*, pp. 105–109.

38. Yasukawa Sadao, "Arishima Takeo to Yosano Akiko," p. 73.

39. Nagahata Michiko has argued that Arishima had an affair with Akiko. For details of the arguments, see Nagahata Michiko, *Yume no kakehashi*, and Nagahata Michiko, *Hana no ran*.

40. Quoted in Kaneko and Momota, *Gendai Nihon shijin zenshū*, vol. 4, p. 72.

41. Chiba, *Gendai bungaku*, p. 66.

42. Morton, *Divided Self*, p. 75.

43. Ibid., pp. 50–51, 73–74.

44. Takamura Kōtarō, *Takamura Kōtarō senshū*, vol. 1, p. 217.

45. Ibid.

46. Sasaki Yasuaki, "Arishima Takeo to Anaakisuto no nakamatachi," pp. 207–219.

47. Ibid., pp. 216–222.

48. Ibid., pp. 207–209.

49. Chiba, *Gendai bungaku*, p. 115.

50. Kaneko and Momota, *Gendai Nihon shijin zenshū*, vol. 6, p. 394.

51. Quoted in Chiba, *Gendai bungaku*, p. 81.

52. Kikuchi Yasuo, *Aoi Kaidan o noboru shijin tachi;* Komata Yūsuke, *"Zeneishi" no jidai—Nihon no 1920 nendai.*

53. Komata, *"Zeneishi" no jidai,* p. 14.

54. Ibid., pp. 33–34.

55. *Arishima zenshū,* vol. 6, pp. 179–180. The line of dots in the poem reproduces the original typography. The notation also appears in the poem "Hand."

56. Nakamura Miharu, *Kotoba no ishi,* p. 267.

57. Sasaki, "Arishima Takeo to anaakisuto no nakamatachi," p. 216.

58. *Arishima zenshū,* vol. 5, p. 508.

59. Ibid., *Bekkan,* p. 876.

60. Yamamoto Tarō, *Yurishiizu,* p. 194. See also a partial translation in Morton, *An Anthology of Contemporary Japanese Poetry,* p. 115.

61. *Arishima zenshū,* vol. 6, pp. 175–176.

62. Blanchot, *Space of Literature,* p. 103.

## Chapter 3: Uttering the Unutterable

"Elm" is quoted in Sylvia Plath, *Ariel,* p. 26. "The Light of Life" appears in Stevie Smith, *The Collected Poems of Stevie Smith,* p. 372.

1. Roland Barthes, "The Death of the Author," pp. 167–172. Note that the romanization "Soh" follows the poet's own usage.

2. For translations of Soh's poetry, see Morton, *Anthology of Contemporary Japanese Poetry,* pp. 55–96.

3. See Wolfgang Iser, *The Implied Reader;* Stanley Fish, *Self-Consuming Artifacts,* and *Is There a Text in This Class?*

4. Michel Foucault, "What Is an Author," p. 208.

5. Ibid.

6. Quoted in Fredric Jameson, *The Prison-House of Language,* p. 185. Further, note that Terry Eagleton in *Literary Theory* argues that "the widespread notion that deconstruction denies the existence of anything but discourse, or affirms a realm of pure difference in which all meaning and identity dissolves, is a travesty of Derrida's own work" (p. 148).

7. Jameson, *Prison-House of Language,* p. 185. Compare the historian Hayden White in his essay "The Absurdist Moment in Contemporary Literary Theory," collected in Hayden White, *Tropics of Discourse,* where he describes Derrida as "the minotaur imprisoned in structuralism's hypostatized labyrinth of language" (p. 280).

8. Jameson, *Prison-House of Language,* pp. 139–140.

9. David Brooks, "Value Judgements and Literature," p. 48. For one perspective on this issue in Japanese studies, see Earl Miner, "Waka," pp. 672–673, where

he writes, "When really intelligent people claim that words produce people rather than the reverse, it becomes time to point out that the critic's new clothes are no longer in fashion."

10. *The Cambridge History of Japan,* vol. 6, ed. Peter Duus, p. 369.

11. Quoted in John Dower, *War without Mercy,* pp. 40–41.

12. Ibid., p. 41.

13. Sō Sakon, "Wadatsumi no itteki," p. 140.

14. George Steiner, "The Hollow Miracle," p. 141.

15. George Steiner, "Silence and the Poet," in his *Language and Silence,* p. 74.

16. Ibid., p. 73.

17. George Steiner, *In Bluebeard's Castle,* p. 48.

18. Ibid.

19. Dante Alighieri, *The Divine Comedy of Dante Alighieri,* trans. Charles E. Norton, p. 19.

20. Genshin, *Ōjōyōshū,* annotated by Ishida Mizumaro, vol. 1, pp. 14–15.

21. Ibid., p. 20.

22. Okudaira Hideo, *Kokuhō emaki,* pp. 32–33.

23. Sō Sakon, *Moeru haha,* pp. 17–18.

24. Ibid., pp. 24–25.

25. Ibid., pp. 28–30.

26. Ibid., pp. 35–37.

27. Ibid., pp. 38–40.

28. Ibid., pp. 47–49.

29. Ibid., pp. 50–57.

30. James E. Young, *Writing and Rewriting the Holocaust,* p. 90.

31. Richard H. Minear, ed. and trans., *Hiroshima,* p. 292. In Soh's case, "breathless" is almost a physical phenomenon, as the repeated use of the phrase "running" *(hashitte iru)* leaves the reader breathless.

32. For details, see Kokai Eiji, *Nihon sengo shi no tenbō,* p. 26.

33. According to Kokai Eiji, "Sengo Nihon no shi undō—'Arechi' no Baai," p. 432.

34. Morton, "Interview with Tanikawa Shuntarō," p. 8.

35. Quoted in Kokai, "Sengo Nihon no shi undō," pp. 434–435.

36. See ibid., p. 432.

37. Yoshimoto Takaaki, *Yoshimoto Takaaki zenchosakushū,* vol. 4, pp. 109–173.

38. Ibid., vol. 13, pp. 5–28.

39. Ibid., vol. 5, pp. 38–119, 317–344.

40. Dvir Abramovich, "Bearing Witness Fiction."

41. John Whittier Treat, *Writing Ground Zero,* p. 163.

42. Ibid., p. 151.

43. Ibid., pp. 185–186.

44. Sō, *Moeru haha*, p. 64.

45. Ibid., p. 76.

46. Ibid.

47. The figure of the fetus represented in the form of a *kappa* is common to many of Soh's collections, but it appears most prominently in *Kappa.*

48. Sō, *Moeru haha*, p. 98.

49. Ibid., pp. 113–146.

50. Ibid., pp. 147–167.

51. Ibid., p. 170.

52. Ibid., p. 190.

53. Ibid., p. 194.

54. Shibusawa Takasuke, "Sakonshi kanken," p. 146.

55. Sō, *Moeru haha*, pp. 199–202.

56. Ibid., pp. 216–221.

57. Jerry Glenn, *Paul Celan*, p. 19.

58. Chalfen is quoted in Sharon Barnett, "Paul Celan and *Todesfuge:* A Legacy of Nazism," p. 4.

59. Paul Celan, *Poems of Paul Celan,* trans. Michael Hamburger, p. 39. See further Leith Morton, "The Paradox of Pain."

60. Treat, *Writing Ground Zero,* p. 193.

61. Ibid., p. 196.

62. Sō, *Moeru haha,* p. 243.

63. Ibid., pp. 269–270.

64. Ibid., pp. 273–277.

65. Ibid., p. 277.

66. Ibid., p. 305.

67. Ibid., p. 307.

68. Quoted in Sakai Tadakazu, *Kokubungaku,* p. 14.

69. Young, *Writing and Rewriting the Holocaust,* p. 132.

70. For details see Kokai, *Nihon sengo shi no tenbō,* pp. 26–37, and also Ōoka Makoto, *Gendai no shijin tachi,* vol. 2, pp. 260–274.

71. Ayukawa Nobuo, *Ayukawa Nobuo shishū,* pp. 48–49.

72. Quoted in Terry Eagleton, *The Ideology of the Aesthetic,* p. 359. Compare this to Shibusawa Takasuke's comments in "Sakonshi kanken," p. 146. Soh is not the only Japanese writer to have foundered on the hard rock of redemption; see Morton, *Divided Self,* pp. 92–95.

73. Søren Kierkegaard, *The Last Years,* ed. and trans. by Ronald Gregor Smith, p. 109.

## Chapter 4: Language as Feminist Discourse

"The Man with the Blue Guitar" appears in Wallace Stevens, *Selected Poems*, p. 72; "Ishtar," in Judith Wright, *Judith Wright: Collected Poems, 1942–1985*, p. 101.

1. The reference is taken from Katie Wales, ed., *A Dictionary of Stylistics*, c.v. "Aesthetics," pp. 12–13.

2. Martin Heidegger, *Basic Writings*, ed. David Farrell Krell, p. 423. Also compare Herder's notion of "world view" in Morton, *Modern Japanese Culture*, pp. 11–14.

3. Quoted in Jan Montefiore, *Feminism and Poetry*, p. 27.

4. Heidegger, *Basic Writings*, p. 411. Italics in original.

5. Heidegger, *Poetry, Language, Thought*, trans. Albert Hofstadler, pp. 196–197.

6. Hans-Georg Gadamer, *Truth and Method*, trans. Joel Weinsheimer and Donald G. Marshall, p. 463.

7. Ibid., p. 470.

8. Ibid., p. 490. Cf. Jacques Derrida, *The Archaeology of the Frivolous*, trans. John P. Leavey Jr., esp. pp. 132–135.

9. From Cixous' essay "Sorties" (trans. A. Liddle), p. 292.

10. Quoted in Toril Moi, *Sexual/Textual Politics*, p. 119. For Moi's discussion of Cixous, see pp. 102–126.

11. Quoted in ibid., p. 146. For Moi's discussion of Luce Irigaray, see pp. 127–150. A variant reading of Irigaray can be found in Elizabeth Grosz, *Sexual Subversions*, pp. 100–184.

12. Both Moi and Grosz discuss Kristeva. But for an early analysis (1974) of language, metalanguage, and intertextual practices, Julia Kristeva, *Revolution in Poetic Language*, provides what is probably the best introduction. For a brief but concise summary of the subject, see the introduction (pp. 1–45) to Michael Worton and Judith Still, eds., *Intertextuality*.

13. Joel C. Weinsheimer, *Gadamer's Hermeneutics*, p. 245.

14. Gadamer, *Truth and Method*, p. 99.

15. Weinsheimer, *Gadamer's Hermeneutics*, pp. 99–100.

16. On the notion of provisional readings of texts, see Morton, "Translating Japanese Poetry," p. 145.

17. For a brief discussion of "male" and "female" linguistic usage in Japanese, see A. E. Backhouse, *The Japanese Language*, pp. 99–100, 167–168. An interesting remark to the effect that distinctions between male and female speech are fairly new, urban, and diminishing is found in Samuel E. A. Martin, *Reference Grammar of Japanese*, p. 921. Masayoshi Shibutani, *The Languages of Japan*, summarizes differences in male and female usage (pp. 371–374). See also Sachiko Ide and Naomi Hanaoka McGloin, eds., *Aspects of Japanese Women's Language*, and, further, Cherry Kittredge, *Womensword*. Janet S. Shibamoto's *Japanese Women's Language* is the most substantial study in English.

18. For a critical feminist reading of Gadamer, see Robin Schott, "Whose Home Is It Anyway?" pp. 202–209.

19. My understanding of "phallocentric' is based on Elizabeth Grosz' definition of the term in *Sexual Subversions,* p. 25 and esp. pp. 104–119.

20. Two autobiographical essays, "Tachiba no aru shi" (1967) and "Shi o kaku koto to, ikiru koto" (1971), are available in Ishigaki Rin, *Ishigaki Rin shishū.* Another autobiographical essay, "Natsu no higure ni," as well as a chronological life history *(nenpu)* compiled by Ishigaki can be found in Ishigaki Rin, *Ishigaki Rin,* ed. Suzuki Shiroyasu.

21. The original text is taken from Ishigaki Rin, *Ishigaki Rin bunko 4: Shishū Yasashii kotoba,* pp. 13–15.

22. Ibid., pp. 18–19.

23. On irony as a feminist strategy, see Moi, *Sexual/Textual Politics,* pp. 34–41; on irony as a trope in Ann Sexton's poetry, see Montefiore, *Feminism and Poetry,* pp. 49–52; for Sylvia Plath, see ibid., p. 32.

24. The reference here is to Isaka's poem "Chōrei" (Morning assembly, 1979), translated in Morton, *Anthology of Contemporary Japanese Poetry,* pp. 291–292. Note that "Yohko" reflects the author's preferred romanization.

25. Moi, *Sexual/Textual Politics,* p. 41.

26. Ibid., p. 38.

27. Ibid., p. 39.

28. Ibid. Italics in original.

29. For Ishigaki's characterization of her own poetic technique, see her "Shi o kaku koto," esp. p. 130. For one commentator's doubts, see Suzuki Shiroyasu's commentary on the poem in Ishigaki, *Ishigaki Rin,* pp. 27–32.

30. The originals of stanzas 6 and 7 are found in *Ishigaki Rin,* pp. 29–30.

31. The last stanza of the poem reads: "Not for the sake of pride or worldly fame but / In order for these things / To be offered to all humanity / To work toward these things with humanity itself as the object of our love."

32. *Ishigaki Rin,* p. 32.

33. Miki Taku, "Ishigaki Rin no shi," p. 141.

34. Tamura Keiji, "Watashi no mae ni aru Nabe to okama to moeru hi to," p. 118.

35. Quoted in Moi, *Sexual/Textual Politics,* p. 156.

36. The original is found in Ishigaki, *Ishigaki Rin,* pp. 88–90.

37. Ibid., p. 123.

38. The original is found in ibid., pp. 122–123. Translations by Leith Morton of all the Ishigaki poems discussed herein can also be found in Tanikawa Shuntarō, ed., *Masters of Japanese Poetry,* pp. 85–111. For other translations of Ishigaki's poetry,

see the five poems translated by Yukie Ohta and Rie Takagi, "Ishigaki Rin: 5 Poems," pp. 723–727.

39. Asō Naoko, *Gendai josei shijin ron;* cf. Ōno Tōzaburō's essay-reminiscences of Tomioka, "Tomioka Taeko no 'Uta no wakare.'" For translations of Tomioka's poetry, see Tomioka Taeko, *See You Soon,* trans. Sato Hiroaki. For a translation of three poems by Ibaragi Noriko, see Naoshi Koriyama and Edward Lueders, trans., *Like Underground Water,* pp. 125–127.

40. Asō, *Gendai josei shijin ron,* p. 268. "Minouebanashi' is available in translation, both by Sato and in Leza Lowitz and Miyuki Aoyama's volume of translations, *other side river,* pp. 203–205.

41. Amazawa Taijirō, "Tomioka Taeko ron no akuru hi," pp. 153–154.

42. Ibid., p. 138.

43. Tomioka Taeko, *Tomioka Taeko shishū,* pp. 34–38.

44. Asō, *Gendai josei shijin ron,* p. 271.

45. Ibid.

46. Quoted in Montefiore, *Feminism and Poetry,* p. 63.

47. Shiraishi Kazuko, "Hachijū nendai to joseishi," p. 65.

48. Asō, *Gendai josei shijin ron,* pp. 273–275.

49. Tomioka Taeko, *Tomioka Taeko shishū,* p. 582.

50. Ibid., pp. 449–450.

51. Quoted in Moi, *Sexual/Textual Politics,* pp. 12–13. Italics in original.

52. Quoted in ibid., p. 168. This text is partially available in translation by Margaret Waller as Kristeva, *Revolution in Poetic Language.* A detailed examination of Kristeva's view of motherwood and feminism is found in Grosz, *Sexual Subversions,* pp. 78–99.

53. Tsuboi Hideto, "Itō Hiromi ron (jō)—Teritorii ron"; "Itō Hiromi ron (chū)—Teritorii ron 1 (sono 1)"; "Itō Hiromi ron (ge)—Teritorii ron 1 (sono 2)."

54. See, for example, Isaka Yohko's comments on the series in Isaka Yōko, "Josei to iu shizen," p. 68.

55. Shiraishi, "Hachijū nendai to joseishi," pp. 68–69. For comments on two feminist poets (Shiraishi Kazuko and Yoshihara Sachiko), see Morton, "Translating Japanese Poetry," pp. 141–181.

56. Quoted in Tsuboi, "Itō Hiromi ron (jō)," p. 24.

57. Ibid.

58. The translation is taken from Morton, *Anthology of Contemporary Japanese Poetry,* pp. 369–370. The original can be found in Itō Hiromi, *Itō Hiromi shishū,* pp. 9–11.

59. Itō Hiromi, *Teritorii ron 2,* pp. 94–95.

60. Ibid., pp. 100–105. Itō lists these texts in a note at the end of the poem (p. 105).

61. Tsuboi, "Itō Hiromi ron (jō)," p. 31.

62. See ibid., p. 32, for details of the analyst's account.

63. Itō, *Teritorii ron 2,* pp. 106–111.

64. Ibid., pp. 142–151.

65. See Tsuboi, "Itō Hiromi ron (jō)," p. 34, for details. Note that one of Itō's culture heroes is the German performance artist Joseph Beuys (1921–1986); in *Teritorii ron 1* there is a poem titled "Koyote" inspired by Beuys' 1972 Action (Beuys' term) "Coyote, I Like America, America Likes Me."

66. For Ayukawa's remarks, see Tsuboi, "Itō Hiromi ron (jō)," p. 33. For a translation of "Killing Kanoko," see Morton, *Anthology of Contemporary Japanese Poetry,* pp. 383–389.

67. Tsuboi, "Itō Hiromi ron (jō)," p. 33.

68. Ibid., p. 34.

69. Itō Hiromi, *Teritorii ron 1.*

70. Quoted in Tsuboi, "Itō Hiromi ron (chū)," p. 49.

71. "Triptych" is the second poem in *Teritorii ron 1.* The book itself is unpaginated.

72. Itō acknowledges in a note at the end of "Otōsan wa burū" her quotations from Sigmund Freud's "Analysis of a Phobia in a Five-Year-Old Boy" (1909), found in *The Standard Edition of the Complete Psychological Works of Sigmund Freud,* trans. and ed. James Strachey, vol. 10, pp. 3–147. For a discussion of the "Little Hans" case, see Peter Gay, *Freud,* pp. 255–261. Tsuboi discusses the disparities between the Freud and Itō texts in "Itō Hiromi ron (chū)," pp. 53–54.

73. Tsuboi "Itō Hiromi ron (jō)," p. 52.

74. Ibid., p. 54.

75. "Vinegar and Oil" is the second to last poem in *Teritorii ron 1.* The complete poem is translated in Morton, *Anthology of Contemporary Japanese Poetry,* pp. 395–397. The lines quoted are on p. 395.

76. Morton, *Anthology of Contemporary Japanese Poetry,* p. 395.

77. Ibid., p. 396.

78. Montefiore, *Feminism and Poetry,* pp. 185–186.

79. From "Women's Time," quoted in Montefiore, *Feminism and Poetry,* p. 187. For the full text, see Julia Kristeva, "Women's Time," pp. 187–211.

80. A discussion of Smith's poetry can be found in Montefiore, *Feminism and Poetry,* pp. 43–49. For a selection of Smith's poetry, see Stevie Smith, *Two in One.*

81. Gadamer, *Truth and Method,* p. 575.

82. Ibid., p. 564.

83. Kristeva, *Revolution in Poetic Language,* p. 101.

84. Ibid., p. 104.

85. For Shiraishi's view of Itō, see Shiraishi, "Hachijū nendai to joseishi," pp.

66–69. An interesting criticism of Itō's work for adopting too directly the "male gaze" can be found in Isaka, "Josei to iu shizen," p. 68.

86. The text referred to is Itō Hiromi (with Ishiuchi Miyako), *Te, ashi, niku, karada/Hiromi 1955.*

87. For some samples of Saga Keiko's poetry, see her *Nō sutoringusu* and *Kusukusu.*

## Chapter 5: Identity in Contemporary Okinawan Poetry

Chapter-opening epigraphs are from Louis Zukofsky, *A,* p. 328, and Charles Olson, *The Maximus Poems,* p. 482.

1. Much research has been carried out on these complex issues of language use in Okinawa; for a discussion of hybrid dialects and interlanguages among the youth of Okinawa, see Ōsumi Midori, "Okinawa no wakamono no gengo to isshiki," pp. 230–235.

2. Hirata Daiichi, "Hazama no sedai ni ikiru."

3. Yamanokuchi Baku, *Yamanokuchi Baku shishū,* p. 130.

4. Takara Ben, "Ryūkyūko de shi o kaku koto," pp. 91–93; Yoshimoto Takaaki, *Zōho sengo shi shiron;* Kokai Eiji, *Nihon sengo shi no tenbō,* p. 277. Takara Ben is a pen name; his real name is Takamine Chōsei.

5. Yoshimoto Takaaki, *Zōho sengo shi shiron,* pp. 172–173.

6. Cited in Ōshiro Sadatoshi, *Okinawa sengo shishi,* p. 209.

7. For translations of prose by Baku, see Molasky and Rabson, *Southern Exposure,* pp. 85–97. For Baku's poetry, see ibid., pp. 46–50, and also Hugh Clarke, "Japonesia, the Black Current and the Origins of the Japanese."

8. For examples of Kishimoto's verse, see *Okinawa bungaku zenshū,* vol. 2, ed. Okinawa Bungaku Zenshū Henshūiinkai, pp. 129–142.

9. Ōshiro, *Okinawa sengo shishi,* p. 218.

10. Ibid., p. 230.

11. Ibid.

12. Ibid., p. 231.

13. For translations of Ichihara's poetry, see Morton, *Anthology of Contemporary Japanese Poetry,* pp. 319–347.

14. Ichihara Chikako, *Umi no tonneru,* p. 130.

15. Yanagita Kunio, *Yanagita Kunio zenshū,* vol. 1, pp. 109–123, 134–155.

16. Ichihara, *Umi no tonneru,* p. 118.

17. Ibid., p. 11.

18. Ibid., p. 18.

19. Ibid., p. 17.

20. Ibid., pp. 16–17.

21. Ibid., p. 13.

22. Ibid., p. 14.

23. Ibid., p. 20.

24. Ibid., p. 40.

25. Ibid., pp. 41–42.

26. Yanagita, *Yanagita Kunio zenshū,* vol. 1, p. 98.

27. Ichihara, *Umi no tonneru,* p. 120.

28. Ibid., pp. 42–43.

29. Ibid., p. 47.

30. Ibid., p. 48.

31. Ibid., p. 49.

32. Ibid., pp. 52–53.

33. Ibid., p. 53.

34. Ibid.

35. Ibid., p. 55.

36. Ibid., pp. 56–57.

37. Iraha Morio, *Maboroshi no mikojima,* p. 92. The word *"miko,"* which I have translated as "female shaman," can also be translated as "female medium" or "shamanic female," or "mantic" or "sacral female." See the excellent study from which I have drawn these translations: Carmen Blacker, *The Catalpa Bow,* pp. 21–31.

38. Iraha, *Maboroshi no mikojima,* p. 80.

39. Nakahodo Masanori, *Okinawa bungaku ron no hōhō,* pp. 202–203.

40. Ichihara, *Umi no tonneru,* p. 63.

41. Quoted in Toril Moi, ed., *The Kristeva Reader,* p. 206.

42. Ichihara, *Umi no tonneru,* pp. 66–69.

43. Julia Kristeva, *Tales of Love,* trans. Leon S. Roudiez, p. 259.

44. Kunimine Teruko, "Joseishi no kōmyaku," p. 152.

45. Ibid.

46. Ibid.

47. Isaka, "Josei to iu shizen," p. 68.

48. Nishiwaki's poem reads in translation: "Morning like an (upturn'd gem) / Someone whispers at the doorway to someone else / Today is the birthday of a god" (Nishiwaki Junzaburō, *Nishiwaki Junzaburō shishū,* p. 14).

49. Ichihara, *Umi no tonneru,* pp. 80–81.

50. Nishiwaki, *Nishiwaki Junzaburō shishū,* p. 14.

51. Kristeva, *Revolution in Poetic Language,* p. 49.

52. Ichihara, *Umi no tonneru,* pp. 88–91.

53. For translations of Isaka's poetry from *Morning Assembly,* see Morton, *Anthology of Contemporary Japanese Poetry,* pp. 291–293.

54. Ichihara, *Umi no tonneru,* p. 103.

55. Ibid., p. 105.

56. Ibid., p. 127.

57. From "East Coker," in T. S. Eliot, *Collected Poems, 1909–1962*, pp. 203–204.

## Chapter 6: Language as Postmodern Expression

Epigraphs from Ezra Pound, *The Cantos*, p. 797; Edward Dorn, *Slinger*, n.p.

1. For translations of Asabuki's work, see Morton, *Anthology of Contemporary Japanese Poetry*, pp. 349–366.

2. Jameson, *Postmodernism*, p. 58.

3. Ibid., p. 62.

4. Ibid., p. 59.

5. Terry Eagleton, "Capitalism, Modernism and Postmodernism," p. 387.

6. Ibid., pp. 395–396.

7. Terry Eagleton, *The Ideology of the Aesthetic*, p. 370.

8. Jameson, *Postmodernism*, p. 411.

9. Ibid., p. 412.

10. Marilyn Ivy, "Critical Texts, Mass Artifacts," pp. 28–29.

11. Ibid., p. 29.

12. David Lodge, in *Modern Criticism and Theory*, p. 107.

13. Quoted in ibid., pp. 121–122.

14. The Frankfurt School was established at Frankfurt University in the prewar period and, led by such thinkers as Max Horkheimer (1895–1973), Theodor Adorno, Walter Benjamin (1892–1940), and Herbert Marcuse (1898–1979), proposed a radical critique of theory that opposed positivism and sought to restructure existing forms of social consciousness or praxis entirely. For a concise account of the school, see chapter 10 of Leszek Kolakowski, *Main Currents of Marxism*, vol. 3, pp. 341–421.

15. Michel Foucault, *The Order of Things*, p. 298.

16. Ibid., p. 300.

17. Ibid.

18. Ibid., p. 384.

19. Ibid., p. 386.

20. Gadamer, *Truth and Method*, p. 490.

21. Ibid.

22. Bruce Andrews and Charles Bernstein, eds., *The L=A=N=G=U=A=G=E Book*, p. 14.

23. Ibid., pp. 33–37.

24. Charles Bernstein, "Stray Straws and Straw Men," in ibid., p. 43.

25. Ibid., p. 39.

26. Andrews and Bernstein, *The L=A=N=G=U=A=G=E Book*, pp. 257–258. For an analysis of McCaffery's work, see Marjorie Perloff, *Poetic License*, pp. 285–297.

27. Michael Palmer, *Notes for Echo Lake*, pp. 22–23.

28. Philip Hammial, *Pell Mell,* p. 25.

29. George Charbonnier, *Conversations with Claude Lévi-Strauss,* pp. 110–111.

30. Perloff, *Poetic License,* p. 133.

31. Ibid., p. 134.

32. For details on the collaboration between Eliot and Pound, see Humprey Carpenter, *A Serious Character,* pp. 399–416.

33. Keene, *Dawn to the West,* vol. 2, p. 323. For details of Nishiwaki's life, see pp. 323–335 and Yasuko Claremont, "Turning Point."

34. *Tabibito kaerazu,* though comprising 168 numbered poems, has been described by Yasuko Claremont as "related thematically in a discrete whole" ("Turning Point," p. 29). Note also that Kondō Teruhiko argues that Eliot's "Four Quartets" (1943) had a decisive influence on the writing of *Ushinawareta toki;* see his *Nishiwaki Junzaburō no shi,* p. 168. For translations of Nishiwaki's poems see Nishiwaki, *Gen'ei: Selected Poems of Nishiwaki Junzaburō 1894–1982,* trans. Yasuko Claremont; see also Hosea Hirata, *The Poetry and Poetics of Nishiwaki Junzaburō.*

35. Some long poems predate Nishiwaki (e.g., Kitamura Tōkoku's "Hōraikyoku," published in 1891, and Oguma Hideo's "Tobu Sori," published in 1938), but none had the impact of Nishiwaki on postwar poets.

36. Partial translations of some of these works are available: for Shiraishi Kazuko, *Seasons of Sacred Lust: the Selected Poems of Kazuko Shiraishi,* and for Yoshimasu Gōzō, *A Thousand Steps . . . and More: Selected Poems and Prose 1964–1984.*

37. Yoshimoto, *Zōho, Sengo shi shiron,* p. 172.

38. Ibid., p. 173.

39. Ibid., p. 216.

40. Ibid., pp. 216–233. For translations of Hiraide's work, see Morton, *Anthology of Contemporary Japanese Poetry,* pp. 309–318. See also Yasuko Claremont, " Hiraide Takashi and the Emergence of Sanbunshi in Contemporary Japanese Poetry," pp. 47–64.

41. For translations of Inagawa's poetry, see Thomas Fitzsimmons and Yoshimasu Gozo, eds., *The New Poetry of Japan,* pp. 149–186, trans. Eric Selland.

42. Inagawa Masato, *Inagawa Masato shishū,* pp. 104–113.

43. Hiraide Takashi, *Hiraide Takashi shishū,* p. 122.

44. Asabuki Ryōji, *Opus,* p. 7.

45. Ibid., pp. 7–12.

46. A brilliant example of what can be achieved by this sort of analysis is found in David Levi Strauss' essay "Approaching *80 Flowers*" (on Louis Zukofsky's *80 Flowers*), pp. 79–102.

47. Asabuki, *Opus,* p. 15.

48. Ibid., p. 16.

49. Ibid., p. 20.

50. Ibid., p. 39.

51. Ibid., p. 14.

52. Ibid., pp. 38–39.

53. Ibid., p. 41. Lineation is difficult in this poem, as the line shapes suggest an attempt at complete enjambment, a "cut" or "slice" from a speech fragment.

54. Ibid., p. 42.

55. Ibid., p. 44.

56. Ibid., p. 45.

57. Compare Don Byrd's comments on Charles Olson's *Maximum Poems*, "parataxis is active, attempting to bring the poem to an immediate coherence by developing concrete associations on multiple planes." "Reading Olson," p. 256.

58. Asabuki, *Opus*, p. 45. Ellipsis in original poem.

59. Ibid., pp. 46–47.

60. Asabuki Ryōji, "Chinmoku/Hakushi ni tsuite," in *Asabuki Ryōji shishū*, p. 127.

61. Ibid., p. 129.

62. Ibid., p. 130.

63. Ibid., pp. 130–131.

64. Ibid., p. 131.

65. Asabuki, *Opus*, p. 60.

66. Ibid., p. 61.

67. Ibid., p. 63.

68. Ibid., pp. 67–69.

69. Ibid., p. 71.

70. *The L=A=N=G=U=A=G=E Book*, p. 22. Watson's statement also revives the debate between "formalistic" analysis of a poetic text such as that advocated by Marjorie Perloff in her treatment of the poetry of Lorine Niedecker and a more content-oriented or ideologically aware analysis, which is, in fact, what Perloff performs. See Perloff's essay on Niedecker in *Poetic License*, pp. 41–51 and especially pp. 50–51, where in her examination of Niedecker's "Paen to Place" she appears to demonstrate the exact opposite of what she advocates.

71. Asabuki, *Opus*, pp. 156–157.

72. Ibid., p. 159.

73. Ibid., p. 160.

74. Ibid., pp. 164–165.

75. Ibid., p. 171.

## Chapter 7: The Limits of Language

Epigraphs are from "my grief, I can see, is deserting to you," quoted in Paul Celan, *Poems of Paul Celan*, trans. Michael Hamburger, p. 337; Adrienne Rich, *The Dream of a Common Language*, p. 18.

1. Tanikawa is probably the best translated of all contemporary Japanese poets.

A list of English translations includes Tanikawa Shuntarō, *Sixty-two Sonnets and Definitions: Poems and Prosepoems,* trans. William I. Elliot and Kawamura Kazuo; Tanikawa, *At Midnight in the Kitchen I Just Wanted to Talk to You,* trans. William I. Elliot and Kawamura Kazuo; Tanikawa, *Coca-Cola Lesson,* trans. William I. Elliot and Kawamura Kazuo; Tanikawa, *Floating the River in Melancholy,* trans. William I. Elliot and Kawamura Kazuo; Tanikawa, *Songs of Nonsense/Yoshinashi Uta,* trans. William I. Elliot and Kawamura Kazuo; Tanikawa, *The Selected Poems of Shuntarō Tanikawa,* trans. Harold Wright; Tanikawa, *With Silence My Companion,* trans. William I. Elliot and Kawamura Kazuo; Tanikawa, *Naked,* trans. William I. Elliot and Kawamura Kazuo.

2. Shimizu Akira, "Fujitsu no bijo—*seken* to jibun to no kakawari," p. 118.

3. Quoted in Takachi Jun'ichirō, "Mozartesque—the Poetic Epiphany of Tanikawa Shuntarō," p. 86.

4. Quoted in Leith Morton, "An Interview with Shuntarō Tanikawa," p. 29.

5. Tanikawa Shuntarō, *Minimal,* trans. William I. Elliot and Kazuo Kawamura.

6. For Sano Yōko's account of the marriage, see Sano Yōko, "Tanikawa Shuntarō no asa to yoru," p. 41.

7. Takachi, "Mozartesque," p. 86.

8. Tanikawa, *Minimal,* pp. 136–137.

9. Morinaka Takaaki, "Kotoba, chinmoku, jiyū—shishū *Tabi* kara *Seken shirazu* e," p. 40.

10. *Tabi* has been translated into English by William I. Elliot and Kawamura Kazuo. See Tanikawa Shuntarō, *With Silence My Companion.*

11. Tanikawa Shuntarō, *Seken shirazu,* pp. 10–15.

12. Kitagawa Tōru, "Roshutsu suru yōki no yō na . . . —*Seken shirazu* no pafōmansu."

13. Nejime Shōichi, *"Seken shirazu,"* pp. 98–101.

14. Yokogi Tokuhisa, "Shijin shirazu no kōzai," pp. 166–167.

15. For "For Sale," see Robert Lowell, *Selected Poems,* p. 44. For "Poem to My Father," see Robert Gray, *Selected Poems, 1963–1983,* pp. 55–60.

16. For "Three Poems in Memory of My Mother," see Les A. Murray, *The People's Otherworld,* pp. 30–36. For "Dream Song 145," see John Berryman, *Selected Poems, 1938–1968,* p. 117.

17. For "Death, an Ode," see John Forbes, *The Stunned Mullet and Other Poems,* p. 43.

18. For "XVI," see Bruce Beaver, *Death's Directives,* pp. 50–53.

19. For a comparative study of Soh and Celan, see Morton, "Paradox of Pain."

20. Tanikawa, *Seken shirazu,* p. 13.

21. For more details, see Booth, *The Company We Keep,* p. 446.

22. On the "implied reader," see ibid., pp. 127–128.

23. Tanikawa, *Seken shirazu,* p. 14.

24. Tanikawa Shuntarō and Tsujii Takashi, "Tanikawa Shuntarō wa 'Seken shirazu' ka?," p. 15.

25. Tanikawa Shuntarō and Inagawa Masato, "Disukomunikēshon wo megutte," esp. pp. 11, 19–21. For details of the language poets, see Andrews and Bernstein, *The L=A=N=G=U=A=G=E Book.*

26. Hiraide Takashi, "Gengoteki yuibutsushugi ni tsuite—shijin ni yoru jissen," p. 165.

27. Ibid., pp. 165–166.

28. Tanikawa and Tsujii, "Tanikawa Shuntarō wa 'Seken shirazu' ka," p. 15.

29. See Tanikawa's postscript in *Mōtsaruto wo kiku hito,* p. 60, and the list of first publications at the end of *Masshiro de iru yori mo.*

30. Suzuki Keisuke, "*Masshiro de iru yori mo*—mō hitotsu no keiretsu no shishū," pp. 105–107.

31. Tanikawa Shuntarō, *Mōtsuaruto wo kiku hito,* pp. 6–7.

32. Tanikawa Shuntarō, *Masshiro de iru yori mo,* pp. 26–27.

33. Takachi, "Mozartesque," p. 87.

34. Tanikawa, *Seken shirazu,* p. 83.

35. Ibid., p. 85.

36. Tanikawa, *Masshiro de iru yori mo,* pp. 82–83.

37. Morinaka, "Kotoba, chinmoku, jiyū," p. 41.

## Epilogue

The epigraphs for this chapter are from Philip Hammial, *Just Desserts,* p. 30; Michael Palmer, *At Passages,* p. 32.

1. Shimaoka, *Shi to wa nanika,* chapters 4 and 6.

2. Chiba, *Gendai bungaku* and *Modanizumu,* in particular the early chapters (pp. 7–39) of the former volume.

3. Kikuchi, *Aoi Kaidan;* Nakano Kaichi, *Modanizumu shi no jidai,* pp. 11–215; Komata, *"Zeneishi" no jidai.*

4. Itō Shinkichi, *Gyakuryū no naka no uta—shiteki anakizumu no kaisō.*

5. See, for example, Perloff, *The Futurist Moment.*

6. Morton, "Interview with Tanikawa Shuntarō," pp. 8, 18–19.

7. Yoshimoto Takaaki, *Masu imēji ron,* pp. 174–203. See also Inagawa's essay "'Wareware' to wa dareka?" pp. 104–113.

8. Mado's work is available in translation in Tanikawa, ed., *Masters of Modern Japanese Poetry,* pp. 113–153.

9. For an attempt at a beginning to this story, see Leith Morton, "A Two-Legged Mongrel," and my essay "Tanka and Haiku" in Sandra Buckley, ed., *Encyclopaedia of Contemporary Japanese Culture.*

10. See Morton, *Modern Japanese Culture,* chapters 4 and 5, for details.

# Bibliography

Abramovich, Dvir. "Bearing Witness Fiction: The Suppression and Evolution of Second Generation Holocaust Literature." *Literature and Aesthetics: The Journal of the Sydney Society of Literature and Aesthetics* 11 (November 2001): 99–116.

Akita Ujaku. "Buronzu no te—(Arishima Takeo kun Tsuitō shuki kara)." In *Arishima Takeo zenshū,* ed. Senuma Shigeki et al. Supplementary volume *(Bekkan).* Tokyo: Chikuma Shobō, 1980–1986.

Amazawa Taijirō. "Tomioka Taeko ron no akuru hi." In *Shinsen Tomioka Taeko shishū.* Tokyo: Shichōsha, 1977.

Anderer, Paul. *Other Worlds: Arishima Takeo and the Bounds of Modern Japanese Fiction.* New York: Columbia University Press, 1984.

Andrews, Bruce, and Charles Bernstein, eds. *The L=A=N=G=U=A=G=E Book.* Carbondale and Edwardsville: Southern Illinois University Press, 1984.

Arishima Takeo. *Arishima Takeo zenshū.* 15 vols. Ed. Senuma Shigeki et al. Tokyo: Chikuma Shobō, 1980–1986.

Arishima Takeo Kenkyūkai, ed. *Arishima Takeo kenkyū sōsho.* 12 vols. Tokyo: Yūbun Shoin, 1995.

Asabuki Ryōji. *Asabuki Ryōji shishū.* Gendai Shi Bunko 102. Tokyo: Shichōsha Bunko, 1992.

———. *Opus.* Tokyo: Shichōsha, 1987.

Ashbery, John. *Flow Chart.* New York: Alfred A. Knopf, 1992.

Asō Naoko. *Gendai josei shijin ron: Jidai o kakeru josei tachi.* Gendai Shijin Ron Sōsho 4. Tokyo: Doyō Bijutsusha, 1991.

Ayukawa Nobuo. *Ayukawa Nobuo shishū.* Tokyo: Shichōsha, 1968.

Backhouse, A. E. *The Japanese Language: An Introduction.* Melbourne: Oxford University Press, 1993.

Barnett, Sharon. "Paul Celan and Todesfuge: A Legacy of Nazism." B.A. (Hons) thesis, University of Sydney, 1988.

Barthes, Roland. "The Death of the Author." Trans. Stephen Heath. In *Modern Criticism and Theory: A Reader,* ed. David Lodge. Essex: Longman Group, 1988.

Beaver, Bruce. *Death's Directives.* Sydney: Prism Books, 1978.

Beichman, Janine. *Embracing the Firebird: Yosano Akiko and the Birth of the Female Voice in Modern Japanese Poetry*. Honolulu: University of Hawai'i Press, 2002.

———. *Masaoka Shiki*. Tokyo: Kodansha International, 1986.

———. "Yosano Akiko: The Early Years." *Japan Quarterly* 37, no. 1 (1990): 37–54.

Berman, Marshall. *All That Is Solid Melts into Air: The Experience of Modernity*. London: Verso, 1990.

Bernstein, Charles. "Stray Straws and Straw Men." In *The L=A=N=G=U=A=G=E Book*, ed. Bruce Andrews and Charles Bernstein. Carbondale and Edwardsville: Southern Illinois University Press, 1984.

Berryman, John. *Selected Poems, 1938–1968*. London: Faber and Faber, 1972.

Blacker, Carmen. *The Catalpa Bow: A Study of Shamanistic Practices in Japan*. London: George Allen and Unwin, 1975.

Blanchot, Maurice. *L'éspace Littéraire*. France: Éditions Gallimard, 1955.

———. *The Space of Literature*. Trans. Ann Smock. Lincoln and London: University of Nebraska Press, 1982.

Booth, Wayne. *The Company We Keep: An Ethics of Reading*. Berkeley, Los Angeles, and London: University of California Press, 1988.

Bradbury, Malcolm, and James McFarlane. *Modernism*. Harmondsworth, Middlesex: Penguin Books, 1976.

Brooks, David. "Value Judgements and Literature." *Literature and Aesthetics: The Journal of the Sydney Society of Literature and Aesthetics* 1 (Spring 1991): 39–59.

Brownstein, Michael. "*Jogaku Zasshi* and the Founding of *Bungakukai*." *Monumenta Nipponica* 35, no. 3 (1980): 319–336.

Buckley, Sandra, ed., *Encyclopaedia of Contemporary Japanese Culture*. London: Routledge, 2001.

Byrd, Don. "Reading Olson." In *The L=A=N=G=U=A=G=E Book*, ed. Bruce Andrews and Charles Bernstein. Carbondale and Edwardsville: Southern Illinois University Press, 1984.

*The Cambridge History of Japan*. Vol. 6. Ed. Peter Duus. New York: Cambridge University Press, 1988.

Carpenter, Humprey. *A Serious Character: The Life of Ezra Pound*. London: Faber and Faber, 1988.

Celan, Paul. *Poems of Paul Celan*. Trans. Michael Hamburger. London: Anvil Press, 1988.

Charbonnier, George. *Conversations with Claude Lévi-Strauss*. Trans. John and Doreen Weightmann. London: Jonathan Cape, 1971.

Chiba, Sen'ichi. *Gendai bungaku no hikakubungakuteki kenkyū—modanizumu no shiteki dōtai*. Tokyo: Yagi Shoten, 1978.

———. *Modanizumu no hikakubungakuteki kenkyū*. Tokyo: Ōfūsha, 1998.

Cixous, Hélène. "Sorties." In *Modern Criticism and Theory: A Reader*, ed. David Lodge. Essex: Longman Group, 1988.

Claremont, Yasuko. "Hiraide Takashi and the Emergence of Sanbunshi in Contemporary Japanese Poetry." *The Journal of the Oriental Society of Australia* 30 (1998): 47–64.

———. "A Turning Point in Nishiwaki Junzaburō's Poetic Career." *The Journal of the Oriental Society of Australia* 20 and 21 (1988–1989): 21–35.

Clark, John. *Surrealism in Japan*. Clayton, Victoria: Monash Asia Institute, 1997.

Clarke, Hugh. "Japonesia, the Black Current and the Origins of the Japanese." *The Journal of the Oriental Society of Australia* 17 (1985): 7–20.

Clifton, Harry. *Night Train through the Brenner*. Loughcrew, Ireland: The Gallery Press, 1994.

Copeland, Rebecca L. *Lost Leaves: Women Writers of Meiji Japan*. Honolulu: University of Hawai'i Press, 2000.

Cranston, Edwin A. "Young Akiko: The Literary Debut of Yosano Akiko (1878–1942)." *Literature East and West* 18, no. 1 (1974): 19–43.

Dante Alighieri. *The Divine Comedy of Dante Alighieri*. Trans. Charles E. Norton. Great Books of the Western World. Chicago: Encyclopaedia Brittanica, 1952.

De Rougemont, Denis. *Love in the Western World*. Trans. Montgomery Belgion. New York: Pantheon, 1956.

Derrida, Jacques. *The Archaeology of the Frivolous: Reading Condillac*. Trans. John P. Leavey Jr. Lincoln and London: University of Nebraska Press, 1980.

Doak, Kevin Michael. *Dreams of Difference: The Japan Romantic School and the Crisis of Modernity*. Berkeley: University of California Press, 1994.

Dorn, Edward. *Slinger*. Berkeley, Calif.: Wingbow Press, 1975.

Dower, John. *War without Mercy: Race and Power in the Pacific War*. New York: Pantheon Books, 1986.

Eagleton, Terry. "Capitalism, Modernism and Postmodernism." In *Modern Criticism and Theory: A Reader*, ed. David Lodge. Essex: Longman Group, 1988.

———. *The Ideology of the Aesthetic*. Oxford: Basil Blackwell, 1990.

———. *Literary Theory: An Introduction*. Oxford: Basil Blackwell, 1985.

Eliot, T. S. *Collected Poems, 1909–1962*. London: Faber and Faber, 1963.

Ellis, Toshiko. "Nihon modanizumu no saiteigi—1930 nendai sekai no bunmyaku." In *Modanizumu kenkyū*, ed. Modanizumu Kenkyūkai. Tokyo: Shichōsha, 1994.

Endō Yū. "Arishima Takeo no shi." *Kokubungaku: Kaishaku to kanshō* 54, no. 2 (1989): 56–61.

Fish, Stanley. *Is There a Text in This Class? The Authority of Interpretive Communities*. Cambridge, Mass.: Harvard University Press, 1980.

———. *Self-Consuming Artifacts*. Berkeley: University of California Press, 1972.

Fitzsimmons, Thomas, and Yoshimasu Gozo, eds. *The New Poetry of Japan: The 70s and 80s*. Santa Fe: Katydid Books, 1993.

Forbes, John. *Damaged Glamour*. Rose Bay, N.S.W.: Brandl and Schlesinger, 1998.
————. *Stalin's Holidays*. Glebe, N.S.W.: Transit Poetry, 1980.
————. *The Stunned Mullet and Other Poems*. Sydney: Hale and Iremonger, 1988.
Foucault, Michel. *The Order of Things: An Archeology of the Human Sciences*. New York: Vintage Books, 1973.
————. "What Is an Author?" In *Modern Criticism and Theory: A Reader*, ed. David Lodge. Essex: Longman Group, 1988.
Freud, Sigmund. "Analysis of a Phobia in a Five-Year-Old Boy." In vol. 10 of *The Standard Edition of the Complete Psychological Works of Sigmund Freud*, trans. and ed. James Strachey. London: Hogarth Press, 1953–1974.
Fukasawa, Margaret Benton. *Kitahara Hakushū: His Life and Poetry*. Ithaca: East Asia Program, Cornell University Press, 1993.
Gadamer, Hans-Georg. *Truth and Method*. 2d rev. ed. Trans. Joel Weinsheimer and Donald G. Marshall. New York: Continuum, 1994.
Gay, Peter. *Freud: A Life for Our Time*. London: Papermac, 1989.
*Gendai shi bunko*. Ed. Oda Kyūrō. Tokyo: Shichōsha, 1968–.
Genshin. *Ōjōyōshū*. Annotated by Ishida Mizumaro. Tokyo: Iwanami Bunko, 1992.
Glenn, Jerry. *Paul Celan*. New York: Twayne Publishers, 1973.
Gray, Robert. *Selected Poems, 1963–1983*. North Ryde, N.S.W.: Angus and Robertson, 1985.
Grosz, Elizabeth. *Sexual Subversions: Three French Feminists*. Sydney: Allen and Unwin, 1989.
Haga Tōru. *Midaregami no keifu: shi to no hikaku bungaku*. Tokyo: Bijutsu Kōrosha, 1981.
Hagiwara, Sakutarō. *Howling at the Moon: Poems of Hagiwara Sakutarō*. Trans. H. Sato. Tokyo: University of Tokyo Press, 1978.
————. *Rats' Nests: The Collected Poetry of Hagiwara Sakutarō*. Trans. Robert Epp. Stanwood, Washington: Yakusha, 1993.
Hammial, Philip. *Just Desserts*. Sydney: Island Press, 1995.
————. *Pell Mell*. Wentworth Falls, N.S.W.: Black Lightning Press, 1988.
Hayes, Carol. "The Influence of a Black Cat on Hagiwara Sakutarō's Poetic Vision." *The Journal of the Oriental Society of Australia* 20 and 21 (1988–1989): 48–69.
Heidegger, Martin. *Basic Writings: Martin Heidegger*. Ed. David Farrell Krell. London: Routledge, 1993.
————. *Poetry, Language, Thought*. Translated and with an introduction by Albert Hofstadter. New York: Harper and Row, 1971.
Heinrich, A. V. *Fragments of Rainbows: The Life and Poetry of Saitō Mokichi*. New York: Columbia University Press, 1983.
Henshall, Kenneth G. "A Call for a Reconsideration of the Japanese Concept of Nat-

uralism." In *Austrina*, ed. A. R. Davis and A. D. Stefanowska. Sydney: Oriental Society of Australia, 1982.

———. *The Quilt and Other Stories by Tayami Katai*. Tokyo: University of Tokyo Press, 1981.

Hijiya Yukihito. *Ishikawa Takuboku*. Boston: Twayne Publishers, 1979.

Hiraide Takashi. "Gengoteki yuibutsushugi ni tsuite—shijin ni yoru jissen." *Gendai shi techō* 34, no. 8 (1991): 162–167.

———. *Hiraide Takashi shishū*. Gendaishi Bunko 100. Tokyo: Shichōsha Bunko, 1990.

Hirata Daiichi. "Hazama no sedai ni ikiru." *Shin Okinawa bungaku* 93 (1992): 27.

Hirata, Hosea. *The Poetry and Poetics of Nishiwaki Junzaburō*. Princeton: Princeton University Press, 1993.

———. "Pure Poetry and Différance: Negativity in Nishiwaki and Derrida." *Journal of the Association of Teachers of Japanese* 26 no. 1 (1992): 5–24.

Ichihara, Chikako. *Umi no tonneru*. Tokyo: Shūbisha, 1985.

Ide, Sachiko, and Naomi Hanaoka McGloin, eds. *Aspects of Japanese Women's Language*. Tokyo: Kurosio Publishers, 1991.

Ishikawa, Takuboku. *Takuboku: Poems to Eat*. Trans. Carl Sesar. Tokyo: Kodansha International, 1970.

Inagawa Masato. *Inagawa Masato shishū*. Gendaishi Bunko 99. Tokyo: Shichōsha Bunko, 1990.

———. "'Wareware' to wa dare ka?" In *Inagawa Masato shishū*. Gendaishi Bunko 99. Tokyo: Shichōsha Bunko, 1990.

Iraha Morio. *Maboroshi no mikojima*. Tokyo: Yatate Shuppan, 1979.

Isaka Yōko. "Josei to iu shizen." *La mer* 14, no. 10 (1986): 64–71.

Iser, Wolfgang. *The Implied Reader*. Baltimore and London: Johns Hopkins University Press, 1973.

Ishigaki, Rin. *Ishigaki Rin*. Ed. Suzuki Shiroyasu. Gendai no Shijin 5. Tokyo: Chūō Kōronsha, 1983.

———. *Ishigaki Rin bunko 4: shishū yasashii kotoba*. Tokyo: Kashinsha, 1987.

———. "Shi o kaku koto to, ikiru koto." In *Ishigaki Rin shishū*. Gendai Shi Bunko 46. Tokyo: Shichōsha, 1971.

———. "Tachiba no aru shi." In *Ishigaki Rin shishū*. Gendai Shi Bunko 46. Tokyo: Shichōsha, 1971.

Ishimoto Ryūichi. "Shizenshugi undō no ryūkō." In *Meiji tanka no bungaku chōryū*, ed. Meiji Jingu. Kyoto: Tanka Shinbunsha, 1996.

Isoda Kōichi. *Rokumeikan no keifu*. Tokyo: Kōdansha Bunko, 1991.

Itō Hiromi. *Itō Hiromi shishū*. Gendai Shi Bunko 94. Tokyo: Shichōsha, 1988.

———. *Teritorii ron 1*. Tokyo: Shichōsha, 1987.

——. *Teritorii ron 2*. 2d ed. Tokyo: Shichōsha, 1988.

Itō Hiromi and Ishiuchi Miyako. *Te, ashi, niku, karada/Hiromi 1955*. Chikuma Shobō, 1995.

Itō Sei. *Nihon bundanshi,* vol. 6: *Meiji shichō no tenkanki*. Tokyo: Kōdansha, 1960.

Itō Shinkichi. *Gyakuryū no naka no uta—shiteki anakizumu no kaisō*. Tokyo: Shichi-yōsha, 1963.

Itsumi Kumi, ed. *"Midaregami" sakuhironshū*. 3 vols. Tokyo: Ozorasha, 1997.

——. *Murasaki zenshaku*. Tokyo: Yagi Shoten, 1985.

——. *Shin midaregami zenshaku*. Tokyo: Yagi Shoten, 1996.

Ivy, Marilyn. "Critical Texts, Mass Artifacts: The Consumption of Knowledge in Postmodern Japan." In *Postmodernism and Japan,* ed. Masao Miyoshi and H. D. Harutoonian. Durham and London: Duke University Press, 1989.

Iwasaki Yukinori. "Myōjō no katsuyaku to romanshugi." In *Meiji tanka no bungaku chōryū,* ed. Meiji Jingu. Kyoto: Tanka Shinbunsha, 1996.

Jackson, Earl, Jr. "The Heresy of Meaning: Japanese Symbolist Poetry." *Harvard Journal of Asiatic Studies* 51 no. 2 (1991): 561–598.

Jameson, Fredric. "The Politics of Theory: Ideological Positions in the Postmodernism Debate." In *Modern Criticism and Theory: A Reader,* ed. David Lodge. Essex: Longman Group, 1988.

——. *Postmodernism or, the Cultural Logic of Late Capitalism*. London and New York: Verso, 1991.

——. *The Prison-House of Language: A Critical Account of Structuralism and Russian Formalism*. Princeton, N.J.: Princeton University Press, 1974.

Kaneko Mitsuharu and Momota Sōji, eds. *Zenshishū taisei gendai Nihon shijin zenshū*. 16 vols. Tokyo: Sōgensha, 1952–1955.

Karatani Kōjin. *Nihon kindai bungaku no kigen*. Tokyo: Kōdansha Bungei Bunko, 1988.

——. *Origins of Japanese Literature*. Trans. Brett de Bary. Durham and London: Duke University Press, 1993.

Kawai Suimei. "Midaregami jidai." In vol. 1 of *"Midaregami" sakuhironshū,* ed. Itsumi Kumi. Tokyo: Ōzorasha, 1997.

Keene, Dennis. *Yokomitsu Riichi: Modernist*. New York: Columbia University Press, 1980.

Keene, Donald. *Dawn to the West: Japanese Literature in the Modern Era*. 2 vols. New York: Holt, Rinehart and Winston, 1984.

Kierkegaard, Søren. *The Last Years: Journals, 1853–55*. Ed. and trans. Ronald Gregor Smith. London: Fontana Library, 1968.

Kikuchi Yasuo. *Aoi Kaidan o noboru shijin tachi*. Tokyo: Seidosha, 1965.

Kitagawa Tōru. "Roshutsu suru yōki no yō na . . . —*Seken shirazu* no pafōmansu." *Gendai shi techō* 36, no. 9 (1993): 50–57.

Kittredge Cherry. *Womensword: What Japanese Words Say about Women.* Tokyo and New York: Kodansha International, 1987.

Kokai Eiji. *Nihon sengo shi no tenbō.* Tokyo: Kenkyūsha Sōshō, 1973.

———. "Sengo Nihon no shi undō—'Arechi' no baai." In vol. 31 of *Kanshō Nihon gendai bungaku: Gendaishi,* ed. Kokai Eiji. Tokyo: Kadokawa Shoten, 1982.

Kolakowski, Leszek. *Main Currents of Marxism.* 3 vols. Oxford: Oxford University Press, 1981.

Komata Yūsuke. *"Zeneishi" no jidai—Nihon no 1920 nendai.* Tokyo: Sōseisha, 1992.

Kondō Teruhiko. *Nishiwaki Junzaburō no shi.* Tokyo: Shinbisha, 1975.

Koriyama, Naoshi, and Edward Lueders, trans. *Like Underground Water: The Poetry of Mid–Twentieth Century Japan.* Port Townsend, Washington: Copper Canyon Press, 1995.

Kristeva, Julia. *Revolution in Poetic Language.* Trans. Margaret Waller. New York: Columbia University Press, 1984.

———. *Tales of Love.* Trans. Leon S. Roudiez. New York: Columbia University Press, 1987.

———. "Women's Time." In *The Kristeva Reader,* ed. Toril Moi. Oxford: Blackwell, 1986.

Kubota Jun et al., eds. *Iwanami Kōza Nihon bungakushi.* 18 vols. Tokyo: Iwanami Shoten, 1997.

Kunimine Teruko. "Joseishi no kōmyaku: josei shi 3." *Gendai shi techō* 36, no. 7 (1993): 152–153.

*Literature East and West: Toward a Modern Japanese Poetry.* Vol. 19, nos. 1–4 (1975): 7–126.

Lodge, David, ed. *Modern Criticism and Theory: A Reader.* Essex: Longman Group, 1988.

Lowell, Robert. *Selected Poems.* London: Faber and Faber, 1965.

Lowitz, Leza, and Miyuki Aoyama, trans. *other side river: contemporary japanese women's poetry.* 2 vols. Berkeley, Calif.: Stone Bridge Press, 1995.

McCaffery, Steve. *Prior to Meaning: The Protosemantic and Poetics.* Evanston, Ill.: Northwestern University Press, 2001.

McCreery, Ruth S. *Shiki and Matsuyama.* Matsuyama, Ehime: Matsuyama Municipal Shiki-kinen Museum, 1986.

Martin, Samuel E. *A Reference Grammar of Japanese.* New Haven and London: Yale University Press, 1975.

Matsuura Hisaki. "Akarui Haibō no kanata e: 80 nendai no shi." *Kokubungaku* 41, no. 13 (1996): 126–131.

Mawatari Kenzaburō, ed. *Gendai shi no kenkyū.* Tokyo: Nansōsha, 1997.

Miki Taku. "Ishigaki Rin no shi." In *Ishigaki Rin shishū.* Gendai Shi Bunko 46. Tokyo: Shichōsha, 1971.

Minear, Richard H., ed. and trans. *Hiroshima: Three Witnesses.* Princeton: Princeton University Press, 1990.

Miner, Earl. "Inventions of Literary Modernity." *Clio* 21, no. 1 (1991): 1–22.

——. "Waka: Features of Its Constitution and Development." *Harvard Journal of Asiatic Studies* 50, no. 2 (1990): 669–706.

Miyoshi, Masao, and H. D. Harutoonian, eds. *Postmodernism and Japan.* Durham and London: Duke University Press, 1989.

Mizutani Akio. *Nihon kindai bungeishi no kōsai.* Tokyo: Ōfūsha, 1971.

Moi, Toril. *Sexual/Textual Politics: Feminist Literary Theory.* London and New York: Routledge, 1985, reprint 1989.

——, ed. *The Kristeva Reader.* Oxford: Blackwell, 1986.

Molasky, Michael, and Steve Rabson, eds. *Southern Exposure: Modern Japanese Literature from Okinawa.* Honolulu: University of Hawai'i Press, 2000.

Montefiore, Jan. *Feminism and Poetry: Language, Experience, Identity in Women's Writing.* 2d ed. London: Pandora, 1994.

Morinaka Takaaki. "Kotoba, chinmoku, jiyū—Shishū *Tabi* kara *Seken shirazu* e." *Kokubungaku: Kaishaku to kyōzai no kenkyū* 40, no. 13 (1995): 37–41.

Morita, J. *Kaneko Mitsuharu.* Boston: Twayne Publishers, 1980.

Morton, Leith. "The Aesthetics of Modernism: The Case of Fin-de-siècle Japanese Poetry." In *Frontiers of Transculturality in Contemporary Aesthetics,* ed. Grazia Marchianò and Raffaele Milani. Turin, Italy: Trauben, 2001.

——. "Akiko, Tomiko and Hiroshi: Tanka as Conversation in Fin-de-siècle Japan." *Japanese Studies: Bulletin of the Japanese Studies Association of Australia* 14, no. 3 (1994): 35–50.

——. "The Canonization of Yosano Akiko's *Midaregami.*" *Japanese Studies* 20, no. 3 (December 2000): 237–254.

——. "The Clash of Traditions: New Style Poetry (Shintaishi) and the Waka Tradition in Yosano Akiko's Midaregami (1901)." In *The Renewal of Song: Renovation in Lyric Conception and Practice,* ed. Earl Miner and Amiya Dev. Calcutta: Seagull Books, 2000.

——. "The Concept of Romantic Love in the *Taiyō* Magazine, 1895–1905." *Nichibunken Japan Review* 8 (1997): 79–101.

——. "Courtly Love in France and Japan: An Introductory Study." In *Variété: Perspectives in French Literature, Society and Culture,* ed. Marie Ramsland. Frankfurt am Main: Peter Lang, 1999.

——. *Divided Self: A Biography of Arishima Takeo.* Sydney: Allen and Unwin, 1988.

——. "An Interview with Tanikawa Shuntarō." *Southerly* 68, no. 1 (1998): 6–30.

——. *Modern Japanese Culture: The Insider View.* Melbourne: Oxford University Press, 2003.

————. "The Paradox of Pain: The Poetry of Paul Celan and Sō Sakon." *Literature and Aesthetics: The Journal of the Sydney Society of Literature and Aesthetics* 1, no. 1 (1991): 82–96.

————. "Sōgō zasshi 'Taiyō' to 'Jogaku zasshi' ni mirareru ren'ai kan: 1895–1905." *Nihon kenkyū* 19 (1999): 293–333.

————. "Translating Japanese Poetry: Reading as Practice." *Journal of the Association of Teachers of Japanese* 26, no. 2 (November 1992): 141–179.

————. "A Two-Legged Mongrel: The Art of Haikai." *Ulitarra* (Sydney), no. 8 (1995): 124–150.

————, ed. and trans. *An Anthology of Contemporary Japanese Poetry.* New York and London: Garland Publishing, 1993.

————, trans. *Mt Fuji: Selected Poems, 1945–1986 by Kusano Shinpei.* Michigan: Katy-did Books/Oakland University, 1991.

Murray, Les A. *The People's Otherworld.* Sydney: Angus and Robertson, 1983.

Nagahata, Michiko. *Hana no ran.* Tokyo: Shinhyōron, 1987.

————. *Yume no kakehashi: Akiko to Takeo yūjō.* Tokyo: Shinhyōron, 1985.

Naka Tarō, ed. *Meishi kanshō: Hagiwara Sakutarō.* Tokyo: Kōdansha Gakujutsu Bunko, 1979.

Nakahodo Masanori. *Okinawa bungaku ron no hōhō.* Tokyo: Shinsensha, 1987.

Nakamaru Nobuaki. "'Monogatari' o tsumugu onna tachi—'shizenshugi' shōsetsu no ichidanmen." *Kokugo to kokubungaku* 74, no. 5 (1997): 20–30.

Nakamura Miharu. *Kotoba no ishi: Arishima Takeo to geijutsushiteki tenkai.* Tokyo: Yūseidō Shuppan, 1994.

Nakano Kaichi. *Modanizumu shi no jidai.* Tokyo: Hōbunkan, 1986.

Nejime Shōichi. "Seken shirazu." *Kokubungaku* 40, no. 13: 98–101.

*Nihon gendai shi bunko.* Ed. Kokai Eiji. Tokyo: Doyō Bijutsusha, 1970–.

*Nihon no shiika.* Ed. Itō Shinkichi et al. Tokyo: Chūō Kōron, 1967–1970.

*Nihon shijin zenshū.* Ed. Katsumoto Seiichirō et al. Tokyo: Shinchōsha, 1966–1967.

Nishiwaki Junzaburō. *Gen'ei: Selected Poems of Nishiwaki Junzaburō, 1894–1982.* Trans. Yasuko Claremont. University of Sydney East Asian Series No. 4. Sydney: Wild Peony, 1991.

————. *Nishiwaki Junzaburō shishū.* Ed. Irisawa Yasuo. Tokyo: Iwanami Bunko, 1991.

Ohta Yukie, and Takagi Rie, trans. "Ishigaki Rin: 5 Poems." *positions* 3, no. 3 (1995): 723–727.

*Okinawa bungaku zenshū.* Vol. 2. Ed. Okinawa Bungaku Zenshū Henshūiinkai. Tokyo: Kokusho Kankōkai, 1991.

Okudaira Hideo. *Kokuhō emaki.* Osaka: Hoikusha, 1962.

Olson, Charles. *The Maximus Poems.* Ed. George F. Butterick. Berkeley: University of California Press, 1983.

Omuka Toshiharu. *Taishōki Shinkō bijutsu undō no kenkyū.* Tokyo: Sukaidaa, 1995.

Ōno Tōzaburō. "Tomioka Taeko no 'Uta no wakare.'" In *Shinsen Tomioka Taeko shishū*. Tokyo: Shichōsha, 1977.

Ōoka, Makoto. *Gendai no shijin tachi*. 2 vols. Tokyo: Seidōsha, 1983.

———. *Tōji no keifu: Nihon gendaishi no ayumi*. Tokyo: Shichōsha, 1978.

Ōshiro Sadatoshi. *Okinawa sengo shishi*. Naha: Henshū Kōbō Baku, 1989.

Ōsumi Midori. "Okinawa no wakamono no gengo to isshiki." In *Fukki nijūgo shūnen dai san kai Okinawa kenkyū kokusai shinpojiumu: Sekai ni tsunagu Okinawa kenkyū*, ed. Fukki Nijūgo Shūnen Dai San Kai Okinawa Kenkyū Kokusai Shinpojiumu Jikkō Iinkai. Shuri: Okinawa Bunka Kyōkai, 2001.

Ōta Seikyū. "Shintaishi no shigeki to waka kakushin." In *Meiji tanka*, ed. Meiji Jingu. Kyoto: Tanka Shinbunsha, 1996.

Paglia, Camille. *Sexual Personae: Art and Decadence from Nefertiti to Emily Dickinson*. London: Penguin Books, 1992.

Palmer, Michael. *At Passages*. New York: New Directions, 1995.

———. *Notes for Echo Lake*. San Francisco: North Point Press, 1981.

———, ed. *Code of Signals: Recent Writing in Poetics*. Berkeley: North Atlantic Books, 1983.

Paz, Octavio, Eduardo Sanguinetti, and Charles Tomlinson. *Renga: A Chain of Poems*. Harmondsworth, Middlesex: Penguin Books, 1979.

Perloff, Marjorie. *The Futurist Moment: Avant-Garde, Avant Guerre, and the Language of Rupture*. Chicago and London: The University of Chicago Press, 1986.

———. *Poetic License: Essays on Modernist and Postmodernist Lyric*. Evanston: Northwestern University Press, 1990.

———. *The Poetics of Indeterminacy: Rimbaud to Cage*. Princeton, N.J.: Princeton University Press, 1981.

Plath, Sylvia. *Ariel*. London: Faber and Faber, 1965.

Pound, Ezra. *The Cantos*. London: Faber and Faber, 1981.

Rich, Adrienne. *The Dream of a Common Language*. New York: Norton, 1993.

Saeki, Junko. *"Iro" to "ai" no hikaku bunka*. Tokyo: Iwanami Shoten, 1998.

———. "'Ren'ai' no zenkindai kindai datsukindai." In *Sekushuarite no shakaigaku*. Iwanami Kōza gendai shakaigaku, vol. 10. Tokyo: Iwanami Shoten, 1996.

Saga Keiko. *Kusukusu*. Tokyo: Kashinsha, 1992.

———. *Nō sutoringusu*. Tokyo: Shoshi Toi, 1988.

Sakai Tadakazu. "Sengo Shijin no shōzō." *Kokubungaku: Kaishaku to kyōzai no kenkyū* 16, no. 13 (October 1971): 10–23.

Sano Yōko. "Tanikawa Shuntarō no asa to yoru." In *Tanikawa Shuntarō*, ed. Hagiwara Sakutarō kinen. Maekawa, Gunma: Maekawa Bungakukan, 1994.

Sas, Miryam. *Fault Lines: Cultural Memory and Japanese Surrealism*. Stanford, Calif.: Stanford University Press, 1999.

Sasaki Yasuaki. "Arishima Takeo to anaakisuto no nakamatachi." In *Arishima Takeo kenkyū sōsho,* vol. 8, ed. Arishima Takeo Kenkyūkai. Tokyo: Yūbun Shoin, 1995.

Seki Ryōichi. "Kindai shiika no akebono." In vol. 9 of *Nihon bungaku no rekishi: Kindai no mezame,* ed. Yoshida Seiichi and Shimomura Fujio. Tokyo: Kadokawa Shoten, 1968.

Schott, Robin. "Whose Home Is It Anyway? A Feminist Response to Gadamer's Hermeneutics." In *Continental Philosophy,* vol. 4: *Gadamer and Hermeneutics,* ed. Hugh J. Silverman. London and New York: Routledge, 1991.

Shibamoto, Janet S. *Japanese Women's Language.* New York: Academic Press, 1985.

Shibusawa Takasuke. "Sakonshi kanken." In *Sō Sakon shishū.* Tokyo: Shichōsha, 1977.

Shibutani, Masayoshi. *The Languages of Japan.* Cambridge: Cambridge University Press, 1990.

Shimaoka Shin. *Shi to wa nanika.* Tokyo: Shinchō Sensho, 1998.

Shimizu Akira. "Fujitsu no bijo—*seken* to jibun to no kakawari." *Gendai shi techō* 36, no. 7 (1993): 118–121.

Shiraishi Kazuko. "Hachijū nendai to joseishi: Fueminizumu undō to heikō shite." *Gendai shi techō {tokushū}: Joseishi saizensei* 34, no. 9 (1991): 64–69.

———. *Seasons of Sacred Lust: The Selected Poems of Kazuko Shiraishi.* Ed. Kenneth Rexroth; trans. Ikuko Atsumi, John Solt, Carol Tinker, Yasuyo Morita, and Kenneth Rexroth. New York: New Directions, 1978.

Silverberg, M. *Changing Song: The Marxist Manifestoes of Nakano Shigeharu.* Princeton, N.J.: Princeton University Press, 1990.

Singer, Irving. *The Nature of Love,* vol. 2: *Courtly and Romantic.* Chicago: University of Chicago Press, 1984.

Smith, Stevie. *The Collected Poems of Stevie Smith.* Harmondsworth, Middlesex: Penguin Books, 1985.

———. *Two in One: Selected Poems.* London: Longman, 1971.

Sō Sakon. *Kappa.* Tokyo: Bunrinsho, 1964.

———. *Moeru haha.* Tokyo: Yayoi Shobō, 1968.

———. *Sō Sakon shishū.* Gendai Shi Bunko 70. Tokyo: Shichōsha, 1977.

———. "Wadatsumi no itteki." In *Sō Sakon shishū.* Tokyo: Shichōsha, 1977.

Solt, John. *Shredding the Tapestry of Meaning: The Poetry and Poetics of Kitasono Katue.* Cambridge, Mass.: Harvard University Asia Center, 1999.

Steiner, George. "The Hollow Miracle." In *Language and Silence: Essays 1958–1966.* Harmondsworth, Middlesex: Penguin Books, 1969.

———. *In Bluebeard's Castle: Some Notes Towards the Re-definition of Culture.* London: Faber and Faber, 1971.

———. *Language and Silence: Essays 1958–1966.* Harmondsworth, Middlesex: Penguin Books, 1969.

Stevens, Wallace. *Selected Poems.* London: Faber and Faber, 1970.

Strauss, David Levi. "Approaching *80 Flowers*." In *Code of Signals: Recent Writing in Poetics,* ed. Michael Palmer. Berkeley: North Atlantic Books, 1983.

Suzuki Keisuke. "Masshiro de iru yori mo—mō hitotsu no keiretsu no shishū." *Kokubungaku* 40, no. 13: 105–107.

Suzuki Sadami. *Modan toshi no hyōgen: jiko gensō josei.* Kyoto: Hakujisha, 1992.

———. *Nihon no bungaku gainen.* Tokyo: Sakuhinsha, 1998.

———. *"Seimei" de yomu Nihon kindai: Taishō seimeishugi no tanjō to tenkai.* Tokyo: NHK Books, 1996.

———, ed. *Zasshi "Taiyō" to kokumin bunka no keisei.* Kyoto: Shibunkaku Shuppan, 2001.

Takachi, Jun'ichirō. "Mozartesque—the Poetic Epiphany of Tanikawa Shuntarō." *Japan Quarterly* 44, no. 3 (1997): 78–89.

Takahashi, Mutsuo. *Sleeping Sinning Falling.* Trans. Hiroaki Sato. San Francisco: City Lights, 1992.

———, ed. *Yoshioka Minoru.* Gendai no Shijin 1. Tokyo: Chūō Kōronsha, 1983.

Takahashi Seori. "Shiteki gengo no genzai." In vol. 14 of *Iwanami Kōza Nihon bungakushi,* ed. Kubota Jun et al. Tokyo: Iwanami Shoten, 1997.

Takamura Kōtarō. *Takamura Kōtarō senshū.* 6 vols. Ed. Yoshimoto Takaaki and Kitagawa Taiichi. Tokyo: Shunjūsha, 1966.

Takara Ben. "Ryūkyūko de shi o kaku koto." *Gendai shi techō* 34, no. 10 (1991): 88–93.

Takeda Nobuaki. "Onna no nichijō/Onna no hinichijō." In vol. 5 of *Kōza Shōwa bungakushi,* ed. Tōgō Katsumi et al. Tokyo: Yūseidō, 1989.

Takumi Hideo. "Meiji 30 nendai ni okeru bungaku to bijutsu kakawari ni tsuite." *Bungaku* 53, no. 10 (1985): 55–68.

Tamura Keiji. "Watashi no mae ni aru nabe to okama to moeru hi to." *Kokubungaku: Kaishaku to kyōzai no kenkyū* 37, no. 3 (1992): 116–118.

Tanikawa Shuntarō. *Coca-Cola Lesson.* Trans. William I. Elliot and Kawamura Kazuo. Portland: Prescott Street Press, 1986.

———. *Floating the River in Melancholy.* Trans. William I. Elliot and Kawamura Kazuo. Portland: Prescott Street Press, 1988.

———. *Kotoba asobi uta.* Tokyo: Fukuinkan Shoten, 1973.

———. *Masshiro de iru yori mo.* Tokyo: Shūeisha, 1995.

———. *At Midnight in the Kitchen I Just Wanted to Talk to You.* Trans. William I. Elliot and Kawamura Kazuo. Portland: Prescott Street Press, 1980.

———. *Minimal.* Trans. William I. Elliot and Kawamura Kazuo. Tokyo: Shichōsha, 2002.

———. *Mōtsaruto wo kiku hito.* Tokyo: Shōgakukan, 1995.

———. *Naked.* Trans. William I. Elliot and Kawamura Kazuo. Berkeley, Calif. and Yokohama: Stone Bridge Press and Saru Press International, 1988.

———. *Seken shirazu.* Tokyo: Shichōsha, 1993.

———. *The Selected Poems of Shuntarō Tanikawa.* Trans. Harold. Wright. San Francisco: North Point Press, 1983.

———. *Sixty-two Sonnets and Definitions: Poems and Prosepoems.* Trans. William I. Elliot and Kawamura Kazuo. Santa Fe: Katydid Books, 1992.

———. *Songs of Nonsense / Yoshinashi uta.* Trans. William I. Elliot and Kawamura Kazuo. Tokyo: Seidosha, 1991.

———. *With Silence My Companion.* Trans. William I. Elliot and Kawamura Kazuo. Portland: Prescott Street Press, 1975.

———, ed. *Masters of Japanese Poetry: Six Distinctive Voices of the Postwar Era.* Rosemont, N.J.: Watchword (The Morris-Lee Publishing Group), 1999.

Tanikawa Shuntarō and Inagawa Masato. "Disukomunikēshon wo megutte." In *Gendai shi techō* 34, no. 7 (1991): 9–27.

Tanikawa Shuntarō and Tsuji Takashi. "Tanikawa Shuntarō wa 'Seken shirazu' ka?—Shi, dokusha, shijin to wa nanika?" *Gendai shi techō* 36, no. 9 (1993): 9–23.

Tomioka Taeko. *See You Soon: Poems of Tomioka Taeko.* Trans. Sato Hiroaki. Chicago: Chicago Review Press, 1979.

———. *Shinsen Tomioka Taeko shishū.* Tokyo: Shichōsha, 1977.

———. *Tomioka Taeko shishū.* Tokyo: Shichōsha, 1973.

Trakl, Georg. *Selected Poems.* Ed. Christopher Middleton; trans. Robert Grenier. London: Jonathan Cape, 1968.

Treat, John Whittier. *Writing Ground Zero: Japanese Literature and the Atomic Bomb.* Chicago and London: University of Chicago Press, 1995.

Tsuboi, Hideto. "Itō Hiromi ron (chū)—Teritorii ron 1 (sono 1)." *Nihon bungaku* 39, no. 2 (1990): 48–57.

———. "Itō Hiromi ron (ge)—Teritorii ron 1 (sono 2)." *Nihon bungaku* 39, no. 4 (1990): 23–33.

———. "Itō Hiromi ron (jō)—Teritorii ron**." *Nihon bungaku* 38, no. 12 (1989): 24–35.

———. "Tassha' o motomete." In *Shōwa bungakushi: Nichijō to hinichijō,* vol. 4, ed. Tōgō Katsumi et al. Tokyo: Yūseidō, 1989.

Uda Notarō, ed. *Meiji bungaku zenshū,* vol. 51: *Yosano Tekkan Akiko shū.* Tokyo: Chikuma Shobō, 1977.

Ueda Hiroshi. "Tekkan to Akiko: Midaregami jojō no genryū wo motomete." *Tanka* 42, no. 2 (1995): 98–105.

Ueda, Makoto. *Modern Japanese Poets and the Nature of Literature.* Stanford, Calif.: Stanford University Press, 1983.

Vidovic-Ferderbar, D. "Hagiwara Sakutarō and Western Literature." *The Journal of the Oriental Society of Australia* 30 (1998): 95–113.

Wada Hirofumi. "Isseiki o koeta Nihon no shishi." In *Kingendai shi o manabu hito no tame ni,* ed. Wada Hirofumi. Kyoto: Sekai Shisōsha, 1998.

Wales, Katie, ed. *A Dictionary of Stylistics.* London and New York: Longman, 1989.

Washburn, Dennis. *The Dilemma of the Modern in Japanese Fiction.* New Haven and London: Yale University Press, 1995.

Watanabe Sumiko. *Yosano Akiko.* Tokyo: Shintensha, 1998.

Weinsheimer, Joel C. *Gadamer's Hermeneutics: A Reading of Truth and Method.* New Haven and London: Yale University Press, 1985.

White, Hayden. *Tropics of Discourse: Essays in Cultural Criticism.* Baltimore and London: Johns Hopkins University Press, 1987.

Worton, Michael, and Judith Still, eds. *Intertextuality: Theories and Practices.* Manchester and New York: Manchester University Press, 1991.

Wright, Judith. *Judith Wright: Collected Poems, 1942–1985.* Sydney: Angus and Robertson, 1994.

Yamamoto Tarō. *Yurishiizu.* Tokyo: Shichōsha, 1975.

Yamanokuchi Baku. *Yamanokuchi Baku shishū.* Tokyo: Shichōsha, 1988.

Yanagita Kunio. *Yanagita Kunio zenshū.* Vol. 1. Tokyo: Chikuma Bunko, 1989.

Yano Hōjin. *Tekkan Akiko to sono jidai.* Tokyo: Yayoi Shobō, 1998.

Yasukawa Sadao. "Arishima Takeo to Yosano Akiko." In vol. 6 of *Arishima Takeo kenkyū sōsho,* ed. Arishima Takeo Kenkyūkai. Tokyo: Yūbun Shoin, 1995.

Yokogi Tokuhisa. "Shijin shirazu no kōzai." *Gendai shi techō* 36, no. 9 (1993): 166–167.

Yosano, Akiko. *River of Stars: Selected Poems of Yosano Akiko.* Trans. Sam Hamill and Keiko Gibson Matsui. Boston and London: Shambhala, 1996.

———. *Tangled Hair.* Trans. Sakanishi Shio. Boston: Marshall Jones, 1935.

———. *Tangled Hair.* Trans. Sanford Goldstein and Seishi Shinoda. Lafayette: Purdue University Press, 1971.

Yoshimasu Gōzō. *Osiris, the God of Stone.* Trans. Sato Hiroaki. Laurinburg, N.C.: St. Andrews Press, 1989.

———. *A Thousand Steps . . . and More: Selected Poems and Prose, 1964–1984.* Trans. Richard Arno, Brenda Barrows, and Takako Lento. Rochester, Mich.: Katydid Books/Oakland University, 1987.

Yoshimoto, Takaaki. *Masu imēji ron.* Tokyo: Fukutake Bunko, 1994.

———. *Yoshimoto Takaaki zenchosakushū.* 15 vols. Tokyo: Keisei Shobō, 1964–1969.

———. *Zōho Sengo shi shiron.* Tokyo: Yamato Shobō, 1983.

Yoshioka, Minoru. *Celebration in Darkness: Selected Poems of Yoshioka Minoru.* Trans. Christopher Drake. Rochester, Mich.: Katydid Books/Oakland University, 1985.

Young, James E. *Writing and Rewriting the Holocaust: Narrative and the Consequences of Interpretation.* Bloomington and Indianapolis: Indiana University Press, 1990.

Zukofsky, Louis. *A.* Berkeley: University of California Press, 1978.

# Index

# About the Author

LEITH MORTON is presently professor at the Foreign Language Research and Teaching Center, Tokyo Institute of Technology. He has taught at the University of Newcastle and the University of Sydney and has been a visiting professor at the International Research Center for Japanese Studies in Kyoto, Kwansei Gakuin University, and Tokyo Metropolitan University. Morton has published extensively on Japanese literature and culture. He is the author of *Divided Self: A Biography of Arishima Takeo* (1988) and *Modern Japanese Culture: The Insider View* (2003) and has edited and translated two poetry collections. He has also published four volumes of his own poetry, including one for children.

Production Notes for Morton/*Modernism in Practice*

Cover design by Wilson Angel

Text design by University of Hawai'i Press production staff using
Garamond 3 and Gill Sans

Composition by Integrated Composition Systems in Quark XPress

Printing and binding by The Maple-Vail Book Manufacturing Group

Printed on 60 lb. Text White Opaque, 426 ppi